Read E-Riches 2.0 to learn about the secrets behind these real life Internet marketing success stories:

▲ How a startup company found 35,000 new friends on Myspace and sold out of its new product in just one week (Chapter 9)

▲ How a New Jersey liquor store owner attracts 80,000 viewers to each episode of his online video wine-tastings and has driven sales through the roof (Chapter 18)

▲ How a North Carolina furniture store profitably captures high-end customers using pay-per-click search engine text ads on Google, Yahoo!, and MSN (Chapter 21)

▲ How an innovative PR exec put Facebook to work to build a new mailing list (and business) with 40,000+ subscribers in just a few months (Chapter 9)

▲ How clever agencies have driven their clients' new web sites and products to the top of the Digg.com and StumbleUpon.com social bookmarking sites (Chapter 11)

▲ How e-mail newsletters published *online* attract business for an *offline* Boston-based tour company (Chapter 3)

▲ The new e-mail-based publicity services that bring press inquiries to your e-mail inbox (and land users placement in the *New York Times*) (Chapter 15)

▲ The practical approach to blogging that helps a business services directory grow its revenues nationwide (Chapter 12)

▲ How *giving away* his products has built a very profitable business for an Ohio accounting consultant (Chapter 17)

▲ How free teleseminars and webinars have helped a disaster recovery firm build recurring audiences and revenues (Chapter 19)

▲ The cost-effective Affiliate Program advertising strategies Buy.com uses to attract a worldwide sales force for its products (Chapter 22)

▲ The article syndication strategy that has helped a Christian stay-at-home mom to attract lots of profitable traffic for her blog (Chapter 16)

▲ The online video strategy that attracted great sales for Vermont Teddy Bear last Valentine's Day (Chapter 18)

▲ How a casual "Tweet" landed an NYC yoga instructor in a *BusinessWeek* cover story (Chapter 13)

▲ *And much more!*

E-RICHES 2.0

NEXT-GENERATION MARKETING
STRATEGIES FOR MAKING
MILLIONS ONLINE

SCOTT C. FOX

AMACOM AMERICAN MANAGEMENT ASSOCIATION

NEW YORK ▲ ATLANTA ▲ BRUSSELS ▲ CHICAGO ▲ MEXICO CITY
SAN FRANCISCO ▲ SHANGHAI ▲ TOKYO ▲ TORONTO ▲ WASHINGTON, D.C.

This publication is designed to provide accurate and authoritative information in regard to the subject matter covered. It is sold with the understanding that the publisher is not engaged in rendering legal, accounting, or other professional service. If legal advice or other expert assistance is required, the services of a competent professional person should be sought.

The author, ScottFox.com, The Liminal Success Institute, or associated persons or entities may have content, promotional, advertising, customer, consulting, or equity relationships with the people or companies discussed or recommended in this book and on associated web sites. Many of the links included in this book and on associated web sites contain affiliate advertising codes, for example. While efforts have been made to identify the best suppliers/vendors in each of these areas, we accept no liability for your use of them. You should use your own independent judgment to evaluate their services and fit for your needs. Nothing herein should be construed as any guarantee of financial success for readers. Prices quoted were accurate when written but may have changed since. All marks belong to their respective owners.

Library of Congress Cataloging-in-Publication Data

Fox, Scott C.
E-riches 2.0 : next-generation marketing strategies for making millions online/ Scott Fox.
    p. cm.
Includes index.
ISBN-13: 978-0-8144-1462-0
ISBN-10: 0-8144-1462-1
1. Small business—Management. 2. Small business marketing. 3. Internet marketing. 4. Electronic commerce. I. Title.

HD62.7.F693 2009
658.8'72—dc22

2009003054

Printing number
10 9 8 7 6 5 4

To my beautiful wife, Katherine.

CONTENTS

. . .

INTRODUCTION

MARKETING YOUR WAY TO E-RICHES

This book is about attracting more customers online so that you can make more money. It covers *what you can do, how to do it*, and, more importantly, *what you should be doing to find your own e-riches.*

Whether your business is Web-based or brick-and-mortar, and whether you're a solo entrepreneur, a partner in a small company, or working in marketing for a multinational corporation, there are new tools online that can help you do your job better, sell more product, and make more money.

If you read my first book, *Internet Riches,* or subscribe to my free E-Commerce Success email newsletters at ScottFox.com, you know that I'm a successful online entrepreneur myself. So my focus in this book is on teaching you how to grow your audience using free and low-cost techniques. These include social networking on Facebook,

MySpace, and LinkedIn, blogs, e-mail publishing, viral video pro-motions, and updates to traditional techniques like word-of-mouth marketing and public relations, plus more technical disciplines like RSS, autoresponders, microblogs like Twitter, podcasting through iTunes, and more.

If you read *e-Riches 2.0*, you'll learn the basics of building your audience using all of these new marketing tools plus smart tips on search engine keyword advertising and affiliate programs, too. (These last two are actually paid advertising strategies, but they are so cost-effective and different from traditional marketing techniques that I want to introduce you to them, too.)

This material is not just me talking, nor is it full of vague theories. *e-Riches 2.0* is full of practical details from my personal experience, *plus* dozens of profiles, case studies, interviews, references, and stud-ies from other real-world experts and real people who are using these new tools successfully. Their success is not just theory but actual (profitable) fact that I want to share with you.

Reading *e-Riches 2.0* will make you a smarter, more modern mar-keter. This includes becoming clever enough with Web 2.0 online marketing tools to:

- ▲ Successfully "do it yourself" in the new world of online marketing

- ▲ Save a lot of money by learning many of the complex-sounding techniques that high-priced consultants will try to charge you for

- ▲ Impress your techie friends, colleagues, and boss

- ▲ Become a better manager of marketing campaigns and employees

- ▲ Learn to be a smarter client if you choose to hire consultants

- ▲ Advance your career by leading the most successful new mar-keting campaigns for your company's products

All of these will help both your career and your wallet.

The Online Opportunity for You

I know you want practical guidance. I wrote my book *Internet Riches* because I was fed up with best sellers that offer only vague strategies for "attracting abundance" as substitutes for a real action plan. *Internet Riches* taught people how to start their own e-businesses based on their personal expertise and interests.

Now I'm back with *e-Riches 2.0*. This book takes the same practical, detailed approach. I've again researched, evaluated, tested, studied, and analyzed all the new marketing tools that I could find online for you. In the space we have available here, I'm going to give you information on the best strategies I have found, plus tools you can use to evaluate and prioritize them depending on your needs and business interests. (And the education continues online at Scott Fox.com, where updates to this book and a worldwide community of fellow marketers and entrepreneurs is available to you 24/7.)

Despite constant media coverage of bad economic news, the Internet Gold Rush is still happening today. Never before in history have you been able to reach so many people so quickly, so easily, and so cost-effectively. So, my question for you is:

What are you doing to profit from the Internet Gold Rush?

There are now more than 1.5 billion people online. That means that no matter how obscure your product or how targeted your pitch, it's likely that there are people on the Web *right now* who want your product.

The trick is for you to reach them cost-effectively. You need to let these potential customers know that your product is the solution to their problems. That's the purpose of marketing and your job as a marketer.

All the new tools available online may sound overwhelming, especially if you are new to the online world, but these marketing techniques are *known and knowable*. I have detailed in this book a set of specific, tactical steps for attracting the *recurring* traffic that your business deserves.

I've even summarized my recommended online marketing philosophies into 9 Commandments for e-Riches Marketing Success and also created a Top 10 List of Online Marketing Success Tips to help you (see Chapter 1). If you follow these steps, you will increase your marketing reach online and learn to make more money.

For additional coverage and updates to these topics, please visit ScottFox.com. Your purchase of this book entitles you to a free trial membership in my online coaching community. (See the front of the book for more details on this Special Offer.)

The Four Audiences for *e-Riches 2.0*

A key factor for success is a desire to be outstanding at Marketing. It does not matter how great your entrepreneurial idea is, you have to be able to convert it to sales. That's why marketing is such a vital skill.

—Chris Cardell, Cardell Media

You should read this book if you are:

1. *A corporate marketer or agency employee.* Your employer needs your expertise in order to compete. If your marketing campaigns are not attracting new customers daily, you will soon lose your job to someone who "gets it" better than you do.

2. *A small business owner or partner.* For the first time in history, small businesses like yours can compete with the "big boys" worldwide. But being good at marketing is a key entrepreneurial success factor that entrepreneurs often overlook. It's naïve to think that just having good ideas and working hard to produce great products will lead to sales success. Don't kid yourself into thinking that you can find success with a product or service without being committed to spending a significant amount of your time promoting it. *Who else is going to do it?*

The huge Internet audience offers tremendous upside if your business can get your product marketing messages out to the right people. This book teaches you how to use inexpensive online marketing tools to do that.

3. *E-business curious.* You may not be a marketer, but you are smart to be curious about the opportunities and challenges offered by the Web 2.0 world. Maybe this is because you want to help your colleagues in other parts of the company (or maybe it's because you have one foot out the door of your current job and you want some advice on how to grow your after-hours hobby into a business online!). Either way, this book will introduce you to online marketing *in plain English*, plus give you a strategic framework that will allow you to better analyze and understand the importance of new media marketing techniques, both to your own life as a consumer and to your career.

4. *Worried about your financial future.* Globalization, uncertain financial markets, technology, and our friend the Internet are combining to restructure the economy to eliminate the long-term security formerly offered by corporate jobs. If you are unemployed, under-employed, unhappily fully employed, or simply looking to upgrade your professional skills, this book can help you retrain yourself for the opportunities of today's "information age" economy.

Internet Marketing Is Your Future

If you don't like change, you're going to like irrelevance even less.
— General Eric Shinseki, Secretary of Veterans Affairs,
former Chief of Staff, U.S. Army

You need to learn to love the Internet! Why? Because it's cheaper and has wider reach than ever before, and because everyone—yes, everyone—is coming online.

Even if you don't see it at the moment, the Web and e-mail are extending further into your life all the time. Mobile browsers bring Google into people's pockets; BlackBerries bring e-mail into the middle of dinner. Tools like RSS feeds and Twitter bring constant updates from people you may barely know.

Just think ten or even five years forward: The screens in your living room will continue to grow, as will those on your desk. In fact, you'll probably have two or more screens soon. Your gadgets will get faster and more powerful so that they combine phone, e-mail, Web browsing, iPod, camera, full streaming video capabilities, and so on all the time everywhere. Soon all this will arrive in your car, on long-haul plane flights, and in your kids' classrooms and pockets, too. This means opportunity for smart marketers who embrace the new platforms and the unique ways in which they can extend brands and messages into people's lives.

The increasingly targeted marketing messages of today are better than ever at anticipating customers' interests. And tomorrow's will be better still. Haven't you been surprised when Amazon.com suggests a book that you already own and love? Imagine that targeted marketing on steroids and working to promote *your* business online!

The tremendous, worldwide reach of the Web has also changed the ways in which customers expect to be able to interact with you and your products. You have the opportunity to take advantage of this increase in customer interaction and two-way feedback to enhance your relationships with your audience, differentiate your brand from competitors, and sell a lot more product.

20th-Century Broadcasting Evolves into 21st-Century Narrowcasting

A marketer's job used to be easier—twentieth-century broadcast-style marketing cast such a wide net that it was presumed that many or even most people who were seeing or hearing your message would not be interested in it anyway. That's why it was called *broad*-casting.

Marketing was generally a one-way blast rather than a personal conversation. Any dialogue that resulted was usually handled by people outside the marketing team, like the sales department or retail store clerks who would close the deals.

Today the Web's millions of web sites, blogs, e-mail newsletters, social networks, podcasts, and video-sharing services offer you inexpensive access to more people than ever before, but the change from traditional marketing is that these audiences are increasingly fragmented. So the best new opportunities are not simply updated versions of broadcast strategies like Super Bowl commercials or editorial coverage in the *Wall Street Journal* or on NYT.com that reach potentially millions of people indiscriminately. Instead, broadcasting is less effective and today's customers are clustered in lots of smaller markets and channels instead of fewer big ones.

Smart marketers are evolving away from simply exposing a marketing campaign to as many eyeballs as possible and toward targeting these more specific and trackable audiences instead. Internet tools offer the modern marketer more efficient and cost-effective ways to reach such targeted communities of potential customers. This creates the opportunity to share more specific marketing messages that are designed to appeal to the specific needs of those communities. In fact, with some online research, you can target your marketing messages to online communities that have *already proved to be interested in your products.*

These online communities may be preexisting, or you, as a marketer, can establish new ones yourself through your web sites, message boards, or blogs. You don't even have to invest heavily in technology today. You can inexpensively piggyback on Internet platforms like Facebook, Ning, or Twitter to attract potential customers to interact with your brand and your products using technology provided by these other companies *for free.*

If you're willing to engage with your customers, the increasingly accurate targeting, 24/7 availability, worldwide reach, low cost of communications, and always growing online population combine to let you relate on a more interactive, personal level than ever before. And because the audiences you reach are more targeted and self-selecting, it's more likely that they are going to want a relationship and a dialogue with you and your products, too.

These opportunities may seem confusing, challenging, and perhaps even threatening, but they offer you huge and highly profitable opportunities.

The good news is that you don't need to figure them *all* out. If you get good at just a few of these Web 2.0 techniques, you'll have made the critical transition from twentieth- to twenty-first-century media maven.

I'm here to help you.

Audiences Are Valuable

Profit in business comes from repeat customers, customers that boast about your product or service, and that bring friends with them.

—W. Edwards Deming, pioneering statistician and author of
The New Economics for Industry, Government, Education

Your audience relationships are 100 percent of your past, present, and future revenues. How your marketing outreach builds relationships with this audience determines the success of your business.

Notice that I didn't just say *customer*; I said *audience*. The distinction I'm making is that you just sell to customers—your relationship is purely transactional. But modern online marketing can be so targeted and inexpensive that you have the opportunity to develop your customers into fans through repeated interaction. By publishing online and participating in digital communities to meet their interests and needs, you can advance casual customers so that they become *fans* of your brand.

Fans bring you deeper and more profitable marketing relationships. And loyal fans don't just buy once; they usually keep buying, are the first to try your new products, and are the first to tell their friends, too. Collecting those fans into an *audience* implies that you have a group of customers interested in hearing more from you.

Serving a loyal audience is more profitable than acquiring new one-off purchasers, and it keeps your audience away from competitors, too. Converting customers to fans and building them into a loyal audience is your goal. Online marketing tools can help you accomplish all of these goals at once and increase your sales.

This reflects an overall shift in marketing strategy from "quantity" of audience to "quality" of audience. Kevin Kelly, the former editor of *Wired* magazine, summarizes this emerging business model in an approach he calls "1,000 True Fans." While only 1,000 customers would never support most big businesses (or the mass marketing budgets needed to build a brand through twentieth-century media), today the Internet changes the economics of both marketing and product delivery so that the *quality* of your customer engagement is increasingly more important than the size of your audience.

This interactive and personal customer service dimension of the "new marketing" isn't all fun and games, however. There are lots of back-and-forth obligations in building any relationship. So you must be ready to cultivate a more personal and authentic approach to fans that includes dialogue. By adding value to the lives/careers of your fans and to the online communities in which you choose to participate, you can develop audiences that are both repeat customers and word-of-mouth evangelizing fans of your products.

And if you make it clear that you are interested in hearing the opinions of your potential customers, you will be rewarded with valuable feedback, greater loyalty, and profitable repeat sales.

Who Am I and Why Did I Write this Book?

I'm Scott Fox. I got started in the online world at Stanford University, in the heart of Silicon Valley, more than 15 years ago. Since then I have founded, grown, or advised more e-commerce businesses than I can remember. I have built businesses online that have sold many, many millions of dollars of goods, services, and information products worldwide.

The success of these businesses today allows me to write and teach full-time. And I donate the profits from my books to charity to fund college scholarships for inner city kids. My mission: To help as many people as possible learn how they, too, can profit from the e-business revolution.

Unfortunately, most of the people who understand Web 2.0 online marketing tools either are so busy making money using them that they don't share their expertise or they have made a business out of selling their expertise to folks like you.

I'm a different type of guy. I want you to succeed. I believe that the new tools of online marketing should be explained as widely as possible.

Why? Because I believe that the benefits of e-business innovation deserve to be shared outside of Silicon Valley. I think that you deserve your shot, and I'd like to help you take it.

A few years ago, a friend was asking my advice on how to start an online business. After I spoke to her for almost 45 minutes straight, she said to me, "Scott, you should write that down." She was right, so I did.

The result was my first book, *Internet Riches*, a practical and detailed guide to help anyone, even people with little technology background or capital, start a business online today. *Internet Riches* has gone on to become a best seller. People from all over the world have been educated and inspired by its original mix of specific, practical business advice; detailed technology recommendations; and motivational support in plain language. I am thrilled to have found an audience for my expertise and even more excited to be allowed to "mentor" so many people and to help them to realize their personal potential.

The success of *Internet Riches* encouraged me to keep writing. I started my blog online at ScottFox.com to respond to the many questions I receive from readers of *Internet Riches* worldwide. And more recently I've opened forums at ScottFox.com that allow my readers worldwide to meet and help one another, too. All the encouraging and questioning inquiries from readers like you (plus a push from my publisher) encouraged me to dive deeper into online marketing. The result is the book you are holding now.

I'm not an early adopter "fan boy" who's charmed by the latest Web gadgets. I'm a businessman who's interested in finding opportunities to make money. Because of this, I can give you *the truth* about much-hyped Web 2.0 online marketing strategies, and help you find money-making promotional opportunities online where marketing industry tradition has failed to keep pace with modern technology.

I also truly understand how difficult it is to pay attention to all of these new "must-have" technologies and online marketing tools. So, I recommend only techniques that I've tried personally.

Accomplishments from my personal use of the techniques in this book include: a widely read blog at ScottFox.com; number-one Google rankings for the search terms that are most important to my marketing; hundreds of "friends," "fans," and "followers" on top social networks; press coverage from sources including the *Boston Globe*, *Orange County*

Register, Philadelphia Inquirer, Toronto Globe & Mail, BusinessWeek.com, MSNBC.com, AOL Money, *Smart Money* and *SUCCESS* magazines, *Los Angeles Business Journal,* and many others; hundreds of radio interview bookings across the United States and internationally; and speaking invitations from Los Angeles to New York City to the U.K.

In short, I have "built an audience," just as I prescribe in this book.

What a Jerk!

I want to apologize now for talking a lot about myself in this book.

I am not doing this to impress you with my own success or intimidate you with my technical knowledge. Quite the opposite: I'm giving you *my own real-life examples* because those are the ones I know best. I think it's important for you to understand that I'm advising you *not based on theory but based on the successful use of these tools myself.* Most importantly, by sharing personal examples, I hope to show you that you, too, can learn modern online marketing: *Successful use of these tools is within your reach.*

My goal is to demystify the Internet so that everyone can understand the amazing financial and personal success opportunities that are enabled by this huge new communications and commerce platform.

Sharing with you examples from my own experience will hopefully help you to see that I'm for real and that I'm leading by example, too. I hope you'll see me as a friend and mentor in your online adventures.

As I have said, I don't do this for the money. I do it to try to help people like you improve their lives. As I said in *Internet Riches:* "I believe that the secrets of prosperity offered by the new generation of Internet business deserve to be shared."

Why? Because the Internet is the greatest self-improvement opportunity in history. The twenty-first century is the first time in history that anyone can afford to start a worldwide business. The tools the Web offers you have permanently altered the risk/reward equation for entrepreneurs like you. This means that anyone, even someone with no capital and little technological knowledge, can now start a business online and market cost-effectively to more than 1 billion people.

The interconnectedness the Internet offers us all liberates human creativity and the potential for collective positive action in ways that we can't even begin to understand yet. If you think Amazon.com, eBay, YouTube, iTunes, Google, and Facebook were interesting, wait until you see what comes next! I'm excited to be a part of the digital revolution, and, if you're reading this book, I hope that you are, too.

This book's marketing techniques are my latest offering to you. *I want to see you succeed.* Use these tools to grow your business. Make more money; create more jobs; help find and share solutions to the world's problems.

I hope that *e-Riches 2.0* helps you build the life you've always wanted.

Let's make it happen!

Scott Fox
Los Angeles, California
www.ScottFox.com

PART ONE

TWENTY-FIRST-CENTURY MARKETING: HOW THE RULES HAVE CHANGED

*Selling to people who actually want to hear from you
is more effective than interrupting strangers who don't.*
—*Seth Godin, author of* Tribes: We Need You to
Lead Us, Purple Cow: Transform Your Business by
Being Remarkable, Meatball Sundae: Is Your
Marketing Out of Sync?, *and many more books*

1

. . .

My 9 Commandments for E-Riches Marketing Success

IT'S A NEW world.

Marketing has evolved from a series of one-way blasts at consumers to a living, breathing, two-way communications thing that needs constant care, attention, staffing, and (ideally) interaction with the customer audience.

The practical implication of this is that marketers need to evolve their thinking beyond focusing on creating eye-catching print pieces, media buys, creative branding, promotions, or even word-of-mouth marketing. Every old technique still exists, but to find e-riches today you need to consider how the Internet has introduced new interactive techniques, given much greater reach (and sometimes unexpected consequences) to old ones, and changed the expectations of your potential customers.

Here are the nine short "commandments" that I recommend you follow to attract maximum customer attention in a Web 2.0 world.

E-Riches Commandment 1:
Don't Worry About the Technology

Don't worry about the technology—focus on your marketing goals instead. I know that Internet marketing technology can be intimidating, especially if you are new to online marketing. But the fact is, all of it is only a *set of tools*.

At its heart, the Internet is really just a communications network. Instead of getting caught up in and distracted (or even intimidated) by the technology, you should feel empowered by the impressive, inexpensive, and powerful marketing tools that the Internet offers you today.

Just as you don't necessarily know how your television or telephone works internally, you don't need to be a technology wizard to put the Internet to good use marketing your products.

Yes, the junior (usually younger) people, the consultants, and, of course, the tech team know lots of buzzwords. They may even know what most of them mean.

But that doesn't mean they know what to *do* with them.

That's the marketer's job. That's *your* job.

No one has yet found a magic formula for marketing online. It turns out that all the technology (as stated above) is really just a set of tools for creating persuasive marketing messages.

You know how to do that part. (And if you don't, this book is full of my guidance and successful examples.)

Focus on the results that each set of new marketing tools offers you— let the techies and consultants use the jargon to justify their billings.

If your marketing strategy is based on "attracting and engaging customers into positive experiences with your products," not just knee-jerk reactions to "Let's start a blog" or "Why don't we have a Facebook page yet?" you'll be prepared for success in any medium, including today's Internet.

E-Riches Commandment 2:
Heed the Interactive Imperative

Many marketers still make the mistake of thinking that web site production and online marketing are simply extensions of traditional print marketing strategies. After all, a web site is just a collection of pages. Why is it any different from a magazine or a brochure?

The difference is that Internet-enabled marketing offers customer *interactivity*. You can use this functionality to draw potential customers into a closer relationship with your products and your brand.

You can treat the Web the same way you have always treated print, but if you do, you'll be missing the huge new marketing opportunities that online marketing offers you (and that the audience increasingly expects).

Here are some obvious examples of how Internet-based marketing can add utility to your traditional approaches.

PRINT-ONLY MARKETING BROCHURE	WEB-BASED MARKETING
Show your address	Add a clickable map and directions
Show a product photo	Enable a larger, more detailed photo to pop up if a visitor clicks on the image
Show a product photo	Add a video of the product in action
Highlight key phrases	Highlight key phrases to help search engine results rankings
Offer product details and photos	Make products clickable for instant online ordering
Promise to deliver in one to three weeks	Make real-time shipping information available online, including tracking
Include footnotes	Include footnotes that link to the original sources

Include information that is valid as of printing date only	Instantly bring information up to date online
Provide a phone number for customer service	Provide online e-mail, chat, and discussion forums

The point here is that traditional print marketing strategies are no longer enough. First generation web sites are usually just "brochure ware," meaning that they take the messaging and creative material from a preexisting sales brochure and adapt them to web pages.

That brochure ware approach is still far better than nothing. (See Chapter 2 for details on the minimum web site presence I recommend if your business is just getting started online.) But to meet today's customer demands for more information, you need to think about using the Internet more and *better*. This means upgrading your Web operation to offer customers more detail and more transparency into your inventory, pricing, and delivery, plus (especially) feedback mechanisms that allow your customers to feel that *they* are in control of the dialogue with you and your products.

Why?

Because customers want this information and increasingly feel entitled to share their opinions. You need to be ready for customer feedback and respond appropriately. There's no longer an excuse for your not putting customer needs first. There's just too much competition in today's marketplace.

If you don't do these things, your competitors will (and in most cases already are!).

E-Riches Commandment 3: Build Customer Relationships—Don't Just Chase Sales

You are no longer in the sales business; you are in the trust, loyalty, attention, and especially the lead generation business online. Today your number one priority as a marketer needs to shift from closing sales as quickly as you can to engaging customers in long-term direct relationships that eliminate as many middlemen as possible.

This paradigm shift is based on simple economics: In the twentieth century, it cost a fortune to reach customers via the media or postal mail. But now that communication via e-mail is so cheap, marketers can afford to keep in touch with customers much more cost-effectively than in previous eras.

This suggests that, although it would be nice to turn every web site visit into a transaction, it's much more important to recruit that potential customer into a relationship *by collecting her e-mail address.*

Because you can keep in touch cheaply via e-mail, it's not as critical as it used to be to "close" a sales prospect right away. Instead, your focus should increasingly be on building a relationship of trust with potential customers. Focus on their long-term value as lifetime partners in your business.

Anyone who signs up for your e-mails is such a sales "lead" and should be encouraged above all else to stay on your email list. As Seth Godin wrote in his classic marketing book *Permission Marketing: Turning Strangers into Friends and Friends into Customers,* you want people's permission in order to engage them in a gradually escalating dialogue from introduction, through engagement, to eventual purchase (and ideally repeat purchases).

Once you have their permission to continue marketing to them, cultivating new prospects to turn them into long-term customers is more cost-effective than ever. The game has changed from talking at customers to relationship building. With millions of competitor web site "channels" competing for customers' attention, treating your customers as valued audience members is the best way to differentiate your business online.

E-Riches Commandment 4: Listen Up! The "Participation Nation" Requires It

Who cares about an angry blogger that's not your customer? Google does.

—Jeremiah Owyang, Forrester Research

Today's online audience is not just passive consumers. As the title of John Battelle's new book *The Conversation Economy* suggests, people are online and they are talking.

Customers talk to each other and also expect to talk with your company representatives about your products. They want to give feedback on the products they use and explain to others why they recommend them (or why they don't). Not all customers are like this, but those in the trend-setting, vocal, active online minority are the critical tastemakers that your brand needs to influence. And even those that don't publicly post their opinions regularly use search engines to research other peoples' opinions before making product purchases.

Their opinions are amplified by the Web's many new communication formats. Note: Even uneducated opinions from people who are not your customers can be influential online. Their online posts, and how you respond to them, are archived forever, too—affecting both your company's reputation cloud (see Commandment 8) and your web site's search engine rankings.

You have the opportunity to welcome such feedback, respond supportively, and even give it an online home as part of your own online product presence (see Commandment 6). Or you can ignore it, and if you do, that customer enthusiasm (or antagonism) will be invested elsewhere.

I recommend that your team engage with your customer audience. Channeling audience enthusiasm into public support for your products is one of the great opportunities of modern marketing, and it can be done more efficiently and cost-effectively than ever before using the many tools explained in this book. This book is full of examples of marketers embracing such dialogue with customers.

At its most successful, this dialogue can funnel audience enthusiasm into participation in your online promotions, publications, and communities—and the audience will more than return the favor by "virally" spreading word of your product's value to their friends across the Web and worldwide.

E-Riches Commandment 5: Your Profit Potential Depends on Being More Personal

What we are communicates far more eloquently than anything we say or do.
—Stephen R. Covey, author of *The 7 Habits of Highly Effective People*

Increasingly personal approaches are expected online. Because so many of the tools (e-mail, blogs, social networks, and so on) were designed to facilitate interpersonal communications, that's what they are best at. So instead of acting like a big company when dealing with customers online, replace your generic and impersonal marketing messages with a more authentic and personal approach. This will help you build relationships and credibility for the long term.

It's also geeky and outdated to hide behind the natural anonymity of the Net—let your personality (or that of your company or products) shine through. This means no more hiding behind fake or anonymous personae. It's time to step out from behind the corporate curtain and be yourself.

Misleading or fake promotions usually get "outed" these days anyway. The online audience is increasingly sophisticated, and lame attempts at "Astroturfing" (faking a grassroots reaction) can lead to serious embarrassment. For example, John Mackey, the CEO of the Whole Foods grocery chain, attracted embarrassing national press coverage and attention from the Federal Trade Commission when it was revealed that he had been active on the Yahoo Finance message boards for years using a fake name and often attacking rival grocery store chain Wild Oats.

The Web's memory is long—maybe forever—so your marketing efforts need to be authentic. Even if you can get away with a sly promo or two today, it's likely that your deception will eventually come out if anybody bothers to look closely. That obviously can damage your brand and your credibility.

Summary: Use only online marketing methods that you'd be happy to explain to your mother. This will help ensure that your online reputation stays clean (and profitable).

> **DON'T WORRY!**
> This is not a theory book. We'll be getting to a specific, action-able discussion of blogs, Facebook, e-mail, RSS feeds, podcast-ing, and so on very soon. I just want to make sure that you catch the big picture first. If you can't wait, just skip ahead to Part 2 to get started with e-mail newsletter publishing strate-gies or Part 3 to get started with my recommended social net-work marketing techniques.

E-Riches Commandment 6: Grow Beyond Your Web Site to a Multichannel Online "Product Presence"

You can see that your web site alone is no longer enough. Your online marketing strategy needs to evolve from being web site–centric to man-agement of what I call your brand's overall "product presence" across all the channels that potential customers use today (see Figure 1–1).

These marketing extensions of your product presence include:

▲ Your web site

▲ Your e-mail newsletters

▲ Your blog

▲ The archives of your newsletters or blog that live on long after their initial publication

▲ Your profile pages on MySpace, Facebook, and LinkedIn

▲ Your friends, followers, and fans on social networking platforms

▲ Your company's listings in online directories

▲ How your brand and your products show up in Google and other search engines

▲ The web sites with which your site exchanges links—and what that says about your business

▲ Your online videos

▲ How your web site looks on mobile platforms like an iPhone or BlackBerry

▲ The archives of your staff's online interactions on message boards, blogs, review sites, and microblogging platforms like Twitter

▲ Your eBay transactions and reputation

▲ Photos your team has shared on Flickr, Photobucket, Facebook, and other media sharing sites

▲ Your online advertising

▲ How distributors and affiliate partners promote your products

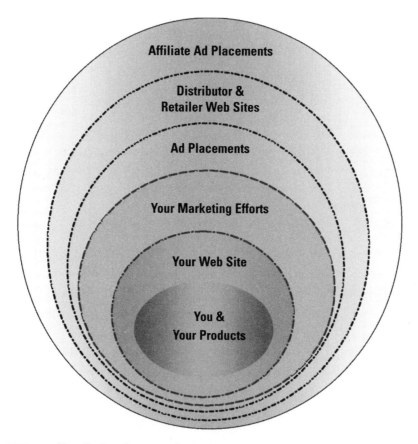

FIGURE 1–1. Your Product Presence: *Product presence starts with the web site that you produce. Then it expands outward through your marketing efforts, advertising placements, and toward less-controlled promotions delivered by third parties. The sum of all your directly controlled marketing is your "product presence."* © *ScottFox.com*

Hopefully you get the idea.

All of these marketing-related activities are produced and promoted by you to present your products and brand to the world. Collectively, they represent a product presence that you need to actively manage to maximize your sales. And the size of this presence suggests that your product presence maintenance and publishing effort needs to be strategized, resourced, and managed constantly.

The fact is that hundreds of millions of customers are online at any moment—and millions of them are literally wandering around with "no particular destination in mind."[1]

This means that both your current and potential new customers are encountering your products right now and making purchasing decisions based on what they find. With the proper marketing product presence online, you could be attracting some percentage of that massive audience to your web site and products literally while you are reading this.

E-Riches Commandment 7: Graduate from Destination Marketing to Distributed Engagement

If you're attacking your market from multiple positions and your competition isn't, you have all the advantage and it will show up in your increased success and income.

—Jay Abraham, author of *Getting Everything You Can Out of All You've Got*

Web 1.0 marketing was about trying to attract visitors to your web site. Today, however, the World Wide Web has gotten so large that there's no single way to reach the majority of Internet users simultaneously. There's no online equivalent of a Super Bowl commercial. Consumers have spread out across the Web to a million different destinations.

This means that "cowboy marketing," where you try to herd everyone to your web site, is no longer enough.

Instead, modern marketers think beyond twentieth-century broadcast marketing or even Web 1.0 web site–centered strategies. They customize their marketing messages to meet the interests of the target audience and *deliver those messages to wherever likely audiences can be found online.*

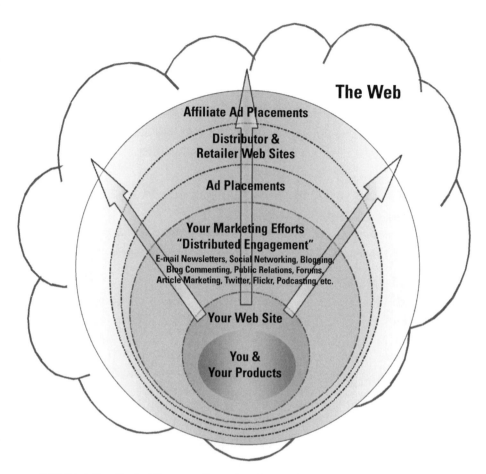

FIGURE 1–2. Your Product Presence Expands with Distributed Engagement: *Reaching out from your initial product presence, distributed engagement expands beyond traditional marketing and advertising through targeted marketing efforts that reach the wider Web of online customer communities.*   © ScottFox.com

This creates Web 2.0–style interaction with potential customers ("engagement") on their turf and on their terms in the niche communities where they are already active ("distribution"). I call this decentralization of your branding and marketing strategy "distributed engagement." (See Figure 1–2.)

It means that you need to stop spending your time and marketing resources just tweaking your own web site. Instead, you need to get on the Web and meet your customers where they are *already* hanging out. Be sure to answer any comments you receive on your blog, visit

Facebook and MySpace to find customers there who share interest in your products, network with potential partners on LinkedIn, host some free teleseminars or podcasts, publish some articles on the niche community sites where your natural customers congregate already, or at least buy some pay-per-click ads to be sure your product presence reaches your customers online *without them having to visit your web site.* (Relax! The rest of this book shows how to do all this.)

E-Riches Commandment 8: Nurture Your Brand's Reputation Cloud

Basing our happiness on our ability to control everything is futile.
—Stephen R. Covey, author of *The 7 Habits of Highly Effective People*

As you advance a strategy of distributed engagement, you will naturally push your product presence out across the Web. Your web site, published materials, advertising, and interaction will naturally invite comment by and interaction with the audience. The collection of customer feedback across these platforms and formats I collectively call your "reputation cloud." (See Figure 1–3.)

The reputation cloud of your brand or products includes all of your traditional offline marketing methods, plus the product presence that your online marketing effort generates. But it also includes the rapidly growing number of customer-initiated interactions, reactions, and responses to your marketing, too.

Shockingly, this reputation cloud includes customer discussions about you, your products, your company, and its suppliers, relationships, ads, and ethics that are *beyond your control.* Your customers, clients, competitors, suppliers, partners, and employees (both current and past in all cases) are growing your brand's reputation cloud online right now *as you read this.*

The new rules of marketing require that you pay increasing attention to this reputation cloud of customer feedback, including:

▲ Your company's appearance in search engine results

▲ Blogs that discuss your products or your company's customer service

- ▲ Customer reviews of your products on Amazon.com, Buy.com, or other review sites

- ▲ Articles about your product, your company, or you personally in directories like Wikipedia

- ▲ Commentary about your company or products in online communities

- ▲ Web sites that link to yours (with or without your permission)

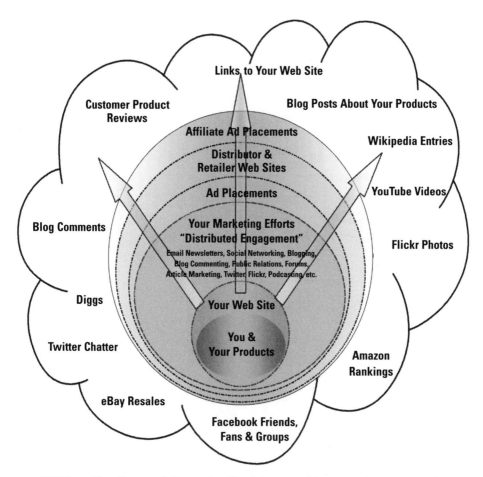

FIGURE 1–3. Your Company's Reputation Cloud: It starts with your product presence but includes your distributed engagement marketing efforts, advertising, and promotions, PLUS customer commentary in all formats. © ScottFox.com

- ▲ Reviews of your products on Amazon.com, Bizrate.com, or other ranking sites

- ▲ Photos of your products, company, or personnel posted online

- ▲ Your company's reputation on city guides like Citysearch, Yelp, Angieslist, or with the Better Business Bureau

- ▲ Video captures of your TV commercials copied, uploaded, or parodied on YouTube.com

To summarize: *The Web has empowered customers to share their opinions about your products. This is feedback that you need to monitor and engage with.*

By becoming active in Web 2.0 communities and tools, you'll be ahead of most brand stewards in positively managing the reputation cloud for your company and its products.

Why does this matter?

Consider this example: Your company web site may show smiling employees cooking tasty pizzas in your wood-burning ovens. But a YouTube search on your restaurant's name might turn up a homemade video of cockroaches in the kitchen posted by a disgruntled former employee. Never mind that the footage is faked, 10 years old, or from another restaurant with a similar name—it's your business that's at risk. And the sensational nature of such a video can easily attract a lot of attention and links, which could then propel the damaging video to the top of the search engine rankings.

The point of the reputation cloud is that you can't control the message completely any more. The Web is bigger than you are. But unless you get involved online, everyone *but you* is contributing to your reputation cloud.

You can choose to manage your reputation cloud to help promote your products and grow your audiences, or you can ignore it and let your customers, suppliers, competitors, and employees create it for you.

Guess which approach I recommend?

TIP: MONITOR YOUR COMPANY'S REPUTATION
CLOUD USING GOOGLE ALERTS!

The free Google Alerts service lets you set keyword searches to monitor both blogs and web sites for mentions of your product name or other key words.

You'll automatically receive an e-mail when new mentions of your targeted phrases are picked up by Google's Web crawlers.

You can use this competitive intelligence to visit and thank positive reviewers and bloggers, and also to step in early if online opinion turns against you.

http://www.google.com/alerts

E-Riches Commandment 9: Publish or Perish

You may not have realized it yet, but all this public customer interaction online means that you are now in the publishing business. Everyone else is, too. From e-mail to web sites to blogs to Facebook to MySpace to Twitter to a hundred other new platforms, you now have the opportunity to interact with your customers better than ever before.

Responding publicly online to customer feedback is one form of publishing. But rethink your marketing approach to go beyond just canned "corporate speak" customer service responses. Embracing the many publishing-style online marketing opportunities that the Internet offers allows you to expand your product presence, target your marketing messages to appropriate audiences (distributed engagement), and differentiate your company's reputation cloud to attract the loyalty of your customers, even if you have a mundane or widely available product.

Publishing content will attract customers into interaction. This content can include free e-mail newsletters ("noozles"), informative web site content, a controversial blog, entertaining bits of Flash animation, or humor—you may need to try all of these to differentiate your products today. You can use this content to entice potential customers into agreeing to hear more from you—attracting web site visitors, blog readers, e-mail subscribers, Facebook fans, Twitter followers, RSS readers, and so on (all tactics we'll discuss soon).

The more you customize your content to stir up a response from your audience ("comment bait") or attract links from other sites ("link bait"), the more traffic you'll attract, and you'll increase your search engine ranking, too.

The content you produce contributes to your product presence. Then, as you distribute this content to customers and they spread it further through your distributed engagement efforts, your reputation cloud grows and you have the potential for a self-reinforcing or "viral" marketing cycle. (See Chapter 8 for more on viral marketing.)

Pursuing these publishing-style goals will get you farther, faster, more cost-effectively than traditional marketing approaches because these strategies engage customers in long-term relationships with your products. They also create long-term loyalty and positive word of mouth, which are less likely to result from traditional sales-focused marketing tactics.

Today you have the opportunity to rise above being just a product supplier/distributor/retailer—the Internet cuts out such middlemen. Your effort to produce content and manage reactions to it (the traditional forte of the publishing industry) can help your brand become a "performer" in its own right.

By this I mean that you can use online marketing tools to attract customers into your online store, entertain them, and encourage them to trust, believe, and start a longer-term relationship with you, your brand, and your products. Instead of trying to close the deal as quickly as possible, the objective of your marketing efforts today needs to be to treat your customers as an *audience* and turn them into *fans*.

The greatest opportunities for marketing success today lie in leveraging the huge reach of the Internet as a common platform. You can put it to work to develop better and more profitable relationships with customers if you are ready to entertain or educate them instead of just pitch at them.

Those companies that recognize this and rearrange their resources to take advantage of it will win. The others will be left wondering where all their customers went.

Conclusion: You're in the publishing business, like it or not.

Congratulations! It's an exciting time to be in marketing, that's for sure.

So what should you do with all this high-minded, business school–sounding marketing philosophy? As my father says, "Let's bring that hay down where the horses can eat it!" Here's a summary of my 10 best specific, practical techniques for attracting the recurring traffic your business deserves. These are "Scott Fox's Top 10 e-Riches Online Marketing Success Tips."

SCOTT FOX'S TOP 10 E-RICHES ONLINE MARKETING SUCCESS TIPS

Here's a 10-point summary of how I recommend that you reorganize your marketing efforts to take advantage of the largest and most cost-effective marketing platform in history: the Internet.

1. **Graduate from web site–centric marketing to "distributed engagement."** *Market your "product presence" across the World Wide Web's many sites, platforms, and communities. Engage with customers to create fans of your brand and a sales-enhancing "reputation cloud" (Chapter 1).*

2. **Reprioritize your marketing tactics to support consistent online content publishing on your web site and across the many new platforms available inexpensively online.** *Today distributed engagement via e-mail (Chapter 3), RSS feeds (Chapter 4), autoresponders (Chapter 7), social networks (Chapters 9 and 10), social news sites (Chapter 11), blogs (Chapter 12), and microblog services like Twitter (Chapter 13) allows you to inexpensively nurture your best customers and recruit new ones into your audience. Start collecting e-mail addresses yesterday, even if you don't have immediate plans to use them (Chapter 3).*

3. **Explore social networks and social bookmarking.** *They can "magically" better connect you to your current customers, introduce you to highly targeted new audiences, and be educational and fun, too (Chapters 9, 10, and 11).*

4. **Blog if you have something to say that will make you more money.** *Otherwise be quiet. Spend your time commenting on other people's* *blogs instead (Chapter 12). If you do publish a blog, use it to publish your noozles, too (Chapter 5).*

5. Learn how the Internet has changed the rules of public relations *(Chapter 14). Don't chase reporters with press releases; use news leads services to make publicity opportunities come to your e-mail inbox automatically (Chapter 15).*

6. Give away as much of your product online as you can afford. *Share your expertise through article marketing (Chapter 16) and "freemium" giveaways (Chapter 17) to attract as many eyeballs as possible.*

7. Leverage new online broadcast platforms. *Online video (Chapter 18), Internet radio and podcasting (Chapter 20), and teleseminars (Chapter 19) offer new promotional "broadcasting" opportunities much less expensively than twentieth-century TV and radio ever did.*

8. Put the huge reach of search engines and affiliate programs to work promoting your business. *Search engine marketing strategies like pay-per-click keyword advertising (Chapter 21) and cost-per-action affiliate programs (Chapter 22) are both cost-effective ways to reach new customers.*

9. Establish key performance indicator (KPI) metrics to measure your traffic and sales growth. *Evaluate your marketing program regularly to ensure the most effective use of your time and resources in growing your online audiences (Chapter 23).*

10. Differentiate or die. *Use online research tools to identify holes in the market that your company's products and marketing messages can fill profitably (Chapter 24).*

Now that I've introduced these strategies, we'll spend the rest of the book explaining the details of how you can implement them quickly, cost-effectively, and profitably.

2

. . .

Quick Start Guide to
Getting Your Business Online

BEFORE WE discuss how you can best apply my 9 E-Riches Commandments and Top 10 Online Marketing Success Tips, let's make sure that your business has addressed the fundamentals of e-commerce success first.

For more details on any of the basic e-commerce topics that follow, visit ScottFox.com. Use the search box there to find my free advice on web hosting, web site design, search engine optimization (SEO), copywriting, domain names, or whatever e-commerce business topic is challenging you.

The Basics of E-Commerce Success

Are you late to the online party and wondering where to start? The rest of this book will overwhelm you if you don't at least have a web site up already.

If yours is one of the millions of businesses that *still* doesn't have an active web site, here's some specialized advice just for you.

You need to get on with it.

Most small business owners are so immersed in their own operations that they forget that it's not obvious to others that they close early on Saturdays or that parking is free around the corner. A web page is a perfect place to share these small insights—they can help bring you more business.

"But I don't sell anything online!"

Even if you don't sell anything online, it's increasingly important that you have a web site. Online is the first place people look for information on businesses today—the Yellow Pages has lost its dominance.

You need to make it as easy as possible for customers to find you and learn about your products. Today, 69 percent of shoppers do research online before making their purchases at the store.[1]

You don't want to miss those sales, do you?

Here's a quick action plan to get you moving toward e-riches:

▲ Buy your best domain name (and variations including common misspellings).

▲ Visit ScottFox.com for my current recommendations on web site hosting services like SiteSell, Typepad, and more.

▲ Use your new domain name to put up a basic site that includes the following:

• Business name and logo

• Three to five sentences about your business specialty

• Details of the geographic areas you serve (be sure to include these if they're relevant)

• Address, including parking info and directions

• Phone number

• Hours

• Three photos:

– A photo of your products—people like pictures.

– A photo of you and your team—people like to see other people.

– A photo of your storefront or building so that people will recognize it when they come looking for you.

Also, you'll then want to visit any online business directories that cover your area or specialty to submit listings of your site and details of your services and products.

Web Site Design

When designing your new web site, I advise that "functional" is more important than "pretty." "Profitable" is even more important than "functional." Design with clear customer purchase paths and conversion goals in mind. *The most important measure of conversion today is collecting e-mail addresses.* Regular publishing to your e-mail list is the best way for you to inexpensively keep in touch with your best customers to improve your relationship and encourage repeat sales.

Get your web site started as soon as you can. Then measure your success at attracting traffic, sign-ups, and sales to find areas for improvement.

Copywriting

Your web site *is* your product today. The image you present there affects almost every other aspect of your business (off-line, too). When a customer arrives at your web site, you have just seconds to persuade her to engage in long-term interaction with your brand. The words on the page are critical in succeeding at this.

Review your web site copy as though it were a direct-response postcard—if the benefits (not the features) of your products don't leap off the page, learn copywriting quickly or hire a professional copywriter.

Search Engine Optimization (SEO)

Your site needs to rank well in the search engines for keywords relating to your products. The basics of search engine optimization (SEO) include correct placement of your targeted keywords in the title, meta, and headline tags of your site.

Links back to your site from established and relevant web sites are even more important to how your web site is ranked by many top search engines.

If your web site has not yet achieved these critical basics (or if you don't know what I'm talking about), please try reading my first book, *Internet Riches*, and visiting ScottFox.com. At ScottFox.com we have Internet marketing discussion sections dedicated to each of these topics where you can meet fellow online marketers at a similar level and get advice from more experienced entrepreneurs, too. (*A free trial membership in this service is yours, since you were smart enough to buy this book!*)

E-RICHES TIP: DON'T PUT ANY INFORMATION ONLINE THAT'S NOT "EVERGREEN."

If it has taken your business this long to get a simple web page set up, it's not likely that you're suddenly going to include weekly site updates into your schedule. So avoid posting anything about your "Holiday Sale" or "Summer Hours" that will soon cause your site to look dated (and therefore unreliable).

This includes a dated copyright notice. Under U.S. law, you do not need to post a year next to a copyright statement—so don't do it. You'll probably forget to change it, and if you do, your site will start looking stale in just a few months.

If you want a quick and basic web site that you can set up yourself to meet these objectives, visit InternetMillionaireDomains.com. It's my Web services store. Domain names are cheap, and the basic "Web Site Tonight" product is only $4.99 per month. InternetMillionaire Domains.com can get you on your way with little tech support needed.

For more detailed recommendations and advanced strategies for starting a more fully-featured business web site that goes beyond this introductory "brochure ware" approach, please read *Internet Riches*.

(You can also visit ScottFox.com for a free download titled "The Web Site Startup Checklist." This special report is available as a free sign-up bonus to my free e-mail newsletter subscribers. It shares the 10 steps that I take personally every time I set up a new business web site.)

PART TWO
E-MAIL: YOUR #1 SALES OPPORTUNITY

3

. . .

TODAY'S BEST E-MAIL
PUBLISHING STRATEGIES

WHAT IS THE by now "old school" technique of e-mail doing as the first major section in a book about Web 2.0 online marketing?

E-mail is the first section because it is the most underappreciated marketing medium in history—and it's still the biggest online marketing opportunity for you.

E-mail offers almost all the benefits of old-fashioned direct mail, but it is cheaper to create, more immediately actionable by the customer, easier to target, easier to track, and essentially free to send. And e-mail is the number one use of online technology—it is still used by 60 percent of Internet users daily, even more people than use search engines (which get a lot more press).[1]

Although it's a Web 1.0 tool, e-mail can distribute your marketing messages directly into the e-mail inboxes of interested customers.

This makes it a critical tool for effective deployment of a Web 2.0 distributed engagement marketing strategy.

You can use e-mail to reach more people more cost-effectively than has ever previously been possible. You can customize your e-mails to create an optimal promotional and advertising platform where you control all the inventory, timing, context, and display—everything you need to maximize customer engagement with your marketing messages. E-mail enables you to target specific customer markets to increase your return on investment (ROI) and generate positive word of mouth that can spread for free worldwide online.

E-mail is not as "cool" as blogs or social networks are today (see Parts 3 and 4), but it is still the workhorse of online marketing. In fact, 69 percent of adults cite e-mail as their primary method of receiving information online.[2] In other words, **the chance that a potential customer is visiting your web site or blog today is dwarfed by the likelihood that she is checking her e-mail.**

So what should you do? Distributed engagement theory says that you should go where the customers are! Extending your product presence by expanding your e-mail marketing is a critical first step in a successful *e-Riches 2.0* distributed engagement marketing strategy.

Publish "Noozles"

The number one opportunity available to you as an online marketer is to exploit the e-mail list that you build.

(The phrase "free promotional e-mail newsletters" is an inconvenient mouthful. So I generally refer to them in my own shorthand as "noozles.")

Regular publishing of noozles is the key to your online marketing success. Especially in today's double opt-in world, the only people on your newsletter list will be people who are actually interested in your product. If you do not use e-mail to reach out and touch them regularly, you are missing a major revenue opportunity.

This approach is based on my simple philosophy that "the easiest customer to sell to is one who has purchased from you before."

Unfortunately, e-mail can be hard work. E-mail newsletters need to be written and published consistently, so their publishing and production is often seen as a distraction instead of being recognized as the most important tool in the modern marketer's toolbox. Responsibility for producing e-mail newsletters often falls in a "gray area"—usually somewhere between the marketers (who are usually more interested in new marketing campaigns, pretty visuals, and ever-cooler web sites with fancier technologies) and operational executives or entrepreneurs (who are busy managing their traditional business or engaging with live customers). *But none of these are good enough excuses to keep you from publishing!*

What E-Mail Publishing Offers to Twenty-First-Century Marketers

Here are some of the many advantages of using e-mail to promote your products.

1. It's inexpensive—there are no printing or postage costs.

2. You get immediate distribution—there's no waiting for the postman to pick it up or deliver it.

3. It has worldwide reach.

4. Customers are self-selected—customers that deliberately ask to hear your marketing messages are likely to be highly profitable.

5. It's targeted—you can segment your lists to increase conversion.

6. It's trackable—you can tell who opened your mail and what they clicked on.

7. It can be automated—you can create noozles in advance and schedule them for automatic delivery later.

8. Easy forwarding and word of mouth allow for explosive viral potential.

9. Audience feedback and participation help to create greater loyalty and more content, too.

The result is wider, cheaper, faster, more targeted, more flexible, and greater reach potential for any marketing communications that you publish by e-mail than was ever possible with traditional print, broadcast, direct mail, or other twentieth-century marketing tactics.

If you want to succeed at distributed engagement marketing, you need to take advantage of e-mail to successfully "distribute" and "engage" your customers. In other words, you should now consider yourself to be in the direct-mail business, even if you never were before.

If you're still not convinced that e-mail newsletters need to be at the heart of your marketing strategy, here is some additional insight as to why an e-mail list is critical to your long-term success.

The Death of SEO

Search engine optimization (SEO) is currently a hotter topic in online marketing than e-mail. E-mail is often seen as "old news." But in addition to e-mail's wide reach and influence today, I believe that the future of marketing is more about e-mail than it is about SEO. In fact, now is the time to focus on developing your publishing skills because SEO may soon be out of your reach.

Search engine optimization is becoming increasingly competitive and expensive, with little end in sight. As "new media" are increasingly becoming just "media" because the media conglomerates continue to take over Web-based news, video, and magazine-type start-ups, SEO is increasingly becoming a game for the big boys, too. This means that small companies and individual entrepreneurs are likely to get priced out of the SEO market in coming years.

Here's why: Companies that have succeeded in achieving a high search engine ranking today will continue to reinvest their profits to maintain their high rankings for valuable keywords. This investment will create new web sites, new software, new training courses, and new technologies specifically designed to attract top search engine results. This is already creating a "new establishment" of online vendors that dominate the search engine rankings for valuable keywords clustered around each target market.

Because humans have limited attention spans and aren't likely to ever click through to the third, fourth, or fiftieth page of search engine listings, those firms that control the first page of results with their top-ranked sites will be difficult to unseat.

This is why you need to start collecting e-mail addresses and publishing noozles *now*. You need to establish and grow your lists today so that you can continue to compete online as SEO becomes harder and more expensive.

Without an active e-mail list full of your company's fans, you will be stuck with either increasingly expensive pay-per-click advertising or word of mouth as your main online marketing tool. Word of mouth is expensive to start if you don't have a list to begin with—but if you start building an e-mail list now, you will soon have it available for marketing.

E-MAIL MARKETING CASE STUDY:
TIM CARTER, ASKTHEBUILDER.COM

Tim Carter runs the home improvement advice web site AsktheBuilder.com. Based on Tim's 20 years of experience as a master contractor, master plumber, and master roof cutter, AsktheBuilder.com offers detailed advice to anyone looking for help with home improvement or remodeling projects. The site offers thousands of pages of information and videos about everything from air conditioning to insulation to plumbing to windows.

This is an advertising-based business model because Tim sells ads around the content that he creates. He's been successful at this, building it from nothing in 1995 to more than $1 million per year today. With only 1.5 employees and no storefront or inventory, AsktheBuilder.com is so profitable that Tim has recently relocated from Cincinnati, Ohio, to a 90-acre woodland in New Hampshire, where he is building a custom home for himself and his wife.

Tim is a big fan of e-mail marketing. He uses e-mail to drive people back to his content-rich web site, where they can also see and click on the advertisements that make him money.

If you think that your business or products are too commonplace or not exciting enough to be worthy of a regularly published e-mail newsletter, here's proof that you are wrong. Here's the table of contents from a typical AsktheBuilder.com noozle:

▲ Granite Countertops and Radon

▲ Composite Decking Announcement

▲ Septic Tank Information

▲ The Stain Solver Warehouse Story

▲ Sandstone and Slate Flooring DVD

▲ Latest Columns and Video

This practical and informative information has helped his e-mail lists reach more than 40,000 subscribers. They are also growing rapidly (adding more than 200 new readers daily when I last spoke with him).

The key to AsktheBuilder.com's e-mail marketing success is the relationship that Tim builds with his subscribers. Building upon this relationship is what leads to increased revenues.

As Tim puts it, "When someone comes to your web site and you convince them to trust you and they sign up for your newsletter, they want to hear more from you. Give them what they expect, and some will become fans. Some will even become zealots for your brand. Then when you give them a call to action in an e-mail, of course they'll buy it from you, too."

He also strives to keep the feeling of a personal dialogue between him and his readers. For example, he constantly asks his list, "What projects are you working on?" or "What would you like to hear more about?" His one full-time employee is dedicated to answering every incoming e-mail request that he receives. This combination of accessibility and expertise creates a unique value proposition for Tim's readers.

He suggests that today's e-mail newsletter is rapidly "taking the place of the traditional handwritten note from a friend. Most of the Web is so impersonal—it's a cocoon of technology. An e-mail newsletter is a chance for you to share a little bit of your life with people who have asked to hear from you."

Tim's success shows that any type of content, even the long-established technologies of home improvement, can be used to create noozles that are valuable to their readers. By mixing solutions to readers' problems with a personal approach, AsktheBuilder.com has a large, loyal, and growing audience.

(See more about AsktheBuilder.com's e-mail strategies in the discussion of autoresponders in Chapter 7.)

How Can You Profit from the E-Mail Publishing Revolution?

As usual, I have several straightforward and cost-effective strategies for you to follow to get started. These basic steps will help to ensure that your marketing outreach begins to take better advantage of the power of e-mail to make you more money.

Here are my recommended steps:

1. Collect e-mail addresses.

2. Decide what to write.

3. Write it well.

4. Start publishing regularly.

Now we'll walk through these steps together. (These basics are followed by more advanced techniques, too.)

The Importance of Collecting E-Mail Addresses

The very, very first thing you should do as soon as you put up a web site is install an e-mail collector.

If you have a web site up and you're not collecting e-mail addresses right now, put down this book and call your Webmaster.

I'm not kidding. Collecting e-mail addresses is by far the most important opportunity for you as an online marketer.

#1 Most Common Web Site Mistake:
Not Collecting E-Mail Addresses!

You need to start collecting e-mail addresses immediately. E-mail is your most cost-effective marketing tool, and you need to start building your customer e-mail list ASAP. Getting started sooner rather than later is critical—you'd rather have your mailing list grow with the Web than try to catch up.

Even if you don't plan to begin publishing e-mail newsletters anytime soon, you should install e-mail collector forms or links to capture the contact info of as many people as possible right from the start. That way, when you are ready to start publicizing your site or your products, you should have at least a small base of subscribers ready and interested in receiving your publicity.

Then the classic network effect of "they tell two friends and they tell two friends and they tell two friends" can kick in. Even without being a mathematics wizard, you can see that the larger your initial e-mail list is to start, the more likely it is that the results will be amplified through online word of mouth initiated by your publishing of attractive e-mail content to your list.

It's also much easier to get business from people who have already bought from you than to attract and convince new customers. If you can continue to keep in contact so cheaply using e-mail, why not do it?

What to Write About:
Top 10 (Plus 1) Easy Noozle Content Concepts
Many marketers overestimate the difficulty of creating interesting content for noozles.

Here are some practical suggestions to make your noozle publishing a consistent and successful routine. People like e-mails to be brief anyway, so just a few sentences on any of the following topics can quickly create a good noozle article.

(Remember, you're not looking to win a Pulitzer Prize here—the point is to be interesting enough to get people to open your e-mails and keep your products in customers' minds!)

1. Monthly updates on your new products and services

2. Regular updates of news from your industry

3. Deal or discount of the week/month/quarter

4. Profiles of or collections of testimonials from happy customers

5. Photographs of recently completed jobs or happy customers

6. Pricing comparison of your services or products versus competitors'

7. Questions from customers answered by your executives

8. Announcement of events at which your company's executives are appearing

9. Birthdays of the month for famous people, industry celebrities, and your customers

10. A free or discounted offer for subscribers to forward to friends

11. Coverage of charity activities by your employees or customers

The best of these tips are 2, 7, and especially 10.
Why?

Because those approaches offer something that is of value to the reader—not just your self-promotions. You'll build a more loyal audience and more of your e-mails will get opened if you use this kind of a "soft sell" approach.

- -

SIX BONUS E-RICHES TIPS
FOR CREATING NOOZLES

1. Jokes get read. *Entertainment content can help ensure that your recipients actually read your e-mails. So include a joke, an inspiring or entertaining quotation, a link to a funny video, or some other entertainment item at the bottom of each noozle.*

For example, Joan Stewart's free Publicity Hound noozle (which you can learn more about at www.publicityhoundreview.com if you'd like to learn more about public relations) always ends with a dog joke. Even on my busiest days when I'm too pressed for time to read the whole e-mail, I rarely delete Joan's noozles. I almost always at least open and scroll to the bottom of her e-mails for a quick chuckle. This means that I see at least some of her noozle's content and product offers every issue.

2. Use my Top 10 Easy Noozle Content Concepts list repeatedly. *Writing a short article on each of those themes will give you enough material for many noozles. Then, when it's time for more, just start at the top of the list again. You'll be surprised at how much new content you can easily create.*

3. Let others contribute. *You don't have to write all the content by yourself. Try inviting coworkers, customers, or industry analysts to contribute, too. It takes work to coordinate contributors, but it takes a lot less work than writing all the material yourself—plus it freshens up the content to have different "voices" and points of view.*

4. Find content online in article banks. *See Chapter 16 for the discussion of these article collection services. These web sites collect articles from experts worldwide and offer them for free republication. You can find articles on almost any topic for use in your noozles.*

5. Don't put ads in your noozles. *Your noozle IS an ad. It should be structured to attract traffic to your web site and upsell readers into engagement and purchases of your products. If you can make more money from ads than from selling your own products, then kill the products and focus on ads instead. A split focus rarely leads to success.*

6. Use these same strategies for your blog. *Publishing a blog is a similar exercise in content creation, so you can use these same techniques as a blogger, too.*

Write It Well: 10 Steps to Better E-Mail Copywriting

Writing for the Web has its own opportunities and challenges, and this is equally true for your e-mail communications. Here are my guidelines to help ensure that your e-mail marketing efforts are rewarded by customer attention, subscription, and sales conversion.

(There is much more discussion of effective copywriting in the forums at ScottFox.com.)

1. *Focus on the subject line.* The subject line is the key. As an active e-mail recipient yourself, you know that the subject line is the most visible (often the only) attribute of an e-mail that a reader uses to make the all-important "open" versus "delete" decision. *The e-mail's subject line is the hook that you need to bait in order to catch the fish.*

E-mail open rates have been dropping for years as more marketers compete for attention in your inbox. E-mail company AWeber says that only 29.7 percent of marketing e-mails were opened in 2007, and that this dropped to 13.6 percent by April 2008. Of course, these are average rates that include many very big lists that are full of stale addresses, but these numbers prove that your subject line must be specific, catchy, and compelling enough to convince the recipient to click on it. Without that opening click, the rest of your clever marketing message will never be seen.

2. *Personalize.* Dale Carnegie (author of *How to Win Friends & Influence People*) said, "Remember that a person's name is to that person the sweetest and most important sound in any language." There's no better place to take advantage of this than in an e-mail marketing message's subject line and introductory paragraph. This is why so many e-mail sign-up forms that you find on the Web require a subscriber's first name as the only other information submission in addition to the e-mail address.

Those marketers know that pretending to be on a first-name basis with a reader is a great way to catch that reader's attention and increase the open rate.

Tom Kulzer, CEO of AWeber, stated on his blog that newsletters sent with subject-line personalization using the subscriber's first name generate an average 40.9 percent open rate, while e-mails without personalization of any type in the subject line generated average open rates of only 28.9 percent.

Most e-mail management programs today will help you automate the insertion of personalization fields, so that you don't have to worry about doing this by hand for a large list.

(Of course, too much personalization can be creepy. As technology continues to advance, we are all receiving increasingly targeted and personalized marketing messages daily. Be careful that you don't overpersonalize your marketing messages—you don't want to come on like Big Brother to your best prospects.)

3. *Pull them in.* Once you have enticed the customer into opening your e-mail, you need to engage her. There are lots of ways to do this, including educating, exciting, outraging, titillating, and even saddening your audience. All of these approaches can be summarized by saying that you need to be entertaining. If your introduction doesn't get people interested, they aren't going to read the rest of the e-mail.

4. *Don't bury the lead.* A classic maxim in the news business, this instruction applies well to e-mail copywriting, too. It simply means that you need to get to the point as quickly as possible. Instead of saying A + B + C, and therefore D, you need to say D! right up front to get the reader's attention. Then you can use the body of the e-mail to explain the supporting arguments A, B, and C that make D such a good offer for that customer.

5. *Promote benefits, not features.* Don't launch into a sales pitch. Your e-mails should focus on the benefits to the reader, not the features of your product. This is basic copywriting strategy—people are only truly interested in "what's in it for me?" Don't waste their time (and yours) talking about the features of your product; tell them how it can make their lives better. Position your products (and the noozle itself) as the solution to their problems.

6. *Be specific.* Avoid vague language and generic-sounding offers. Today everyone is too busy, and there is far too much spam e-mail, for anyone to waste her time figuring out what you meant to say. The more specific you are in your subject line and in the details of your offer, the more quickly and positively customers will react.

7. *Offer incentives.* Bribery works. If you can afford to offer incentives to encourage the behavior you desire, by all means do it. This can be discounts, "forward to a friend" bonuses, or free downloads.

(See Chapter 17 for my interview with Bill Jelen, who has built his whole business by giving away free samples of his products by e-mail.)

8. *Propose a clear call to action.* Once you have succeeded in attracting and engaging your readers, you need to give them specific direction. A clear call to action is a requirement. It's amazing to me the number of e-mails I receive that lack this. Be sure you put a prominent "buy here" button or link several times in every issue.

9. *Keep it short (or very long).* My favorite e-mails—and probably yours, too—are the short ones. Strive to be concise yourself and you'll be rewarded with much higher open rates from readers who know that you won't waste their time.

You can also try just using "teaser text" as the body of your e-mail. Such teaser text is usually a summary of the first few lines of a longer article, plus a link back to your web site. This approach is needed if you really want to get the reader out of her e-mail inbox and onto your web site to generate page views, but it is obviously risky because the teaser text alone may not be enough to fully engage the reader into clicking.

Unfortunately, many topics require lengthy discussion to explain or convince. This is why you see very long "sales letter" type e-mails in your inbox and similar Web pages all over the Internet. Sometimes length is necessary to close the sale. The appropriate length is up to you, but always be aware of the value of your readers' time and edit accordingly.

P.S. Yes, there are 10 steps here! *Use the "postscript"—what most of us call the "p.s."—at the end of the e-mail.* Did you know that the p.s. is the second most read part of any letter? Use this to your advantage to reinforce your call to action.

Review these e-mail copywriting guidelines and take them to heart every time you publish. The more you use them, the easier they will become for you to follow. Consistently implementing them effectively will reward you with higher open rates, clickthroughs, and sales.

How to Publish E-Mail Newsletters

Writing a marketing noozle is really not much different from writing a few quick e-mails.

You want to determine how many articles to include in each issue. Then you (or a contributor) write the articles. Thinking of noozles as collections of small articles instead of the larger whole that you need to produce can make the publishing chore less daunting. Compiling those articles into a consistent, unified format is what creates your noozle.

The easiest way to do this is to use an e-mail newsletter template. You can copy and paste your articles into the appropriate boxes of the template. The reason to use a template is that it will apply formatting to your text. The headlines, subtitles, font styles and sizes, and appropriate colors are all determined by a good template so that you don't need to worry about them. That's important so that you can focus on writing good articles instead of having to worry about graphic design, too.

Figure 3–1 shows a screenshot of an e-mail template from the Constant Contact e-mail management service.

The editing tools available are similar to those in Microsoft Word or Outlook. So, by typing (or copying and pasting) your articles into appropriate boxes, then adding your company logo to the top of the template and hitting "save," you can quickly produce a nicely formatted noozle.

From: E-Riches Reader <info@scottfox.com>
Subject: News from Your Online Business
Reply: info@scottfox.com

News from Your Online Business
Newsletter Subtitle

In This Issue	Issue: #	Month/Year

ARTICLE HEADLINE

Dear Scott,

Quick Links

Register Now
News
Related Topics
More On Us

Your introduction sets the tone for your newsletter and encourages the recipient to read further. Your style may be warm and casual, or technical and no-nonsense depending on your audience.

Join Our List

Join Our Mailing List!

ARTICLE HEADLINE

Article Subheading

Know your target audience. Who are your most important customers, clients or prospects, and why? Know what is important to them and address their needs in your newsletter each month. Include a photo to make your newsletter even more appealing.

YOUR IMAGE HERE
Click to change
in edit mode.

100 x 100
pixels

Insert a "read on" link at the bottom of your article to drive traffic to your website. Links are tracked, allowing you to see which articles create the most interest for your readers.

Use this area to provide your subscribers information about your organization.

Sincerely,

Your Super New Online Business

**Save
25%**

If you are using a special coupon or promo code, include it here. Or, indicate if the coupon must be printed and presented in person. Is the coupon transferable? If so, encourage recipients to share the offer with friends and family to maximize the viral effect of the coupon. Add a "Register Now" link to your website with more information.

Offer Expires: Enter Expiration Date here

Forward this email to your friends!

✉ **SafeUnsubscribe®**
This email was sent to info@artfaircalendar.com by info@scottfox.com.
Update Profile/Email Address | Instant removal with SafeUnsubscribe™ | Privacy Policy.

Email Marketing by

Constant Contact®
TRY IT FREE

Your New Online Business | 12368 Autumn Lane | Santa Monica | CA | 90021

FIGURE 3–1.

If you are using an e-mail management service, it will usually have dozens of templates like these from which to choose. An easy way to get started is to select one that offers colors similar to those of your company logo or web site.

You can also buy preformatted templates online or commission your own designers or tech team to create a custom layout for your repeated use.

Additional items to pay attention to when producing an e-mail newsletter:

1. The subject line of your e-mail is the number one factor in determining the open rate for e-mails.

2. Your "To" and "From" fields are also critical: Be sure to set up your account so that the "from" address/name is how you want to be represented and doesn't look like spam. For example, your e-mail should appear in my inbox as coming from "John Smith, the best plumber in Kansas City" or "John's Plumbing, Inc.," not as coming just from "John." It's especially distracting and spamlike if the from field shows just your first name and all in lowercase, like this: "john."

3. Be sure to produce a text-only version of your noozles, too. Many people read much of their e-mail on mobile devices like BlackBerries, which don't display HTML formatting or images well, if they display them at all.

E-Mail Publishing Frequency

The "right" publishing frequency is different for every business. It is dependent on a combination of your resources, the complexity of your newsletter content, subscriber expectations, and many other factors. Regardless, you should try to reach out to touch your customers via e-mail at least once a month as a general rule of thumb.

You can also publish "special edition" noozles when you have "breaking news" that highlights specific newsworthy items *that are of interest to the audience* (not just interesting to you). This is a great way to get extra attention for special product offers, for example.

The other reason to put your noozle list to work frequently is that if you don't use it regularly, the e-mail addresses it contains will go "stale." People change e-mail addresses much more frequently than they do postal addresses.

If you sit on your e-mail list without using it for more than a year, you are likely to find that 30 percent or more of its addresses have become undeliverable or are no longer used.

Those are customers who asked you for more information, and you have failed them by not following up. That's not a technique I recommend for growing your revenues.

WHAT'S THE BEST DAY OF THE WEEK TO SEND YOUR E-MAILS?

Controversy rages over this point. Experts from all sides claim that different days of the week are "best" to attract the attention (and clickthroughs) of e-mail subscribers.

There is no one best answer, however. The best day and time to send e-mails depends on the type of business you are marketing.

For example, e-mails offering business info to professionals are usually best sent on Tuesdays. This is the day when the most work gets done in the corporate world, so if your business targets those folks with professional services, Tuesday may be best for you.

For my own e-mails, subscribers seem most receptive later in the week or on the weekend. This is because many of my readers are interested in starting their own businesses on the side, so Thursdays and even Sundays work well.

The best way to find out what your audience prefers is to test. Try splitting your list into parts. Send half of your noozles on Tuesday and half on Saturday. Repeat using the other days of the week as well. Careful analysis of open rates and clickthroughs will help you decide which day of the week is best for your business to send out its e-mails.

This same approach applies to determining the best time of day to send your e-mails (midnight, early morning, lunchtime, and so on).

E-MAIL MARKETING CASE STUDY:
CINDY BROWN OF BOSTONDUCKTOURS.COM

You don't have to run an e-commerce business to profit from many of the strategies in this book. The Internet can help you grow your business even if you have a minimal Web presence.

In fact, one of the major waves of opportunity about to hit the world of e-commerce is the arrival of many brick-and-mortar businesses that have so far had little presence on the Web.

Here's an example of a "real-world" business that finds itself increasingly involved with Internet marketing.

BostonDuckTours.com is a Boston-based tour company. Founded in 1994, the company has grown from 4 employees to over 100. Its unique specialty is providing tours of Boston's historic sites in restored military amphibious landing craft from World War II. (These vehicles were code-named "DUKW" and are commonly called "ducks.") In 2008, the company served more than 600,000 tourists with its unique presentation of Boston's sights. This is a company that is about as far offline as you can get!

The company's general manager, Cindy Brown, told me about its Web strategy. The company's first web site was started in 1997—but mostly as an afterthought. At first the company struggled with how best to use the Web. Its site was even down for more than a month in 2001 without anyone fixing it.

In 2000, the company added the ability to sell its tour tickets online. Today, Cindy estimates that 40 percent of the company's business is affected by the Web and approximately 30 percent of its tickets are sold online.

Replacing its postal postcards with an e-mail management service called Constant Contact was a big step forward for Boston Duck Tours. The decreased costs, increased immediacy, and professional presentation offered by e-mailing customers have been a big help to the company's business. Today the company has to print brochures only for on-site distribution at hotels and other tourist spots or for use in group gift bag promotions.

Even though it is not an online company, Boston Duck Tours uses e-mail marketing in three ways:

1. *Business-to-consumer e-mail marketing.* The company regularly sends noozles offering specials like holiday deals, especially to increase sales during slow periods, such as the late fall. With a list of more than 125,000 interested tourists, this can obviously generate a lot of sales.

2. *Business-to-business e-mail marketing.* Boston Duck Tours has almost 4,000 industry subscribers, segmented into various groups, such as travel group leaders and tour operators. These audiences receive different types of e-mails on different schedules as determined by the Boston Duck Tours marketing team. Because of these e-mail tools, the company now targets customers better than its competitors, and this has contributed significantly to the company's growth.

3. *Employee e-mail communications.* A use of the e-mailing system that surprised me was the company's use of e-mail for internal employee communications, too. Because the company has more than 100 employees spread across various locations (many of whom rarely visit the head office), e-mail has proved to be a useful tool to ensure that everyone in the company receives consistent information about tour updates, HR issues, holidays, staff changes, and other such matters.

Choosing an E-Mail Publishing Vendor

There are many competing services available to help you collect e-mail addresses and manage their subscriptions. The key functionality that you need includes:

▲ Reliable mass e-mail sending with high delivery rates

▲ Easy-to-install e-mail collector code for your web site

▲ Supporting services that allow your subscribers to subscribe and unsubscribe easily 24/7 without your involvement

Additional services that can be important include:

▲ Customizable design templates to help you make your e-mails look attractive and match your branding.

▲ Management of multiple lists targeting different segments of your audience.

▲ Web-based reporting that shows frequently updated details of your subscribers' activity, including open rates, click-throughs, and subscribe/unsubscribe requests.

▲ *Bonus:* Autoresponders—for easy follow-up with subscribers, it can be very helpful to automate more follow-up messages or offer series such as tutorials or tips. (More on autoresponders soon!)

Spam Filters and Deliverability

A key criterion for evaluating any e-mail service provider for your business is its deliverability rate. *Deliverability* measures the percentage of e-mail messages sent by a service that are successfully received by subscribers.

While this sounds like an easy and obvious requirement for an e-mail service, the vast quantities of spam e-mail make it difficult to be certain that every e-mail you send actually reaches your subscribers.

E-mail delivery problems are largely the result of the spam filters that are now imposed at several levels of the e-mail deliverability chain. E-mails that you send may be blocked or filtered by your own Internet service provider when you send them, blocked or filtered as they travel across the network, blocked or filtered again when they reach your subscriber's Internet service provider, blocked or filtered again when they reach the firewall that guards the network that your subscriber uses, and then blocked or filtered once again when the e-mail is actually downloaded to your subscriber's mail program. And there may be additional settings in your subscriber's e-mail inbox (or Web-based service like Gmail or Yahoo mail) that prevent the delivery or proper display of your e-mail there.

All of this blocking and filtering is the Internet software industry's attempt to reduce unwanted e-mail spam. Unfortunately, all these hurdles mean that only 75 percent of the e-mail that is sent is generally received by the intended recipients—even if the e-mail is legitimate and has been requested by the subscriber.[3] In fact, 16 percent of permission-based e-mails are delivered directly to the user's junk or bulk folder.[4]

This issue of deliverability is one of the major reasons I do not recommend that you try to operate your own e-mail list or run your own e-mail server. For a few dollars per month, you can subscribe to one of the services I recommend instead and let its trained technology personnel battle spam filters for you.

Unless you have a tech support team with specialized expertise in e-mail "white listing" and deliverability, bulk e-mail management and sending is much better outsourced.

Double Opt-In Verification

If you have subscribed to any e-mail newsletter lately, you have probably gone through a double opt-in process yourself. This is simply the process where you provide your e-mail address to the online publisher at its web site and later receive a confirmation e-mail. You must click on the confirmation link in the e-mail before you will receive any of the publisher's noozles. This is done to verify that you are a real person and not some sort of software bot trying to compromise the publisher's e-mailing system.

Unfortunately, this "best practice" of double opt-in is terrible for e-mail sign-up conversion rates. Many users never click on the link in the confirmation e-mail to complete their subscription opt-in. Nevertheless, double opt-in is increasingly the standard for online marketing. This is because it helps reduce spam, increases compliance with the federal CAN-SPAM Act of 2003, and helps consumers better manage the volume of e-mail that they receive.

Oh, well.

On the positive side, double opt-in does yield more strongly motivated subscribers because they have gone through multiple steps to ensure that they get to receive your e-mails.

Testing Your E-Mails

You should test your e-mail campaigns regularly before sending them out. You'll want to try sending your noozles to people who have e-mail accounts with different service providers (like AOL, EarthLink, corporate accounts, international accounts, and so on) to make sure that they can receive the e-mails that your service is sending.

When your e-mails are received, you'll want to check their appearance upon arrival. You should view your e-mails to make sure that they look the way you intended them to in different e-mail programs. For example, try Microsoft Outlook, Gmail, AOL, and Mac clients such as Entourage. You might even try mobile e-mail platforms to ensure that your marketing messages are conveying what you intended and appearing the way you intended.

Unfortunately, standards for e-mail delivery and display are still far from settled, especially with the arrival of mobile platforms, so you need to repeat this step regularly.

Collect E-Mail Addresses Anyway

Even if you don't have *any* plans to *ever* publish a noozle, you should still collect e-mail addresses.

Why? Because you can use them to make money by promoting other people's products.

You can e-mail information on related services or use affiliate ads for well-known products, as discussed in Chapter 22. You'll receive a commission on each sale generated. There are many marketers online who make a profitable full-time business simply out of promoting other people's products this way.

Too much of this, especially if the offers are poorly matched to your audience, will alienate your subscribers. But if you choose offers that will appeal to your audience, readers can actually see such product e-mails as a service. This is a "service" that can keep your brand in customers' minds, keep your e-mail list fresh (and growing), and make you money, too.

Remember—it's spam only if they're not interested!

E-Mail Delivery System Vendor Recommendations

This leaves you with three types of e-mail list management and publishing services.

1. *Self-hosted.* You can install software on your own PC or servers to send your mass mailings and to manage the subscribe/unsubscribe dialogues with customers.

Unless you are both technically qualified and have plenty of extra free time to spend on setting up the e-mail servers, ensuring deliverability to ISPs worldwide, and constantly managing customer subscribe/unsubscribe requests, I am certain that your time will be better spent on projects with higher ROI—like writing compelling noozle content that attracts more sales.

Simply put, the services available online today are simply too good and too affordable to ignore.

2. *Web-based custom newsletter e-mail management services.* Many companies today offer fully featured e-mail management services that handle the production of noozles, administration of subscribers, and the distribution of your newsletters for you through a Web browser interface. These are cost-effective and take most of the headache out of publishing noozles. (This was the approach recommended in Chapter 21, "Small Budget Marketing Secrets," of my book *Internet Riches*.)

Leading vendors for online e-mail management and publishing include:

Constant Contact: http://www.constantcontact.com

Vertical Response: http://www.verticalresponse.com

Exact Target: http://www.exacttarget.com

iContact: http://www.icontact.com

NetAtlantic: http://www.netatlantic.com

3. *Feed-driven e-mailers.* Driven by the rise in the popularity of blogging and feeds, a new type of e-mail delivery service has emerged since I wrote *Internet Riches.* This is e-mail delivery services powered by RSS. This is my recommended strategy today. I'll explain what RSS is in the next chapter, and my feed-driven e-mail services vendor recommendations follow in Chapter 5.

4

. . .

RSS FEEDS

THE REVOLUTION IS

BEING SYNDICATED

"**REALLY SIMPLE** Syndication" is a revolution that is making the distribution of information easier than ever before. Things have changed since the twentieth century, when a newspaper article, a TV broadcast, or a book was defined as much by its format as by its content. Today RSS extracts underlying information (usually a text-based article) and allows it to be easily reformatted and shared in other formats and on other delivery platforms. The spread of RSS and similar cross-platform "feeds" is even harmonizing the quagmire of compatibility problems presented by PC vs. Mac, Internet Explorer vs. Firefox vs. Safari vs. Chrome Web browsers, and different mobile devices.

Simply put, feeds like RSS take any information that has been posted online and package it for automatic redistribution. Posts that you write on a blog, MP3 recordings of your band that you post online, a string of business e-mails (or love letters), links to photos from your vacation, new product updates, or any similar series of digital information can be packaged and sequentially delivered to subscribers using RSS feeds.

You may be using RSS without even knowing it. For example, on any news-oriented web page, you usually see regularly updated headlines. On NYTimes.com, they are probably selected by a *New York Times* editor. But on your My Yahoo page, you choose from which sources you want information displayed. And on Facebook, you automatically receive feeds of what your friends are doing. In all these cases, the delivery of that information is probably based on a feed similar to RSS. RSS grabs information posted in one place and delivers it to other platforms, web pages, and devices in whatever formats and lengths are required by that platform.

Many people today collect RSS feeds from all their favorite news sites and blogs and feed them into a Web browser–based "news aggregator" or "blog reader" program. An increasing number of people (especially early adopters) use these programs to read content online instead of receiving it in their e-mail inboxes. This creates a centralized custom news source where they can quickly and efficiently keep up with the latest on their favorite topics. Popular browser-based RSS readers include My Yahoo, Bloglines, Google Reader, and Netvibes.

Feeds: The Magic of Really Simple Syndication

The magic of RSS is that it allows you to publish your content online just once. RSS lets your content easily "feed" into other services, like Facebook and other social networks, because it uncouples your information from the format in which it was created. Then users can consume the content (read, listen, or watch) wherever and whenever they wish and on whatever device they request its delivery to.

Because feeds help make it more convenient for users to consume content, you can understand the rapid increase in the use of feeds for spreading information around. Today, you need to offer RSS feeds of any regularly updated content you produce so that it can reach the widest audience. Posting your content (or at least summaries, teasers, and introductions of the content) to a blog will automatically create an RSS feed that you can offer to your readers for free.

Where can you create an RSS feed for yourself? Easy; just start a blog (see Part 4). Most blog software automatically packages any content posted into a feed.

Any public blog's feed is automatically available to the many users of blog readers (software that collects posts from different blogs into an inbox-type interface for easy browsing). The folks who use this technology are usually early adopters and often are bloggers themselves, so they are well worth serving. To reach the even wider audience of e-mail readers, you can also use an RSS feed to automatically produce e-mail noozles from your blog articles, as detailed below.

YOUR ATTENTION, PLEASE!

Using feed-based e-mail noozle services can cut your noozle production time in half (or double your output). Regular publishing of noozles is the cheapest and most cost-effective way to monetize your customer base, so this section has significant revenue upside.

Please pay extra attention here and check ScottFox.com for updates.

Techie, Web 2.0 people: I know that you love your RSS feed readers. But don't ignore the e-mail market—convenience rules! You want to engage with customers anywhere, any way that they want. Unfortunately, longtime bloggers and social media early adopters are so accustomed to RSS that they use blog readers all the time, often neglecting e-mail and Web browsing entirely for reading blogs.

If you're smart, you'll cater to both audiences. You can offer your content via an RSS feed for your audience members who read using blog readers, and also use that feed to create

---

e-mail noozles automatically for your more traditional e-mail-reading customers.

What Do RSS Feeds Have to Do with E-Mail?

RSS is where the Web 1.0 online marketing of e-mail crosses into Web 2.0. You can use an RSS feed to create and send your noozles automatically. Simply by directing your feed into a feed-driven e-mail system, you can create an e-mail newsletter from any content you post on a blog. For example, if you're posting on your blog once each week, any modern blog software will automatically offer those posts in an RSS feed format. You can take the URL for the feed and use it to automatically turn your blog posts into e-mail newsletters that are then sent out to your subscriber list. Automatically!

This is awesome because it frees you from having to produce noozles separately. You can focus on producing high-quality content instead of copying and pasting and formatting back and forth between content posted on your web site or blog and whatever noozle publishing system you are using.

5

. . .

FEED-BASED E-MAIL SERVICES
CUT YOUR PRODUCTION
TIME IN HALF

ALERT! The following is a discussion of a breakthrough type of service that you need to know about! If you're not clear on what "feed-based" means here, please review Chapter 4 where I define and discuss RSS feeds.

Feed-based e-mail newsletter services can automate the production and sending of your e-mail newsletters. By taking a Web 2.0 view of newsletter content as just another syndicate-able piece of content, these services can make publishing e-mail newsletters much easier.

Feed-based e-mail newsletter services take the posts from your blog and automatically insert them into an e-mail template that you can customize. You no longer have to retype or copy and paste your content into the e-mail template yourself, as you need to do to use the Web-based custom newsletter e-mail management services discussed earlier.

The systems will then *automatically* send out the resulting collection of your blog posts as an e-mail newsletter on whatever schedule (hourly, daily, weekly, etc.) meets your publishing needs.

The services even include subscriber address management tools. This means that they will manage the subscribe/unsubscribe function for you, much like the Web-based custom newsletter services discussed in Chapter 3.

Finally, these services also take responsibility for deliverability. This means that they use their own servers for the bulk mailing and also maintain the whitelisting/blacklisting spam filter optimization that we discussed in Chapter 3.

All of this means that you can post your content just once on a blog and the blog's RSS feed allows you to easily repurpose the content many times, including instant and automatic production and distribution of e-mail noozles to your entire mailing list.

Note: These services work only if you have a feed to feed to them. Most popular blog software will create a feed of your recent blog posts for you automatically, so this is not difficult, but it is a prerequisite for this strategy.

Conclusion: Feed-based e-mail services are an amazing timesaver and a significant breakthrough for any marketer smart enough to be using e-mail newsletters.

The Best Feed-Powered E-Mail Services

Here are the three leading providers of feed-based e-mail publishing services. Because of the tremendous utility offered by these services, there are sure to be new competitors entering the market soon, as well as improvements by the existing players (none of which are yet perfect). Be sure to check ScottFox.com for the latest updates and recommendations on the best vendors to help you market your business using these new tools.

ADSENSE FOR FEEDS (FORMERLY KNOWN AS FEEDBURNER)

Google offers an impressive suite of services to help you manage, promote, measure, and advertise in the distribution of your content by feeds.

This system was known as Feedburner, but is now part of Google's online advertising service called AdSense. It takes feeds in any format (e.g., RSS, Atom, and others) and attaches several services to them. By registering for a free account, you can "burn" the feed from your blog. This means submitting the feed from your blog into the AdSense for Feeds online system. It will reconfigure your feed and enable you to:

- ▲ Measure the number of subscribers to the feed and their activity levels.

- ▲ Offer the feed by e-mail instead of readable only in news aggregator RSS readers.

- ▲ Display on your web site a "chicklet" that shows how many subscribers your feed has.

- ▲ Even help you automatically insert money-making ads from Google Adsense if that's appropriate for you.

And did I mention that all this is free?

Google's purchase of Feedburner and its integration into AdSense suggests that the service will be around for a long time. Unfortunately, it also means that improvements to the service are slow to arrive and customer service is basically nonexistent. Luckily, the user interface is pretty logical, and it's difficult to complain too loudly about a free service.

The biggest objection I have to the service is that it will not allow you to import existing subscriber lists. This means that if you want to use AdSense for Feeds effectively as an e-mail publishing tool, you have several bad choices:

1. Start your own e-mail list from scratch by allowing users to register one by one (that's OK if you're new to e-mail marketing, but it's problematic for anyone with a preexisting list).

2. Manually type in and resubscribe all of the subscribers on your list (and subject them to another round of double opt-in verification).

3. Run two concurrent e-mail lists, one using your previous service and another using Feedburner. (I've tried this—it's a recipe for confusion among your customers.)

4. "Burn" your feed using the Feedburner tools in order to gain some of its many helpful reporting and optimization tools, but also run it through another provider in order to send out the e-mails and have full e-mail subscriber management capabilities available to you. (This is what I do and recommend.)

AdSense for Feeds' lack of subscriber list importing is a surprising and frustrating omission from an otherwise excellent service. Continued requests to the Google help desk have resulted in no assurances that this would be fixed anytime soon.

Unfortunately, there is also little customization of e-mail graphic templates in the system. You are limited to changing font sizes and colors and adding a logo. This is enough to roughly "brand" the e-mails as coming from your site, but there is no access to the underlying HTML or CSS, so you can't match your official branding or site look.

The other big problem with AdSense for Feeds is its limited scheduling options. The system just sweeps your blog each day to pick up any blog posts that were new in the last 24 hours, so it will send a noozle every day that you post on your blog. It can nicely target (within two-hour time blocks) what time each day you'd like your e-mails sent out, but they go out every day that you post, like it or not. This can be problematic if you are trying to create a weekly noozle or one that contains specific posts and omits others.

FEEDBLITZ

Feedblitz is another blog feed to e-mail publishing automation solution. As with Google's AdSense for Feeds, you can sign up for a free account and use the feed from your blog to power automatic distribution of your blog updates to an e-mail subscriber list.

Feedblitz goes beyond Google's service by offering the ability to import subscriber lists. It also includes:

▲ More customizable e-mail templates, including full HTML access so that you can match your web site branding

▲ Scheduling tools that allow you to package batches of your articles into a weekly or monthly "digest" or "best of" newsletter

▲ The ability to pick and choose which of your blog posts you want included in each newsletter instead of having a constant daily update of everything you post

▲ Lots of formatting capabilities and customization settings

▲ The ability to set sending to just once per week or "on demand"

▲ Subscriber import/export tools that can help you manage your e-mail contact list far better than in Feedburner

The other feature of Feedblitz that I really like is that you can offer subscriptions to multiple noozles on the same page. This allows you to cross-sell different lists at just the right moment, when a visitor is in a signing-up mood. A good way to get a new newsletter to attract its first subscribers is by including its sign-up opportunity on the same page as one of your more highly trafficked lists.

Feedblitz also has its own advertising network. So if you want to allow its ads to be displayed in your e-mail newsletters, the service can be free for you. If you want no ads or your own ads, the pricing runs from $1.49 to more than $600 per month, depending on how many subscribers you have on your list.

Cons of the Feedblitz system include:

▲ Very confusing web site user interfaces and menus

▲ Ugly sign-up and confirmation pages, full of distractions for the subscriber

▲ Difficult to read reporting

▲ Impossible to use demographics collecting

▲ Few customer service resources (although much better than Google's Adsense for Feeds)

I'm sure that Feedblitz will continue to improve its services, however, so it's definitely worth investigating. Visit www.Feedblitz Review.com for my latest review of the Feedblitz service.

AWEBER BLOG BROADCAST

The third blog feed to e-mail solution is AWeber.

AWeber is mostly known for its outstanding autoresponder service, which is profiled in Chapter 7. Here we're going to focus on the "blog broadcast" service that is included in an AWeber subscription. This blog broadcast service is similar to the services offered by Google's AdSense for Feeds and Feedblitz in that it allows a blog feed to be automatically packaged and distributed as a noozle. Automation of e-mail-related marketing is the company's specialty. (Its name, AWeber, is a contraction of Automated Web Assistant.)

The blog broadcast service is part of a larger suite of tools that offers a lot of functionality for good prices; however, the overall AWeber service is not free. Current pricing ranges from $19 per month (for up to 500 subscribers) to $150 per month (for lists of up to 25,000).

I think it is more than worth the money.

Like the other feed-driven e-mail services profiled here, the blog broadcast part of AWeber allows you to enter the URL of your blog's feed to automatically create and send out e-mail newsletters.

The service offers a variety of design templates that you can use to customize the look and feel of your noozles. This includes WYSIWYG editing and access to the underlying HTML, so you can fully customize the look to match your company branding or web site.

The site also is laid out logically and is fairly easy to use.

If you have any difficulties, the most impressive part of the AWeber service is its customer support. The company offers e-mail, live chat, and phone support at no charge (in addition to the standard FAQ and searchable database of questions and answers). Its reps are friendly and knowledgeable, too. This customer service is truly differentiating when compared to Google's complete lack of customer service and Feedblitz's sporadic support.

Reporting tools are available that track the percentage of your e-mails that get opened and the clicks that each link attracts. Using these reporting tools to identify your most responsive subscribers can help you create mailing list subsets that are optimized for profitability.

AWeber makes it easy to segment your subscribers into such lists, as well as split your subscribers into groups to test different designs, copywriting, and special offers, to uncover which approaches most improve your conversions and sales.

Lastly, AWeber offers several options for you to use to collect e-mail addresses from your subscribers. This includes standard text links and small forms with entry boxes. It also includes a very useful set of JavaScript codes that you can use to easily install fancier e-mail collection pop-ups and animated e-mail collection widgets on your site. (These tools alone are worth the monthly expense.)

Unfortunately, AWeber's Blog Broadcast system does have a few significant drawbacks:

The biggest of these drawbacks is that noozles produced by AWeber's Blog Broadcast tools do not include the formatting from your blog posts. The bolds, font sizes, colors, and spacing are lost when the posts are imported into AWeber. You can customize the e-mail template, and you can modify your post formatting by hand after they are imported into the Blog Broadcast tool, but the system does not import the formatting you already did on your blog when you originally wrote the post! This means that you are forced to choose between sending out plain text articles in customized templates (ugly!) or re-doing all the formatting you already did once on your blog post (twice the work, and this often doesn't work in my experience anyway).

In extensive correspondence with AWeber's CEO and Help Desk, I could not get them to see the difficulty that this presents to users. Hopefully by the time you read this, they will have realized that their competitors (Google and Feedblitz) both import blog post formatting just fine. Unless you are happy with plain text e-mails, being forced to reformat every imported blog post manually greatly reduces the appeal of this tool unfortunately.

The other complaints I have about AWeber's system are that its sign-ups are limited to one e-mail list at a time—Feedblitz's or Constant Contact's ability to offer multiple lists on one sign-up page is a great cross-selling tool. Also, you can't easily rearrange articles in your newsletters (as you can in Feedblitz) without manually cutting and pasting (which usually upsets the formatting of your template). Visit www.email-review.com for my updates to this review of the AWeber service.

■ ■ ■

All three of these services assume that you already have a reasonable level of technical ability, so their FAQ and Help sections are pretty minimal. AWeber backs up its system with superior customer service, though.

Blog feed-based e-mail noozle services are a big step forward for entrepreneurs because they can greatly increase your publishing productivity. As you can see, however, we are once again on the cutting-edge of new web tools bececause none of these providers yet offers a perfect solution. If Google's AdSense for Feeds would offer more customer service and list importing, if Feedblitz was easier to use, or if AWeber's Blog Broadcast didn't ignore imported blog post formatting, any of these services would be a real winner. Competitive market pressure (and repeated e-mails from me!) are likely to improve these services, so be sure to check ScottFox.com for updates.

Why Bother Sending Blog Posts by E-Mail?

In the "real world," most people have never heard of a blog reader, much less use one on a daily basis the way so many online marketers do today. You can't presume that everyone even knows how to subscribe to an RSS feed or use an RSS reader.

Even more importantly, you can't count on people to visit your site regularly—everyone (especially anyone with money to spend on your products) is too busy.

For example, I recently made a new acquaintance who runs a popular blog. I visited his site and liked his work, so I wanted to sign up to receive his many blog updates by e-mail. He had no e-mail sign-up available!

I was floored—this is an online marketing guru who is basically ignoring anyone who doesn't use an RSS reader.

Of course, when I e-mailed him about it, he said that he had "forgotten" about this when he recently redesigned the site. Maybe that's true, but it's a poor excuse.

The moral of this story: You need to make your content available in any format that *the customer* (not *you*) wants. (See my note about Scott Fox's Convenience Principle below.)

The bottom line?

None of the feed-driven e-mail newsletter services is perfect yet. But any small business that doesn't use them is *crazy*. They can greatly reduce your work load and simultaneously increase your contact with your best customers.

Because these services all have their own problems, there's likely to be continued development and competition among them. Please be sure to check ScottFox.com for updates on feed-based e-mail services before you get started using them because there may be new competitors or improvements that are important to your decisions.

SCOTT FOX'S CONVENIENCE PRINCIPLE

If it's not convenient, customers won't do it. It's your job to make it as easy as possible for customers to receive your information and make purchases from you.

My point?

Don't presume that all your customers use the Web the same way you do. To keep up with news, for example, many will use e-mail programs like Outlook, but many others today use RSS blog readers or mobile devices. You need to accommodate all of these preferences if you are going to maximize your online product presence.

A distributed engagement strategy (as discussed in Chapter 1) means making your content available as feeds (which is easily done by posting your articles into a blog) so that it is convenient for your audience to consume your updates wherever it wants to and in whatever format it prefers. The easier you make it for your customers, the more likely that they'll reward you with increased attention and sales.

E-MAIL PRODUCTION CASE STUDY: ME!

Here's how I've evolved my own noozle production process—hopefully you can benefit from the many time-saving tips my team has developed.

Like many small businesses, I started my newsletter mailings almost accidentally. I was simply e-mailing updates to friends, family, and colleagues from my desktop-based Microsoft Outlook program.

When *Internet Riches* was published, I began publishing more regularly. Readers from all over the world began e-mailing me questions, so I set up an account with Constant Contact. This enabled me to centralize the e-mail list management and provided design templates to make my e-mails look professional. That service also took care of the bulk mailing and was whitelisted with the many ISPs of my readers, so that my e-mails were not labeled as spam.

I found Constant Contact to be a reliable and useful tool. I especially liked how easy it is to set up multiple lists, segmenting customers and business contacts into different contact groups for appropriate mailings. For example, readers were a group, students who had attended my seminars at the Learning Annex were another group, and publishing industry contacts were still another. This enabled me to easily mail to all of them simultaneously or to pick and choose, depending on the message.

Once I started my blog, however, I found that I was spending a lot of time duplicating effort. I would write a post for the blog. Then I would also have to copy the post into Constant Contact for use in the newsletter (or at least part of it as a teaser). This required a lot of going back and forth and reformatting of material as I moved between the blog and the e-mail management system. Wasted effort really.

This explains why I was so pleased to discover the feed-driven e-mail systems that I'm recommending to you. They allow you to write your content just once (in your blog); the e-mail construction, formatting, and sending all follow automatically. Aaah . . . what a relief! This is much more efficient.

MY CURRENT RECOMMENDATION

Use a Feedburner (Google AdSense for Feeds) feed and run it through AWeber if you have the budget to pay AWeber's monthly fees. If not, try using a Google's AdSense for Feeds feed through Feedblitz's free (ad-supported) service.

This approach gets you the many useful services offered by Google's AdSense system, but also gives you the editing and template customization flexibility of AWeber (like autoresponders—see Chapter 7) or the multiple list sign-up capabilities (at no additional cost) of Feedblitz.

I assume that other Web-based custom newsletter e-mail vendors like Constant Contact and Vertical Response will soon add this feed-driven e-mail production functionality, too. So check ScottFox.com, FeedBlitzReview.com, and email-review.com for updates on these recommendations.

E-RICHES TIP: CUSTOMIZE YOUR E-MAIL TEMPLATES

Be sure to customize the e-mail templates that the blog feed-driven e-mail newsletter services provide.

I regular receive the e-mail edition of a top online marketer who uses Feedblitz to distribute his blog posts by e-mail. Every single time I almost delete his noozle because it has no customization and looks like spam!

It takes only a few minutes to reset the "from" address on your e-mails from "Feedblitz" to your company or blog name and to customize your e-mail subject lines to pick up your blog post titles. And changing the colors and logo to at least roughly match your branding is just a few mouse clicks more. (Not customizing your noozle template can also cause Feedblitz to group your blog posts in together with articles from other blogs—an ugly result sure to confuse your readers!)

There are top names in online marketing (some of whom are even quoted in this book) who have told me that they neglect this branding opportunity because they "have only a couple of thousand e-mail subscribers."

Does that sound like a good excuse to you?

6

. . .

WINNING E-MAIL LIST
BUILDING STRATEGIES

ALL OF THE preceding information about why and how to become a successful e-mail marketer is useful only if you have an e-mail list, right? So how do you build a robust e-mail list of your own?

What You Should Do to Build Your E-Mail List

The longest journey begins with a single step.

—Lao-tzu, author of the *Tao Te Ching*, founder of Taoism

Yes, it's a "chicken and egg" conundrum—how can you get sign-ups for your e-mail list from your web site when no one yet visits your site? In this case, you need to heed Lao-tzu's advice—take the initiative yourself and start anyway. Even the biggest e-mail lists started with just one subscriber.

There are no quick fixes for building an e-mail list. There are, however, *lots* of tactics that you can execute on a daily basis to gradually build a significant and profitable audience for your marketing messages.

As with most of the strategies in this book, I have personally used all of these techniques to build e-mail lists of thousands of subscribers worldwide.

Also note that not all subscribers need to be "new." What many of the tools this book discusses are best at is helping you collect, organize, and administrate contact with people who are *already* interested in your products. Any successful business has hundreds of previously satisfied customers who traditionally have had little or no way to express their enthusiasm for its brand or products before. Effective use of Web 2.0 technologies can make it easy for them to sign up and spread the word.

E-Mail List-Building Success Steps

Here is a list of proven subscriber attraction strategies:

- ▲ Start with friends and family—invite them to subscribe to your e-mail list and ask them to invite others, too.

- ▲ Ask for sign-ups on your web site. Prominently feature a sign-up form on every page of the site—even before the "official launch" of your site if it is new. Clearly state in your sales copy what you are offering. Present the benefits to the subscriber and make it easy and quick for her to join your list.

- ▲ Build visitor traffic to your web site by exchanging links with other related web sites.

- ▲ Create and offer incentives, such as free e-books, that are only available upon subscription.

- ▲ Partner with other sites to cross-promote—offering folks free publicity is generally a good way to get attention.

- ▲ Periodically ask your current subscribers to forward your noozles to friends. Offer prices to top referrers.

▲ Participate in online forums and communities. When you find people with similar interests, make friends and invite them to your site and your list.

▲ Take advantage of .sig files for both you and the rest of your company (.sig files are the couple of lines of info that you insert at the bottom of each e-mail to identify yourself). If you and everyone in your company adds a few lines like this to the bottom of all outgoing e-mails and discussion forum posts, the cumulative effect can be impressive:

```
Julie Jones
Account Administrator
Gee Whiz, Inc.

Visit GeeWhizProducts.com to sign up for our
free e-mail newsletter. Download a free
research report on industry trends and
receive special discounts!
```

(Note: Don't overdo your .sig file by putting in too much information, smiley faces, or irrelevancies. BlackBerry and mobile users in particular don't appreciate really long .sig files that use too much of their tiny screen space.)

▲ Include a special offer on your business card that is available only to noozle subscribers.

▲ Comment on relevant blogs (politely including your URL when appropriate) to attract the attention of potential customers.

▲ Write guest posts on other blogs to demonstrate your expertise and attract customers.

▲ Become active on social networks like MySpace and Facebook, plus online communities targeted to your customer demographics, to find more friends and offer invitations.

▲ Send press releases (not necessarily to get press coverage, but to build links back to your site—see Chapter 15 for a discussion of current press release tactics).

▲ Get free publicity by responding to press inquiries, using tools from Chapter 15.

▲ Write product reviews on Amazon.com and similar sites. Include links to your site and mention of your noozle offers where appropriate.

▲ Write and syndicate informational articles with similar links and offers (see Chapter 16).

▲ Buy keyword ads promoting your list and its benefits to subscribers. (See Chapter 21 for more information on search engine marketing and keyword advertising strategies.)

▲ Set up promotional joint ventures with people at the next level of success (those with larger lists), and offer value to them for promoting you. For example, you could write an e-book and offer it to a potential partner as a freebie for its readers. (Many "gurus" currently pitch expensive courses about this approach.)

Most especially, you need to write what people want to read. Be informative and interesting, and provide actionable steps that readers can take to meet the needs that inspired them to read your publication in the first place. If you write high-quality content (or hire others to do so) that you would want to read yourself, it builds trust and leads to both purchases and positive word-of-mouth marketing.

The key is to offer value in a concise and entertaining way to encourage subscription and forwarding.

WHAT *NOT* TO DO TO BUILD YOUR E-MAIL LIST

▲ Do not spam your friends.

▲ Do not fall for offers promising a CD with 1 million "clean" e-mail addresses for only $39.95.

▲ Do not fill your e-mails with self-promotion, advertising, or other pitches.

> ▲ Do not try to send a mailing list of any size from your personal computer.
>
> ▲ Do not fill your e-mails with large image files or attachments.
>
> ▲ Do not add anyone you meet (online or off) to your list without getting her permission first.
>
> ▲ Do not ask for too much information to initiate a subscription.

Brick-and-Mortar Business E-Mail List-Building Tips

If you have a real-world business, any time you see customers face to face, you have additional opportunities to build your e-mail list for free that are not available to online-only marketers.

For example, your real-world restaurant, hair salon, oil-change shop, shoe store, or plumbing supply outlet should:

▲ Have a clipboard next to your cash register for every customer to leave her e-mail address.

▲ Add e-mail list sign-up cards to every bill or invoice.

▲ Offer prize drawing entries at trade shows to anyone who will sign up.

▲ Insert flyers promoting your web site and e-mail noozles into your packages if you are shipping goods.

▲ Train your staff to finish every phone call with an offer to add the caller to your e-mail list.

▲ Display your web site address prominently on your building signage, on staff uniforms, on your delivery vans, and anywhere else it makes sense.

Even if you don't have a brick-and-mortar business, you're still liable to meet groups of people at association lunches, the county fair, your child's school play, or any number of other public events. Don't be obnoxious about it, but whenever you can, you should get out your clipboard and collect more e-mail addresses from interested potential customers.

E-MAIL SIGN-UP CONVERSION STRATEGIES

Once you attract visitors to your web site, be sure that you don't miss the opportunity to capture their e-mail addresses.

▲ Make your web site's e-mail collection link obvious—the bigger the better. *The e-mail subscription link or sign-up box is the most important item on your entire web site.* Don't listen to Web designers who want to minimize it into a corner graphic or a small link on your site's navigation menu.

▲ Present the benefits of subscribing—clearly answer the "what's in it for me?" question.

▲ Reduce the subscription sign-up info required to a minimum—despite your interest in knowing everything, extra questions will reduce your sign-ups.

▲ Try offering multiple different lists on one sign-up page. This can help entice visitors into multiple sign-ups just when they are in the mood for signing up for things.

▲ Offer an incentive like a discount or a "free report" to encourage them to sign up now. Even better is if your incentive is good enough that new subscribers forward it to friends. See Chapter 17 for more details on "freemiums"—how giving away your products by e-mail can help grow your e-mail list and revenues.

Building Your E-Mail List Won't Happen Overnight

The truth is, it can take time to build an e-mail list.

It won't get you rich quickly, but one proven strategy is simply to build up your list over time before you commit resources to trying to turn it into a business. For example, you might start a blog about your hobby, whether it's making mint-flavored desserts or collecting Star Wars memorabilia, and just post to it occasionally for months or years.

As long as you installed an e-mail collector right from the start and took the other introductory steps I outlined earlier, your list should gradually grow over time.

Then, when you are ready and the site has proven that it has profit potential, you will already be armed with a list of hundreds or thousands of e-mail addresses.

And remember: Every e-mail list starts with just one subscriber.

(See Chapter 5 on automated publishing of blog noozles to learn how you can publish your own promotional newsletters automatically and cost-effectively.)

Online Advertising for E-Mail Collection

Advertising can also be an effective traffic driver. Pay-per-click keyword advertising is the most common strategy for this online. See Part 7 for more details.

E-RICHES TIP: IDENTIFYING TARGET CUSTOMER GROUPS

Find potential customers online by setting up a Google Alert to track interest in your products. You can enter search terms exactly the way that customers ask questions when searching for your type of products. It takes only seconds and is free.

You'll get results directly into your e-mail box that will include message board posts from people who are looking for products like yours. You can often join such discussion forums for free in order to respond. Message boards generally discourage self-promotion, but these very targeted communities can offer you the opportunity to reach out and start relationships that can lead to more sign-ups for your noozles.

7

. . .

Automatically Make More Money with E-Mail Autoresponders

WHILE A WEB site can be called a "sales force that never sleeps," autoresponders are even better—they are a sales force that continues to follow up with your customers repeatedly. You enter your sales or follow-up marketing messages once, then the service repeatedly e-mails your sales prospects to keep generating sales even while you are asleep or on vacation.

As any successful sales professional will tell you, following up with customers is key to growing your revenues. The challenge is finding the time to follow up consistently. Automating your customer follow-up by e-mail is therefore a winning approach to monetization of your customer base.

Autoresponders are a solution to this problem, and also to another problem that many companies don't even realize they have: *an overemphasis on acquiring new customers at the expense of better monetizing existing customers who may be more profitable.*

An e-mail autoresponder can be used to automatically send repeated follow-up e-mails to any customer or potential customer who gives you her e-mail address. It is a great way to increase the follow-up, frequency, and targeting of your marketing.

Surprisingly, there's a great real-world example of this strategy that you probably have been receiving but underestimating for years: *your dentist.*

Your dentist sends you postcards reminding you of your semi-annual checkup, right? An autoresponder is the modern, online version of this proven marketing technique.

To use an online autoresponder, you simply load your e-mail contacts list into the program or web site to start. Then you can write a series of "evergreen" e-mails to those customers and schedule them to be sent automatically at a future date.

For example, if you register for my free e-mail noozles at ScottFox.com, you will receive a "welcome" e-mail that says something like this:

```
Hello {first name},

Thanks for your recent subscription to my "E-
Commerce Success" e-mail list. I look forward to
helping you build and market your business bet-
ter online.

I know that the online world can be a bit over-
whelming, so I hope that the information we share
is helpful to you.

I'm always interested in comments and feedback.
Please visit ScottFox.com any time to ask a ques-
tion or contribute to the discussion.

As your first step with us, how about visiting
ScottFox.com to tell me what you're looking for?
Share a little about your online goals and we'll
try to help!
```

I look forward to helping you build YOUR online success. Don't be shy—this is supposed to be fun!

Scott Fox
Author, *Internet Riches* and *e-Riches 2.0*

Then three days later you'll get another e-mail from me that looks like this:

Hello {first name},

Thanks again for your recent subscription to my "E-Commerce Success" e-mail list. Since you've just joined us, here are a few resources you might want to check out:

1. My first book is called *Internet Riches*. Learn more here any time: http://www.scottfox.com/internet-riches-book.html.

2. Did you know that I have a free online radio show and podcast? I interview "e-commerce success stories" every week to share the secrets of their online marketing success with you. Here is the Podcast Archive of past shows—it's full of useful info, and you can listen any time from your PC for free: http://www.ScottFoxRadio.com.

3. Please visit my blogs any time to COMMENT or ask questions. I want to help and hear from you. Please take part in the online community we're building. It can help you make more money. http://www.ScottFox.com.

I look forward to hearing about YOUR online success! Don't be shy!

Scott Fox
Author, *Internet Riches* and *e-Riches 2.0*

Then eight days after that you'll get another e-mail. This third one will contain some additional special offers based on whatever I'm promoting currently. I'm sure you get the idea.

It's important to note that this autoresponder follow-up series is *in addition* to the weekly e-mail newsletters to which people are subscribing. I am using the autoresponder functionality to personalize my outreach to you and encourage your integration into my subscriber community. By creating these e-mails *far in advance* of your subscribing, I am still able to give you, a potential customer, the sense of welcome and enthusiasm that I have for your joining the ScottFox.com online community. To respond like this to each new subscriber personally and manually would of course be more than I could do. The autoresponder thus greatly increases my reach while also making you feel good about your choice to subscribe by hearing more from me.

If you want to use autoresponders for a harder sell, you can easily adopt the same approach, but insert copy that promotes limited-time special offers to drive sales more directly.

AUTORESPONDER MARKETING
CASE STUDY: ASKTHEBUILDER.COM

Tim Carter of AsktheBuilder.com (profiled previously in Chapter 3) is also a big fan of autoresponders. He uses them to send out free "online courses."

These educational tools provide subscribers with a series of instructional steps to help them learn how to make home-improvement repairs themselves. The courses have titles like "Foundation Waterproofing," "Ceramic Tile Installation," "Driveway Repair," and "How to Get Rid of Mold." The courses usually have three or four installments. They are e-mailed in sequence to subscribers automatically by his autoresponder service over a period of several days.

Some of these courses are purely promotional (helping to attract more subscribers to AsktheBuilder.com and more clicks on its ads), while others also offer recommendations for products that Tim sells in his online store. For example, in the "How to Get Rid of Mold" e-mail class that I tested, Tim recommends a bleach-based product called Stain Solver. This is both a useful recommendation for the reader and a marketing placement for that product, which Tim sells in his online store.

In Tim's case, the e-mails that the autoresponder sends don't actually contain the course material. Instead, the e-mails link back to AsktheBuilder.com. This obviously creates more visitors to the web site, more potential clicks on ads, and more cross-selling opportunities.

Using an autoresponder service to deliver e-mail courses makes their administration easy. The system automatically keeps track of subscriber requests and timing, so that each person gets the appropriate e-mails in the series that she requested in sequence and on time. Since Tim is sending out thousands of such courses, with new subscribers starting sequentially every day, you can see how an autoresponder's scheduling capabilities are valuable. As Tim puts it, the autoresponder solves the potentially very complicated problem of "whom am I supposed to be sending which lesson to today?"

Tim has been so pleased with the response to his autoresponder courses that he is counting on the strategy for more revenues. His goal for next year? A 10 times increase!

Four Popular and Effective Uses of Autoresponders

Autoresponders can also be used very effectively without an accompanying newsletter. They can be set up as:

1. A series of e-mails simply reminding customers about your products

2. Periodic notifications of scheduled sales or discounts (think "holiday specials")

3. Reminders of back catalog products that customers may not have seen or may have forgotten about (this can help to keep your inventory turning over profitably).

4. "Courses" that deliver installments of knowledge or marketing materials to subscribers at predetermined intervals

Combining these strategies with whatever other e-mail marketing outreach you have planned can be very effective.

As we've now discussed extensively, e-mail is such a cost-effective way to reach a wide audience that it cannot be ignored. Adding the power of automated follow-up by using autoresponders can compound the effectiveness of e-mail and turn it into a systematic revenue-generating process.

Autoresponders can be tremendously profitable tools because they keep your products in front of your most likely prospects—people who have already demonstrated their interest in what you offer by giving you their e-mail addresses.

AWeber is the leading autoresponder service. (Learn more details at www.email-review.com.) I use it and the newer one recently offered by Feedblitz, too. Larger customer relationship management systems also sometimes offer autoresponder services, but usually at much higher prices as part of a larger software package.

SPECIAL (HIDDEN) BONUS!

Congratulations! If you're reading this, you are on your way to online marketing success.

As a free surprise gift (available only to readers of this page!), I invite you to subscribe to a free e-mail course that I'm not publishing anywhere else.

It's full of tips for building and marketing your online business.

To subscribe, just send me an e-mail with the subject line "Hidden Book Offer" to specialreaderoffer@scottfox.com.

(And don't tell your friends—this is our secret! Thanks for reading so closely.)

E-Mail Strategies: Conclusion

My goal is not to turn your existing business into a publishing company. Our shared goal, however, is to make you more money online. Publishing is the key to this.

The easiest customer to sell to is one who has purchased from you before. This is why I insist that you dedicate more of your resources to noozle publishing as soon as you can. E-mail marketing is your best opportunity to make more money by interacting with new customers and by reminding existing customers to purchase your products again.

PART THREE
SOCIAL MEDIA MARKETING
SUCCESS STRATEGIES

8

. . .

ONLINE VIRAL MARKETING

SOCIAL MEDIA OFFERS WORD
OF MOUTH ON STEROIDS

One of the coolest things about the Web is that when an idea takes off, it can propel a brand or company to seemingly instant fame and fortune. For free. Whatever you call it—viral, buzz, word-of-mouse, or word-of-blog marketing—having other people tell your story drives action. One person sends it to another, then that person sends it to yet another, and on and on.

—David Meerman Scott, *The New Rules of Viral Marketing*, p. 8

VIRAL MARKETING is what makes Internet marketing different. The massive worldwide reach and inexpensive distribution of the Web and e-mail mean that promotions and publicity efforts can spread like wildfire if you capture the audience's attention. This section of the book is about Web 2.0 marketing techniques that take advantage of online viral marketing's explosive potential.

Viral marketing is an Internet-powered version of what everyone used to call word-of-mouth marketing. Generating positive word of mouth is still an important goal for any marketer because it's much less expensive to have customers telling each other about your products than for you to advertise so much that they all hear from you directly.

Positive word of mouth or "buzz" generally starts as a result of simple enthusiasm for a product. Customers who are fans start spreading the word—and they tell two friends, who then tell two friends, and so on. Good marketers will watch for and encourage such positive word of mouth whenever they can. This is usually done by giving encouragement, recognition, free samples, or other support to positive word of mouth wherever it is found, and especially to influential community trendsetters or celebrities who use (or can be convinced to use) the product.

What's different about word-of-mouth marketing today is that the Internet can greatly magnify it. The constant web of communications via e-mail, instant messaging, online videos, message boards, blogs, newsletters, and so on means that any idea can spread really, really rapidly and widely. If you are trying to promote a product, you want to put this viral nature of the Web to work for you.

The first popular example of viral marketing was the explosive growth of Hotmail. Founded in 1996, the start-up company offered free e-mail accounts. This was a very popular product in a day when e-mail accounts were mostly offered one at a time through a dial-up modem–based Internet access account. By merely inserting a small promotional line of text at the bottom of each e-mail users sent from the Hotmail system that said, "Get your free e-mail at Hotmail.com," Hotmail created the first widely recognized "viral loop"—a self-spreading and self-reinforcing virtuous cycle of customer adoption. The more users there were who used the Hotmail service, the more others saw the attractive offer and signed up. Then those new users started sending e-mails and even more people saw the offer and started using Hotmail, and so on. Hotmail grew from nothing to more than 12 million users in just 18 months. (And this was in an era when the Internet's audience was a fraction of what it is today.) The company was acquired by Microsoft in 1998 for an undisclosed price, probably in the hundreds of millions of dollars.

The viral characteristics that the Hotmail example demonstrates are what you want to recreate with your online marketing: Try to build incentives into your pitch, or into the product itself, that are spread and reinforced by the customers' natural behavior. Doing so can allow the product message to be spread virally through their daily activity. (This is the same way a cold virus spreads from one person to others through common daily interactions.)

Today YouTube is often used as a viral platform because people enjoy sharing funny videos with one another. Online games, tools, or promotions that encourage you to participate and forward the promo to your friends are viral marketing, too. Such games and tools often live on their own web sites or are packaged into "widgets" or "apps" for easy sharing and installation on social networks like MySpace and Facebook.

Some well-known examples of viral marketing campaigns include:

- ▲ OfficeMax's popular Elfyourself.com web site (which attracted more than 100 million users in 2008 by allowing them to paste photos of their faces onto an animated dancing Christmas elf's body and forward it to friends)

- ▲ Paltalk's "Ever Dream of Running for President?" video, which allowed you to insert your own name into a fake TV newscast about candidates for the 2008 U.S. presidential election at www.news3online.com

- ▲ Intuit's QuickBooks software promotion that helps small business owners enter a virtual recording studio to create their own advertising jingle at www.thejinglegenerator.com

- ▲ An ad from a Canadian forklift company at www.pimp-mylift.com that allows users to outfit a forklift with hot rod–type accessories

All of these promotions went viral because they were entertaining and they inspired users to forward them to friends. For a more current list, try visiting the "most popular" listings on YouTube.com or Google Video, or visit ScottFox.com and click on the "Cool Sites" or "Viral Marketing" categories to see a bunch more.

Viral promotions don't all have to be fancy games or videos, however. The explosive growth of Hotmail was based simply on text-based e-mail promotion, and social networks like those we'll discuss shortly grow because friends invite friends to come play with them there. *And those e-mails you get every few months saying that Bill Gates is donating $1 for every e-mail forwarded? Those are viral, too, aren't they?*

You can see that each of these examples offers similar things to users: entertainment or utility that is enhanced by sharing it with others. Unlike traditional media, which were largely one-way, today's social media are based around *sharing* information, entertainment, and experiences with friends online. That's why social media are such a rapidly growing marketing opportunity for your business.

So, next time you're cooking up a promotion, don't just think in terms of informing or entertaining one potential customer at a time. Think ahead to the next step: Take advantage of the Internet's interactive, inexpensive, and international nature to offer an activity that rewards your target customers for *sharing* your promotion with others. Then the worldwide leverage of the Internet can help your marketing go viral, too.

Understanding Social Media

Social media is the collective term for the second wave of Internet-powered web sites and tools that help people connect and interact. Also called "Web 2.0," these tools help people extend their personal lives, further their careers, and create communities by facilitating the sharing of information, feedback, and media with one another online, on their mobile phones, by e-mail, or in other digital formats. The use of these tools for business promotions is called *social marketing.*

Social media tools are great for developing relationships with customers. This is revolutionary because they can cut out many layers of distributors, retailers, and salespeople to allow direct customer interaction. For most marketers, that's an exciting opportunity because it can lead to increased sales, increased customer loyalty, and useful customer feedback.

Common applications of social media include:

▲ Social networks like MySpace, Facebook, and LinkedIn that help users share personal information, meet new people, and easily keep in touch with others

▲ Social news aggregator and bookmarking services that allow users to vote for and share recommendations for news stories at web sites like Digg, StumbleUpon, Reddit, deli.cio.us, bizSugar, and Propeller

▲ Sites that allow users to submit their own writings, videos, photos, or other contributions for community consumption, ranking, or collaboration

▲ Online communities that host discussions or other social interactions (see Chapter 10)

▲ Blogs and microblogging tools that help individuals (and increasingly companies, too) easily publish updates (see Chapters 12 and 13)

▲ Public display of customer feedback and reviews as part of a web site's content (as seen all over the Web today such as on Amazon.com, eBay.com, etc.)

▲ Easy redistribution, broadcast, and syndication of content between users and groups, often using feeds that update content across platforms and devices automatically (see Chapter 4 about feeds)

Because most of these Web 2.0 services were started for social reasons, so far marketing through social media is most successful for individuals or small businesses that grow on relationships. Marketing commodity products or large company brands that lack a "personality" fits less easily into the self-promotional paradigm that most social marketing tools were built to support. This is rapidly evolving, however, as the companies behind many of these tools come to recognize how much money can be made by helping large companies promote their products.

If your company truly has little need or desire to engage with its customers, social media may not be important for you. But it's a rare business that doesn't have customers, even if they are just a few business-to-business, well-established wholesale relationships.

A "presence" on social media sites can improve relationships with those customers and help you expand your reputation cloud to attract new customers, too. Of the 60 percent of Americans who use social media, *93 percent believe that a company should have a presence in social media.* An overwhelming 85 percent of those potential customers also believe that a company should not only be present but *should also interact with its customers* through social media.[1]

The numbers don't lie: Facebook has over 200 million users, MySpace's Tila Tequila has more than 1 million "friends," a mention of your web site on the front page of the social bookmarking web site Digg.com can overload your servers with traffic, both employees and employers spend increasing amounts of time online investigating (or avoiding) each other, and even politicians are now using social network tools to raise money and get elected.

But, although social media are all the rage, like most of the other techniques discussed in this book and in my blogs, they are just a tool. *You don't use a hammer for every job; that's why they make screwdrivers.*

Does social media offer a good set of tools for expanding *your* product presence?

Now let's turn our attention to choosing which of these new social networking tools are worthy of your valuable time and attention.

9

. . .

SOCIAL NETWORK MARKETING USING FACEBOOK, MYSPACE, AND LINKEDIN

CURRENT BUZZ positions social networks as the exciting frontier in marketing. MySpace, Facebook, LinkedIn, Friendster, Bebo, Hi5, and hundreds of other social networks crowd the online marketplace today.

About 40 percent of active U.S. adult Internet users now belong to social networking web sites,[1] and of those who use them, 39 percent of U.S. adults access social networks at least once every day.[2]

Social networking is a worldwide phenomenon. As an example, consider QQ, which today has 300 million active accounts (and 700 million total) in China, or Mixi's 15 million users in Japan (a much smaller country). Vkontakte.ru and Odnoklassniki.ru dominate the former Soviet states, Cyworld is the social network of choice for Koreans, Skyblog is number one in France, and Orkut, although started by California-based Google, is now primarily used by Brazilians.

But what are these social networking tools? And are they appropriate for your business? Here's how social networks (including details on Facebook, MySpace, and LinkedIn) can be helpful to you in marketing your business online.

The Digital Divide

If you are not active in social networks, you probably still don't "get" these tools. And that's even more likely if you are over 40 years old, just as your parents or grandparents may never have completely gotten the hang of e-mail. For example, most baby boomers are not using social networks much at all yet. In fact, 58 percent of adults worldwide do not yet even know what online social networking is.[3]

In 2008, I even wrote a blog post (luckily never published) complaining about what I called a social networking "bubble." While I still think a bubble may exist for the too many start-up companies trying to compete in the social networking marketplace, I have come to appreciate the power of social networks. Social networks offer you excellent tools to spread your marketing messages, establish a wider product presence, and manage your company's reputation cloud.

Just as e-mail and the Web brought unanticipated efficiencies in communications first to the early adopter "digerati" and later to wider segments of the population, social networks started with early adopters, but they are now on their way to increasing mainstream acceptance. This means customers are there waiting for you. . .

The Magic of Social Networks

Social networks are for networking. Not networking of the computer "cables linking to routers and switches" kind, but networking of the old-fashioned, twentieth-century "meeting people to make new friends and get to know them better" variety. This means building relationships to attract new customers and increase purchases by existing customers.

Social networks are essentially specialized tools for helping you meet people and maintain your relationships more easily; they automate much of the legwork of traditional networking. While they can be very useful, social networks still require basic steps like being friendly and meeting people. They help facilitate that process by amplifying your ability to meet new people, find common interests, and keep in touch. So unless you're going to buy a bunch of advertisements on their web sites, the way to use social networks successfully to market your products is to "network." In fact, much of the magic of social networks is simply the automation of the process of meeting new people and the filtering of friends to find those with whom you have the most in common.

All the social networking sites/systems/services offer you some version of a "profile page" where you can share info about yourself. With millions of people sharing their personal characteristics and interests online through such profile pages, the social networks are essentially huge databases of self-updating résumés. (I say "self-updating" because your contacts keep their own info current, and this is automatically available to you.) This means that social networks are great for contact management because they largely eliminate time-consuming "keeping in touch" tasks like sending update e-mails, sharing photos, updating Rolodexes, and so on.

Social networks serve the age-old human desire for social interaction, validation, and entertainment by helping their members find one another and connect based on common interests. The result is that instead of individuals being stuck with whatever community they happened to have been born into in the real world, social networks help people make new connections and find new friends based on common social or professional interests. Not all of their features are needed by everyone, but some of the basic functionalities discussed here are quickly becoming indispensable features of business communications and marketing today (not to mention dating, politics, religion, and more).

As a marketer, this means that social networks offer you unprecedented efficiency in finding and tapping into previously established

and self-selected online communities that are likely to be enthusias-
tic about your products. The trade-off is finding the time and choosing which ones to participate in, because just like real-world
communities, you get out of social networks what you put into them.

The Top 10 Reasons You Need
to Be on Social Networks

Online networks are the twenty-first-century version of the Yellow
Pages phone directories. (Sorry, I know, you are just getting used to
the idea that your business needs a web site and a presence on
search engines!)

But while your web site's search engine placement continues to be
key, in coming years, any company that doesn't also distribute its
product presence to at least a few key social networks as well will be
losing business. The audiences that are active on these sites are now
too large to be ignored, especially since you can target your marketing efforts very effectively to those users who are most likely to be
potential customers for your products.

Here are the 10 top reasons that your business needs to be on
social networks today:

1. Your customers are there.

2. Your competitors are there.

3. Your customers are looking for you there.

4. Your customers are looking for your competitors there.

5. If you don't establish a presence soon, someone may imper-
sonate you or your company. (This is a critical part of managing your reputation cloud.)

6. Being there will improve your search engine rankings: A
presence on a social network creates more links to your main
web site (demonstrating authority and credibility to the
search engines), which creates higher search engine rankings
and more traffic for your web site.

7. By collecting "friends," you allow your best customers to demonstrate their loyalty publicly, leading to more branding and viral spread of your message as the "friends" of your "friends" investigate each others' interests and see your marketing messages.

8. Your employees are there. You should start a group to include them, encourage their interaction with the brand, and (presuming you have their good will) employ them as viral marketing agents. Many companies have employee groups on Facebook, for example (authorized or, more often, unauthorized).

9. You want to get the URL or yourcompanyname user name that most clearly matches your brand so that users of that service can most easily find you.

10. Journalists are looking on social networks for story leads and experts to quote. A large part of a reporter's job is finding the "right" people to interview for stories, so social networks are a great tool for them, but only if you are there to be found.

E-RICHES TIP: FREE ENGINEERING TALENT

By participating on social networks, you automatically get the benefit of those companies' large and cutting-edge software engineering teams. They are spending millions to create easy-to-use promotion tools that you get to use for free!

Your company or product's mere presence on a social network shows that you are interested in speaking with the network's users. You don't have to become an expert or spend lots of time on updating your social network profiles. But it is increasingly important that you are visible. It demonstrates that you are current and credible, especially to the influential younger audiences who take social networks very seriously.

Today, your company needs a presence on the top social networks, just as your store needs to take credit cards in addition to cash.

A FREE TRADE SHOW INVITATION

What would you do with the following offer?

A new trade show for your industry is coming to your town— right down the street from your office. Its attendees will include probably half of your current customers. On top of that, *all* of your competitors will be exhibiting and staffing their booths 24/7.

But, for just a one-hour investment of your time, I could offer you a booth at this highly targeted trade show, *and* it would be *free*.

What would you do? You'd jump to sign up for that exhibition opportunity, wouldn't you?

Well, that's the value proposition that social networks offer to you today!

But you're still too busy?

Getting Started in Social Networking

Not only is your profile the page that you have the most control over, it's the place where you can most deeply and authentically express your passion for the brand, company, or product you want to promote. Your profile page is an opportunity to craft a credible real-world story around the reasons your products or services are so valuable. Take advantage of Personal Info, Work Info, Photos, and applications to tell bits and pieces of your narrative as it relates to your brand.

Justin Smith, InsideFacebook.com

All social networks offer you some version of a profile page. This web page is where you enter and display whatever personal characteristics you want to share with others in the community. The basics generally include your name, credentials, and identifying photos.

You can then customize your profile page to also reveal your personality to visitors based on the content you choose to display. This content may be badges of affiliation with different hobby, professional, alumni, or geographical groups, for example. Or it can be links to other web sites or blogs that you like.

By creating a profile page on a social network, you are creating a twenty-first-century version of a résumé, business card, photo album, yearbook listing, phone book entry, and references list all in one. At a glance, a potential customer or business prospect can size up your credentials, relationships, appearance, or education—whatever you choose to display. This is true both for you personally and for your company or product.

But because you can choose what information to reveal (or make up) on that page, you control the way others perceive you and the role you play in that social network's community more flexibly than in real life. For example, depending on the type of interaction on that network, your profile page may be factual and businesslike, representing your real-world personality, or it may be an anonymous or fictional persona that you inhabit only in that community.

This ability to experiment with different social approaches and learn how others perceive different online personas is part of the fun of social networks, especially for young people who are still deciding what personality to grow into as adults.

It also offers you the chance to personalize your brand by emphasizing the characteristics that you think are most appealing to your target audience.

Choosing the Best Social Networks for Your Marketing

Here are my strategic guidelines for exploring where and how to best spend your marketing energy on social networks:

1. Investigate several social networks—bounce around to test MySpace, Facebook, LinkedIn, and any social network that you know that people in your own industry actively use. Use fake names and an anonymous e-mail address at this point just to get familiar with the systems. You're just looking, and you don't want to leave embarrassing tracks or misconfigure

an important but irreversible setting (like your profile name or URL).

2. Use this exploratory phase to find a network that seems to suit your personality, marketing needs, and technical capability best. (Again, a good bet here is to find out which networks others in your industry use the most.)

3. Pick one or at most two social networks to join for real. Yes, it would be nice to be everywhere, but you'll never have the time. I'd suggest simply starting with a Facebook company "fan" page account and a personal LinkedIn account.

Quick Setup Steps for Your
Social Networking Profile Page

Prepare the following information, and establishing a basic presence on almost any social network will be painless and quick:

▲ Create an account. Be careful which e-mail address you use because it may be publicly displayed, and it is likely to receive a lot of traffic from "friend requests" and status updates.

▲ Have a Web-ready headshot photograph or other personal image available as a small jpg or gif file. (Additional images of your products can also be very useful.)

▲ Prepare a short text description of yourself.

▲ Prepare a list of interests to share that reflect appropriately on you.

▲ Prepare an initial list of friends or contacts and their e-mail addresses to contact once your account setup is complete. You can use the list to quickly to start building your network by inviting those "friends" to link to your new online profile.

Pimp Your Profile: Top Tips for
Business Use of Social Networks

A social network profile page is an increasingly important part of your company's overall digital product presence. So you'll also want to set up a new profile page that is an extension of your company web site and marketing materials.

The account setup process outlined above applies to anyone setting up a profile on a social network. If you are looking to use the network for business purposes, you should take some additional steps to optimize your presence for marketing outreach.

Many of these are steps that casual or personal users of social networks can afford to forget or skip, but as a businessperson you want to be sure to follow these guidelines to maximize the marketing potential of your time spent social networking. (Most of them are quick, one-time setup chores, too.)

These steps include:

- ▲ Put up a "real" profile following the guidelines discussed once you have decided in which network(s) to invest your effort. Give some careful thought to the professional image that you hope to project, both for yourself and for your products or brand. Social networks are about demonstrating who you are by publicly displaying your affiliations and certain selected information. *Don't be intimidated—your new profile page doesn't have to be perfect; it just has to exist to get you started.*

- ▲ Enter complete business contact info so that viewers can see that you are real and are also open to hearing from them. This should include street address, phone numbers, and e-mail addresses that demonstrate your professional commitment to the business.

- ▲ If your business has a real-world retail location, be sure to post store hours, directions, and parking instructions, too.

- ▲ Concisely state who you are and what your products are about. Be casual and friendly—avoid corporate-speak.

▲ Be specific about your specialties so that both customers and potential partners can quickly understand what you have to offer. (Extra points if these are phrased as keywords that others might use to search on.)

▲ Also be specific about what you have to offer the online community you have just joined and what you are looking for, both in customers and in partners. *The more you share, the more potential customers will be able to self-select and come to you with the targeted business you want.*

▲ If the network's pages allow it, display your company logo and use the color codes that match your company's branding so that customers can quickly identify your page. MySpace allows lots of customization; Facebook and LinkedIn allow much less.

▲ If there's a limit, specify the geographic area you serve. Remember, the Internet is global. No need to waste time fielding inquiries from 2,000 miles away if you're a gardener or hair salon.

▲ Build your online profiles to be evergreen if finding time for online marketing is challenging. By this I mean include only info that doesn't distract you by requiring regular updating.

▲ Produce a steady stream of updates to share with your network of friends. This is even better than posting evergreen information. These updates can include photos, news items, blog posts, event invitations, press releases, personal updates, videos, or whatever is appropriate for your audience. *You want to keep your network thinking about your business as regularly as you can without being intrusive or presumptuous.* (You'll see that this advice applies to all of the publishing-style marketing strategies in this book, including blogging and e-mail marketing.)

▲ If you set up profiles on multiple social networks, refer inquiries you receive from your multiple online profiles back to one central profile, e-mail account, or, ideally, your company web site. This is where you can put your more timely info—that way you only really have to update one place. This approach will help keep you from getting overwhelmed by distracting maintenance chores on different sites. The magic of feeds (discussed in Chapter 4) will help you distribute your content to multiple sites automatically.

▲ Post a link asking for e-mail addresses. Anyone who visits your profile has already demonstrated an interest in your products or services. Most social networks allow you the ability to "message" your friends within the system. But ideally you should collect the actual e-mail addresses these contacts use in the real world, outside the system, too. This will allow you to continue to communicate with them cheaply even if they (or you) stop using the social network where you met. Then, in addition to keeping in touch through the network, use the e-mails also by sending an occasional "special offer" or discount to your subscribers by e-mail.

Follow these steps and the social network will go to work for you, offering your contact information and products to the millions of social network users looking for solutions to their life's problems 24/7.

How to Succeed in Social Networking

The currency of real networking is not greed but generosity.

—Keith Ferrazzi, author of *Never Eat Alone*

Succeeding in social networking is actually more about "people" skills than technical ones.

The steps in the previous section will get your basic social network presence established, but it's how you *behave* in the social network's community that will decide the success or failure of the time you invest there. Regardless of which social networks you choose to use (or which are popular by the time you read this), each community has its own norms for behavior, just as in the real world. You need to learn and respect those norms if you want to be actively included in the community.

Once you have your basic social network profile established, here are my ten recommended steps to begin using it as a marketing tool.

1. Invite a half-dozen or more friends to get your network started. Practice using the tools of the social network to communicate with them. For example, you can "add" friends on MySpace, "poke" or "write on the walls" of Facebook connections, or respond to some questions in the LinkedIn "Answers" section.

2. Start engaging, publishing, and interacting. Get to know some people—that's why you're here.

3. Be authentic. A big part of being authentic is letting the "real you" out to play. Nobody wants to play with a "suit," so don't be afraid to be yourself (within professional and legal limits, of course!). Mixing the personal and business sides of your life is more common than it used to be.

4. Only try to connect with others with whom you really do have common ground. Indiscriminate friend requests are "friend spam." They are no more appreciated than e-mail spam or junk mail in the real world. (And if people you don't know start linking with you, your own network will soon be less valuable, too.)

5. Ask for help. Most social network users are online to be social, and most are happy to help by sharing their knowledge about how the systems work.

6. Use the feeds we discussed earlier to keep up with your friends' activities and broadcast your own. Posting your own status constantly and cleverly is a great distributed engagement marketing tactic.

7. If you have a blog, feed its posts into your profile page. This will automatically help keep your pages fresh and share your writings with a new audience, too.

8. Join some groups—learn the lingo and the tools of the network by using them and observing how others use them, too. Joining groups will also begin to create a natural dialogue with other users that will grow over time.

9. Be a good and involved citizen in those groups to cultivate new friends. There's no better way to gain the respect of any community than adding value by sharing info, support, or companionship—and these tools will amplify the effect. If you are an expert, social networks are a great way to spread your reputation cloud for that expertise.

10. Create your own group. Once you are comfortable, start a group around your product or brand. Position yourself as an expert resource and offer to help and facilitate community. Members usually proudly display the names of the groups to which they belong on their profile pages. This can lead to lots more clicks (and members) as others see your group's name or logo on friends' pages and in their feeds.

These steps will help you make friends on social networks and begin to position you and your brand to attract more attention. If you participate in the parts of your chosen networks that are populated by your most likely customers, your product presence and reputation cloud will start to spread.

However, just as it's difficult to make cocktail party conversation about a commodity business like selling socks, it can be difficult to get audience attention on Facebook or MySpace if your products are less chatter-worthy. Read the opposite way, however, this same analysis suggests that there is a big opportunity for the first sock retailer, bakery, or tax preparation firm to make a splash on social networks if it can find an appealing angle. (See the Bacon Salt example later in this chapter for a great example!)

Two factors can help speed the growth of both your personal reputation cloud and your marketing messages:

1. Creative or unusual products that are worth talking about, at least among enthusiasts

2. A conscious effort to entertain the audience and encourage word of mouth

You will soon see that my case study examples of successful social network marketing have both of these important factors in common.

WHAT IS A "FRIEND"?

The most common measure of "success" on social networks is the number of "friends" you display.

The word *friend* has taken on new meaning in the social networking age. It still means someone with whom you have friendly relations, but those relations may be quite thin by historical standards. The (in)famous Tila Tequila is a young woman who is famous mostly for having several million friends on MySpace, for example.

Competing to acquire lots of these friends is a top activity on many social networks. As a member yourself, acquiring friends will also be a large part of your goal in using social networks because the number of friends that you display is the easiest way for others to judge your importance in and commitment to the community. Collecting these friends and fans and followers of your brand is also your goal as a marketer because these friends are really a new audience of potential customers and product evangelists.

The social network's software will help you collect, organize, and communicate with these friends very efficiently. It's then up to you to entertain or otherwise "feed" them to encourage their continued interest, positive word of mouth, and purchasing.

Note: Social networks were started to help individuals socialize. As they've grown, marketers have begun targeting their huge and attractive audiences. But because social networks were designed for one-to-one interpersonal networking, they don't yet always have great tools for companies or brands to promote themselves. Consequently, most of the advice here is about how to market yourself as an individual or how to squeeze your product or branding message into the social network platform tools that exist today (not always a perfect fit).

By the time you read this, there will doubtless be more tools developed to help online marketers spread their messages through social networks. Check ScottFox.com for updates.

Using Facebook
FACEBOOK STRATEGY GUIDE

Facebook was started in 2004 as an offshoot of a Harvard University project. Conceived as an online equivalent of the paper-based "face books" that show students photos of their classmates and faculty, Facebook is the current reigning champion of the social networking scene.

Facebook started by connecting Harvard students to one another and later expanded to include other colleges in the Ivy League. Adoption was swift because college students are among the most socially open age groups. (Half the student body at Harvard signed up in just two weeks!) The service soon expanded to include any university student, then high school students, too. By late 2006, Facebook had opened its services to anyone aged 13 and over, regardless of university affiliation.

If you join Facebook, you can connect with friends across the world for free. This allows you access to your friends' profiles and the ability to see their friends, too. You can also join networks or groups. Networks are generally organized by city, school, company, or other obvious affiliations. Groups are generally sponsored by one or more individuals or by a company to attract members who share common interests. Groups offer discussion boards, photo sharing, video posting, and e-mail list management, too. In each of these cases, the point is to meet and keep in touch with friends from around the world, using the tools that the Facebook platform provides for communication and interaction.

The principal features of Facebook include a profile page like that found on MySpace, LinkedIn, or most other social networks. A major difference with Facebook is that others cannot see the details of your profile page until you have approved them as friends. This restricts friend links on Facebook to people with whom you have at least some connection, as opposed to MySpace, where indiscriminately collecting as many friends as possible is a popular sport. (See Figure 9–1 for my personal Facebook page.)

Activities on Facebook include updating one's profile, sharing updates on one's daily activities through "status" posts that your friends can see, visiting the profile pages of other friends to write messages on their "Walls," sharing photos and videos, posting event announcements, or blogging, as well as interacting on message boards that are often hosted by different groups or networks.

Facebook has also had pioneering success by allowing software developers to create small applications ("apps") that enable users to play games, send each other gifts, or engage in other small recreational activities through the network.

With more than 200 million members worldwide, Facebook today offers profiles, networks, groups, and apps on any subject imaginable.

FACEBOOK MARKETING EXAMPLES

Like most social networks, Facebook's fundamental architecture is designed more to help its members socialize than to promote corporate marketing messages.

Facebook is more marketing-friendly than MySpace, however, primarily because it offers easy-to-use ways for companies and even individual products to establish profile pages.

Individuals can create their own profiles; celebrities, companies, or products can create "fan pages" (or fans can create them independently); and easy-to-use group pages are available to help users congregate around shared interests.

Creating these pages requires little graphic expertise (unlike in MySpace) because Facebook pages are all standardized in one generic blue-and-white template.

FIGURE 9–1.

Of course, more expensive and complex advertising opportunities are available, too. Facebook is attracting major agencies and brands to its site, including Microsoft, Absolut, Coca-Cola, Travelocity, Vodafone, and many more. Many of these placements are integrated opportunities that include deployment of customized widgets and apps that include interactive capabilities like polls or games. The best of them are, of course, then widely used, commented upon, and forwarded within the huge (and easily distracted) Facebook community.

A post I found on Neil Patel's Quick Sprout blog gives nice insight into how an active but noncommercial user uses Facebook. A reader named Laura said:

> Facebook has allowed me to create groups of my own to network more than just my friends. I teach a girls' class in church on Sunday mornings, and I've found that Facebook lets me know what's going on in their lives, keeps me up to date on whatever might happen. We have a group together on Facebook that lets us remind each other about service projects or certain bible studies. Also, it's a great forum for a more uninhibited discussion. The girls will post difficult questions that we all weigh in on and then we discuss those in class.
>
> Also, Facebook applications keep you invested in Facebook. You come back for the online Scrabble game or the other games going on, which in turn introduces you to new people who also want to play a little. I've met people in Australia and people in my own city.[4]

I share this example to demonstrate how users see Facebook as a social platform. If your marketing plans include Facebook (and I think they should), keep this example in mind. Laura is not there looking for your marketing pitch; she's there to keep in touch with her friends and entertain herself. If you can tailor your marketing to her interests and those of her network of friends, users like Laura will be much more receptive than to traditional marketing pitches.

At the other extreme are big company marketing successes: Victoria's Secret's PINK line of women's sportswear has been a hit on Facebook. By setting up a profile on Facebook and populating it with regularly updated photos, video, and news about its clothes, PINK has collected more than 500,000 friends.

This means that more than half a million people have voluntarily endorsed the products and agreed to hear updates from Victoria's Secret about the PINK line's new styles, sales, and events. Thousands of them also visit the page to participate in discussions on the PINK message boards, display PINK widgets on their own Facebook pages, and spread the PINK brand message throughout the Facebook community daily with their interactions.

And popular Comedy Central TV personality Stephen Colbert's Facebook group is famous for having grown from zero to over 1 million members in just nine days!

Here's an example of an "in-between" Facebook success story—a successful business use of Facebook, but one that has been accomplished by a single entrepreneur:

FACEBOOK CASE STUDY:
PETER SHANKMAN'S HARO

"Help A Reporter Out" is a Facebook success story that I love because it so clearly demonstrates the explosive potential of Internet marketing. HARO, as it's now commonly called, is a publicity service founded by Peter Shankman, a PR wizard and entrepreneur.

Peter, a public relations professional himself, recognized the difficulty that journalists have in finding the best sources to validate and quote in their articles, especially because they are so often under difficult deadlines. HARO grew out of the repeated requests that Peter received from journalist friends asking if he knew people who could supply background or quotes on various topics they were covering. So, he turned to Facebook to help out his reporter friends.

Peter had had a personal Facebook page for a few months, but in late 2007, he started a new group on Facebook. (Starting groups on Facebook is free.) He called the group "If I Can Help a Reporter Out

I Will." This new group created a virtual meeting place where Peter could collect and post inquiries from his friends who were journalists—many of whom were becoming active on Facebook.

Peter started the Facebook group by inviting a few friends from his personal Rolodex—people that he knew were already using Facebook. This included both reporters and expert sources. He asked the reporters to submit story research requests. Then the sources could respond with pitches targeted to each reporter's needs. He wasn't expecting much, but he was optimistic that Facebook would help him "help some reporters out" because the platform made it so easy to collect and redistribute information.

Each day Peter collected the inquiries from reporters, copied and pasted them into an e-mail, and then used the Facebook e-mail system to blast them out to anyone who had joined the group. If the reporter was looking for information on a topic that you knew (or that your clients knew), then you could respond to the reporter, offering assistance in hopes of being mentioned in the story. This made it easier than ever for reporters and sources to connect with one another—and PR folks loved being in the middle of this new process.

If you were a member of Facebook and you joined Peter's new group, each day you could see the journalist inquiries that he received and posted.

Facebook is built around sharing information and personal updates. Peter found a way to put that personal network to work by providing a business service that all of his friends (and their friends and their friends and their friends) found useful. The Facebook platform enabled the virtual word of mouth to spread rapidly because the primary activity on Facebook is visiting constantly and checking out what friends are doing. When Peter gave his fellow PR professionals a reason to check Facebook even more often, and for good business reasons, adoption in the public relations industry was swift.

This new service also was well received because it has traditionally been difficult for journalists to find new, credible, and interesting sources to use when researching their stories. (It also certainly helped that it was free.) Within a few weeks, Peter's Facebook group had grown to 600 members.

Fast-forward a couple of weeks more and the "If I Can Help a Reporter Out I Will" group took off. Within just a few months, Peter's experiment had exceeded the then-current limit for group membership of 1,200 members. (Facebook raised that limit soon after.) Clearly he had found a vein of unfilled demand in the world of public relations.

The snowballing demand for the new service soon forced Peter to leave Facebook and start a separate web site to support the traffic. In less than six months, HARO had more than 40,000 subscribers and was sending out dozens of inquiries daily from reporters at qualified, often nationally recognized publications. (Peter is also making real money from his free service because the audience has grown so rapidly that he can now sell ads in each day's e-mail announcements.)

(See Chapter 15 on public relations to learn more about using the HARO service yourself.)

The lessons to be learned here are a combination of traditional business smarts and modern online marketing. Peter obviously found a valuable niche in brokering introductions between journalists and experts. Every marketer wants more publicity, just as the reporters want better sources. This classic win-win situation was facilitated perfectly by Facebook's easy-to-use group e-mail tools.

Additionally, because Facebook is obviously a Web-based platform, the audience is full of early adopters. This meant that a cool new service like HARO spread rapidly as the audience competed to both share knowledge of the new tool and help out Peter, who was simply offering to help them do their jobs better for free.

This is classic viral marketing. Because the service's growth helped them, too, the audience spread the word about the HARO service for free as a natural part of their daily work.

Note: While not every marketing campaign or product can hope to take off as explosively as HARO has, the same principles of using Facebook to collect people with common interests into manageable (and therefore marketable) groups apply. The key is targeting groups with appropriate offers, not just blasting promos at everyone who is dumb enough to sit still for spam.

HOW TO CHOOSE BETWEEN PERSONAL AND COMPANY PROFILE PAGES

If your brand, product, and personality all use the same name, choosing between a personal profile and a company- or product-focused social network profile is pretty straightforward. Joe's Plumbing and Terry's Law Firm are both run and marketed by Joe and Terry, respectively. These folks can easily set up profile pages using their own headshots and fill in the profile page setup questions using their own names, birth dates, city, and so on.

But if you market products for a larger company, you are forced to choose how to present yourself on social networks. On LinkedIn, which is focused on individual professionals, you really only have one choice: to complete your profile page using your work title, such as Marketing Manager or VP Sales for Company XYZ.

But MySpace or Facebook profile pages do not support developing relationships and an audience for your company and your products as well as they do for yourself. It can be awkward to squeeze a product or company profile into the profile page formats they offer which were designed for use by individuals. For example, date of birth or gender don't really apply for a company or service you may be promoting. (And this can be even more complicated if you already have a personal profile active on the network. Family and high school friends are just as likely to visit your new profile as your business marketing contacts are—a recipe for confusion that could hurt your business!)

What to do?

I recommend using Facebook. On Facebook, you can set up your profile (or a second one if you want to avoid the business/social conflicts I just mentioned) as an individual professional. Fully explain your role as a member of the marketing, sales, or other department for XYZ Corporation.

Then, you can also set up a "fan page" on Facebook separate from your personal profile. A fan page will allow you to highlight your brand or your products instead of yourself. These fan pages are amped-up profile pages that are more customizable than typical Facebook personal profiles. You can add HTML, Flash, or other Facebook applications to increase their visual appeal and functionality. Then you can become the first "fan" of your products and administrate and promote that page to attract other fans of your company's products (while also keeping that activity separate from your personal presence). (See Figure 9–2 for my fan page.)

Facebook fan pages also show up nicely in search engine results. Because they are visible to non-registered users, a fan page can both

FIGURE 9–2.

help you to attract search engine traffic and also publicly demonstrate your company's involvement in social media.

Fan pages also offer traffic reporting (called "insights") that neither personal nor group pages do. You can view the number of visitors to your fan page and their demographics easily and for free. This can be helpful in measuring the success of any marketing or advertising you do which drives traffic to your Facebook presence.

This fan page strategy may sound odd if you are not used to thinking of your products or company as celebrity material, but there are plenty of fans of mundane products on Facebook. These include Pop-Tarts (six fan groups with 18,589 total fans), Chevy trucks (six fan groups with a total of almost 11,000 members), or Nikon cameras (one group of 40,782 fans), plus millions of fans for more obvious celebrity products and personalities like bands, movie stars, or *Star Wars*.

Additionally, you should consider setting up a group on Facebook. Groups are designed for community interaction, so their features (many of which overlap with the personal and fan pages previously discussed) include discussion forums, member messaging, and similar promotional tools.

Facebook groups are generally organized around a topic or shared interest rather than around the promotion of a specific product or company. But you can still target the group toward the products you market by setting up a group for your industry or product type. This approach allows you to attract other enthusiasts (potential customers) into your marketing orbit. An example might be to start a snowboard group that is open to all snowboarders because you are a sales rep for Burton snowboards.

FACEBOOK CONCLUSIONS

As an individual, you should have a Facebook page to build your own network, regardless of your career intentions. As a marketer, you can see how Facebook can help the rapid spread of a useful service, product, or idea. Sign up for and use Facebook for a few weeks or months to get the hang of it. With over 200 million active users, there's got to be a way for you to position your products to attract their attention.

A winning way to do this is to provide a valuable service (as Peter Shankman did), but even if you can't do that, you can probably mimic the other aspect of HARO's success more easily: a constant stream of updates. As with our previous discussions of e-mail and blogs, by consistently publishing interesting, informative, or actionable "status updates," you can broadcast your marketing messages widely and inexpensively to any of your fans or friends who choose to receive them.

E-RICHES TIP: FACEBOOK UPDATES BY E-MAIL

If you don't plan on becoming a regular Facebook user, visit the "Settings" section of your Facebook page. There you can set your "Notifications" so that you receive updates of relevant Facebook activity by e-mail. That way you can save time—Facebook activity updates will come to you right in your e-mail inbox.

Using MySpace

MYSPACE STRATEGY GUIDE

MySpace.com was the hottest social network of 2005 and 2006. MySpace.com users come from all demographic groups, so it is difficult to summarize the vast community of more than 100 million people worldwide without generalizing.

Despite the commercialization of social networking, MySpace has remained primarily focused on social interaction rather than business-to-business activity. This means that your marketing opportunities are primarily paid advertising placements or clever promotions that encourage users to share marketing messages virally through graphics, online videos, games, or web site widgets.

Here are some examples.

MYSPACE SUCCESS PROFILES

MySpace allows its profile pages to be used in many ways. The most common use is for individuals to meet other individuals. But there are also millions of bands, companies, products, clubs, and random crazy stuff on the network, each with its own profile page and list of friends.

Although there are plenty of examples of those marketing themselves through MySpace, I found a few examples of more mainstream consumer product-driven MySpace marketing successes to share with you. As you'll see, each of these businesses has an offbeat product or approach that struck a chord with the MySpace audience. Try to imagine using techniques like these to market your products using MySpace.

MySpace Marketing Example 1: Birds Barbershop. Birds Barbershop is a "rock & roll hair place" with two locations in Austin, Texas. In addition to its web site (BirdsBarbershop.com), it started using MySpace to drum up interest in its first shop even before it opened. It uses MySpace to maintain one-on-one relationships with its friends and customers. Erin, one of the owners, says, "MySpace enables us to respond to customer feedback quickly while getting the word out on our promotions, live music, etc. to both our stylists and fans in one easy post!"

http://www.myspace.com/birdsbarbershop

MySpace Marketing Example 2: Seneca Lake Wine Trail. The Seneca Lake Wine Trail promotes tourism in the wine country of upstate New York. It started marketing its events, products, and brand via MySpace in early 2008 and was pleased with its initial success:

- ▲ Its MySpace profile has more than 2,800 friends, an overwhelming majority of whom live within a short drive of the trail and claim to like wine.

- ▲ There were more than 10,000 page views of its MySpace profile, which is substantial given how targeted the traffic is.

- ▲ At least 10 percent in extra ticket sales to the group's annual Golden Nose event resulted from MySpace.

▲ A "MySpace Party Photo Shoot" event provided a terrific batch of free models, photos of whom are being used in a variety of marketing collateral.

▲ Posting a proposed print ad campaign to its MySpace page allowed the group's thousands of friends to critique the ads. This impromptu focus group generated extensive, surprisingly valuable feedback.

Executive Director Paul Thomas told me that the key thing for the Seneca Lake Wine Trail is reaching the 21–31-year-old market. He said, "Rather than spattering them with traditional media ads, which that demo is uniquely capable of tuning out, or not even being exposed to in the first place, we are using MySpace, and to a lesser extent other social sites, to try and create a viable community with whom we interact and build lifelong relationships with."

http://www.myspace.com/senecalakewinetrail

MySpace Marketing Example 3: Bacon Salt. Believe it or not, my last MySpace example is the MySpace marketing campaign for a product called Bacon Salt. (Yes, it's salt that tastes like bacon.) More importantly, it's a lot more popular than you might expect, thanks largely to the company's marketing work on MySpace.

Here's a quick interview with Dave and Justin, the "Bacontrepreneurs" of J&D's Down Home Enterprises, the company behind Bacon Salt.

SF: Hello, Dave and Justin—can you give my readers a brief introduction to your "Bacon Salt meets MySpace" story?

J&D: Sure. We're definitely an example of a company that has used MySpace to impact our business. We launched our product with a web site, a MySpace profile, and a Facebook group and ended up selling out within a week. On MySpace we added everyone we could that had "I love bacon" on their MySpace profiles—there are actually 35,000 of them, believe it or not—and got tons of traffic and word of mouth from it.

SF: How did you find people with "I love bacon" on their profiles? Is there some sort of site-wide search?

J&D: Yes, you can do a search in MySpace to find profiles that have specific keywords.

SF: What did you do to convince them to friend you?

J&D: Just asked them, with a note to the effect of "we're trying to make everything taste like bacon. Want to come?" We also joined groups like Jews for Bacon (our product is kosher).

SF: Any other numbers or specifics you can share?

J&D: We sold all 3,000 of our jars in the first week, which shipped to people in 5 countries and 25 states. We were unprepared, to say the least—we only had 25 boxes and a roll of packing tape ready in my garage when the crush of orders started.

Today we're in over 7,000 stores around the country, have shipped our product to 47 countries, and have been featured on *Good Morning America*, ABC News, NPR, Fox News, the Food Network, Fox Business News, and the *Wall Street Journal*, sold out on QVC, and a lot more. It started with MySpace, spread to blogs and forums, then started to get picked up by traditional media.

It turned out that MySpace was the ultimate vehicle to promote a food company with zero budget because it allowed us to connect and engage with people who shared our love of bacon and brand our new product.

Using MySpace as a platform to launch a guerrilla marketing campaign worked very well, to say the least.

(Please note the absurdity of the initial marketing technique that led to Bacon Salt's success. Who would have thought that there were more than 35,000 people on MySpace who publicly displayed their love of bacon! This is great evidence of my "Nobody Demand" theory. See Chapter 12 for details of how almost any concept can find customers online.)

MYSPACE CHALLENGES

Although these stories are inspiring, MySpace is not the easiest social network to use if you are new to the online marketing arena.

One drawback of MySpace.com that has hurt its adoption by business users is that optimizing one's profile page is time-consuming. Unlike with LinkedIn.com or Facebook.com, for example, if you are a serious MySpace user, you need to invest some time before your page can compete with the millions of profiles that have already been established there.

This work falls into two categories: collecting friends and customizing your profile page.

1. *Collecting friends.* One of the reasons for MySpace.com's huge success was that it turned the age-old ritual of competing for popularity into a quantifiable commodity. It does this by displaying on each person's profile page how many friends have accepted links to that profile page. This encourages everyone on the network to compete to add as many people as possible to demonstrate his or her popularity to visitors.

2. *Customizing your MySpace page.* MySpace pages are usually heavily customized by regular users. This includes using HTML and CSS to personalize the color and graphics of your profile page, including lots of widgets, videos, and other graphic eye candy. This means that most pages on MySpace have different looks—and often even have different navigation methods. This chaotic visual environment is fun, but it's also challenging to brand managers who want to present a specific image.

Everybody starts from zero, of course, but to be taken seriously on MySpace, your page ideally needs to display a lot of friends, and also demonstrate some of this graphic customization. (See my MySpace profile page in Figure 9–3.)

Both of these activities are time-consuming and have an uncertain ROI. I recommend establishing a MySpace presence and customizing it enough to prove that you and your products "get it." But most

FIGURE 9–3.

professional people who use the site today do it for social reasons and/or drive whatever customer interest or business leads are generated there back to their more complete presences on their own web sites or other, more business-friendly social networks like LinkedIn or Facebook.

Using LinkedIn

LINKEDIN STRATEGY GUIDE

LinkedIn is a professionally oriented social network with more than 30 million members. Founded in 2003, it has risen to become the leading network for professionals who are interested in business networking. It is most commonly used to meet other professionals for personal career advancement, for sales or business development discussions, or simply for keeping in touch.

It's especially useful and appropriate for independent professionals, such as consultants, accountants, sales reps, attorneys, or PR professionals. These folks find the professional contacts particularly useful in marketing their services.

This focus on individual professional relationships means that LinkedIn is not an obvious platform for mass-market consumer marketing. Instead, it's most helpful to individual professionals and small B2B firms that attract a lot of their business by referral.

LinkedIn is also the most formal of the major social networks. Behavior and discussion topics are more professional than you'll find on MySpace, for example.

LINKEDIN.COM QUICK SETUP GUIDE

LinkedIn is designed to help professionals find each other and keep in touch. This means that its focus is on sharing credentials and qualifications that demonstrate its members' capabilities to one another. It does not allow companies or products to have their own profile pages. So, to set up your LinkedIn.com profile page, you mostly need to be ready to type in your personal career history to use as the basis for networking outreach.

Here's how to get started:

1. Sign up for a free LinkedIn account.

2. Post your résumé-style work history. It's up to you how much detail you want to share. It's generally a good idea to at least list your employers, the years you worked there, and the title you held in each of those positions. Disclosing this top-level data will allow other LinkedIn users (including former colleagues and executive recruiters) to most easily find and connect with you.

3. Begin building a network by inviting people to join your network. You will want to start with the easy invitations. These are people whom you know well and expect to be in touch with for the long term and who are already using the LinkedIn service. This may include both coworkers and family, but be careful about mixing your personal and business lives too much.

4. As soon as you have five or ten friends, other people on the network are likely to start seeing your name. This is because your listing will show up on your friends' pages as a friend of theirs, as well as in the search engines that LinkedIn uses inside its own site to help users find each other. This visibility will lead to additional invitations to "link" from other people. Those whom you know are then easy to accept and stay in touch with. (Those whom you don't know are worth a moment of research before you accept them.)

5. By establishing your profile with this initial short list of contacts, you have now entered LinkedIn's social network. To maintain and grow your network, all you will have to do is return to the site occasionally to accept (or deny) new link requests. (You can set your profile to automatically e-mail these requests to you, too.) Over time, your network will grow naturally as additional acquaintances offer to link to you. And if you put any time into it by seeking out and

inviting additional contacts, it will grow even faster. (See my LinkedIn profile page in Figure 9–4.)

LINKEDIN MARKETING TOOLS

LinkedIn Answers. The most direct tool for marketing on LinkedIn is its "Answers" section. On this part of the LinkedIn.com web site, members pose questions for other members to answer. Categories are as diverse as the fields in which LinkedIn users work. From IT to travel to nonprofits to startups, fashion, and sustainability, there are active LinkedIn members trading expert advice 24/7/365.

The dialogue on LinkedIn Answers is professional and mature, with most questioners receiving many thoughtful responses.

This forum obviously offers you a chance to position yourself as an expert, if that's helpful to your marketing approach. Many of the most active answer providers on LinkedIn.com are consultants or service providers of various types, for example. They answer questions to demonstrate their expertise and ask other questions to drum up new business leads or promote topics that are useful to their own businesses.

You can participate in these discussions for the same reasons. Ask questions for market research or promotional reasons, and answer questions where you can add value and attract business (or at least a LinkedIn connection) from new partners.

LinkedIn Recommendations. You can also post short "recommendations" of friends and colleagues on LinkedIn, and they can return the favor. These recommendations appear in text on both of your profile pages. These public displays of affection can help build credibility for an individual's work history or expertise. Especially if you are new in a field or are trying to make a career transition, it can be helpful to have public recommendations from former colleagues that say things like "Susan was a strong leader who helped us bring in the project on time and under budget."

LinkedIn Groups. LinkedIn also offers "groups" tools. These allow users to organize themselves into smaller communities targeted

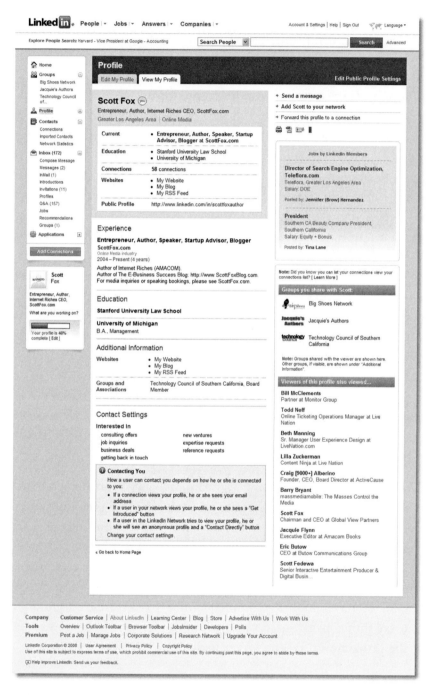

FIGURE 9–4.

toward shared interests. Examples include associations (the Technology Council of Southern California), corporate groups (IBMers), alumni associations (the University of Michigan), nonprofits (Wildlife Habitat Council), and many, many smaller groups focused on special industry or other networking interests.

Group members benefit by meeting other professionals with similar interests and keeping in touch easily through the LinkedIn system. Joining or starting a LinkedIn group is free.

LinkedIn groups can be valuable for keeping in touch with your customers or other industry contacts. Here's an example of a company that uses LinkedIn well, including groups.

LINKEDIN CASE STUDY: BIGSHOESNETWORK

Big Shoes Network is a job-posting web site for entry- to senior-level professionals within the fields of advertising, communications, graphic design, marketing, public relations, and Web design. Its market focus is on the upper midwestern states of Wisconsin, Illinois, and Minnesota.

The company's founder, Jeff Carrrigan, told me the company's LinkedIn story:

> Since our launch on October 1, 2006, we've served almost 1,000 companies in Wisconsin, Minnesota, and Illinois. Some of those companies include American Girl, Children's Hospital, Harley-Davidson, Johnson Controls, Kohl's, Manpower, and Northwestern Mutual.
>
> Big Shoes Network (BSN) has a presence on Facebook, LinkedIn, Namyz, and Twitter. Of these, we feel LinkedIn is the best fit for what we do. It has proved useful in the following ways:
>
> 1. *Business development opportunities.* By using LinkedIn's "Advanced Search" function, I'm able to identify and solicit key human resources and/or marketing-oriented potential clients at agencies, corporations, and nonprofits. These are individuals I never would have had access to in the past.

2. *Big Shoes Network Group.* We don't do recruiting ourselves because it would pose conflicts with our job advertisement posting clients. But by creating a group on LinkedIn, we've been able to help clients with their recruiting needs. For example, in the greater Milwaukee area, about 20 of the top 25 ad agencies use BSN to advertise their open job positions. If we started recruiting people from these same firms, it could be damaging to our ongoing relationship with them. Thus, we created the BSN Group on LinkedIn so that employers could privately initiate contact with potential recruits, and whatever happens, happens separately from our job posting business.

3. *Exposure.* BSN utilizes a Web analytics program that shows us where visitors are coming from. LinkedIn is an ever-present source of referrals, usually in our top 10. For example, already this week, we've received dozens of visits from LinkedIn. Now, these could be existing subscribers, but more likely they are new to our site thanks to our activity on LinkedIn.

As you can see, LinkedIn is an excellent resource for job seekers and for small businesses seeking new customer contacts.

For salespeople, LinkedIn is even more valuable on a day-to-day basis. As a former salesperson myself, I know that the hardest part of sales is often finding the right decision maker within a large organization. LinkedIn allows you to search by company name or industry to find the key players who are the decision makers for your sales or business development deals.

Your presence on LinkedIn can also be seen as "insurance" against the day you might need to find a new job. If you have followed the casual steps given here and grown your network over time, on that fateful day when you are let go from your position, you will have a list of at least dozens and possibly hundreds of people that you can reach with a few clicks of your mouse. Those folks will be a targeted audience, most likely in your same industry, who are members of LinkedIn for exactly the same reasons that you are there.

LinkedIn members are generally open to facilitating introductions and answering questions. This is the sort of networking tool that can greatly leverage your reach (and with a lot less work) at the critical moment when you need to call in favors, meet new people, and reposition your career.

Both of these uses of LinkedIn can directly affect your bottom line. I recommend spending an hour today to set up your LinkedIn profile if you don't already have one. And if you do, why not drop by its web site and update your contacts or answer a question or two in your field of expertise? It's a good investment.

HOW TO DETERMINE WHOM TO INVITE
OR ACCEPT AS A FRIEND

As soon as you become active on a social network, you are confronted with the rather awkward question of who is and who is not an appropriate friend.

Answering this correctly is a function of how you intend to use the social network. If you are using MySpace, Facebook, or any of the many other social networks we've discussed purely for social reasons, then you can add anyone who catches your fancy.

Using a social network for business purposes, however, means that it becomes part of your product presence. This suggests that you should be a little more strategic in how you build your network. Your list of friends is the social network equivalent of your subscriber mailing list in direct mail, with the addition that they might mail you back! That means that ideally you want to collect friends who are potential customers or business partners.

Most marketers on social networks are generous with their friending. For example, I accept pretty much every friend or link request that I receive on MySpace or Facebook. (Visit me on Facebook!) The more people who express interest in you and whatever product or brand you're representing, the better, right?

I do try to avoid accepting friend links from people who seem to be either cuckoo or extremist. However, that is not always possible to ascertain up front, given the wide reach of the Web, the low degree of actual contact, and the fact that people can change from someone you were happy to do business with to something else over the course of years.

On the flip side of the same coin, you will want to invite people to be your friend. It's obvious that the friends who can be most helpful in expanding your reputation cloud are those who are most socially influential. Their influence is, if anything, magnified online because of these tools.

These key influencers, or "mavens," to borrow a term from Malcolm Gladwell's best seller *The Tipping Point*, can differ from the real world. Instead of necessarily being the most attractive or "coolest," the most influential folks online are those who really know their chosen topics and choose to share their knowledge and passion with others. They are often experts at communicating online with a clever sense of humor that makes their writing (or videos) entertaining.

There are also differences among the social networks in terms of how valuable a friendship is. On MySpace, for example, users commonly collect thousands or even hundreds of thousands of friends. Obviously they don't really know most of these people. A friendship in this context simply represents a shared enthusiasm.

On Facebook, however, you can't even see much about other people unless they have already accepted you as a friend. This means that networks are built either truly through friends and friends of friends, or else by just blindly accepting almost anyone who expresses an interest in becoming your friend.

In LinkedIn's social network, which is more oriented toward professional business networking, people tend to be a bit more selective (as I am), since their presence there is designed specifically for career advancement.

The major danger of *overfriending* **is the potential mixing of your business and personal lives in inappropriate ways. If you are sharing personal details about your life or your family or sharing personal photographs, you can quickly distract your friends from the business-oriented marketing messages you are also trying to share through the network.**

My advice: Draw some lines in your head about the purpose of your membership in any social network sites you join. Use separate e-mail addresses, and post your private material in some places and your business material in others. There are more and more stories about people losing their jobs or being "uninvited" to job interviews because of inappropriate disclosures on social networks. You don't need to let that happen to you or the products you are trying to market.

E-RICHES TIP: HOW TO TURN DOWN A FRIEND REQUEST

One of the most awkward occurrences in social networking is when someone you know offers to link to you or become your friend, but you don't want to associate further with him. This can be because of social or professional issues, but it happens all the time. Unfortunately, there's no easy way to politely say "leave me alone" in cyberspace.

The result: If you do not want to become linked, you can usually simply ignore the invitation. This is a passive way of saying, "No, thank you." It is more commonly used than responding directly by saying no, which is obviously awkward and often can lead to problematic further dialogue.

Using Status Feeds: "What Are You Doing?"

The most interesting new tool enabled by the near-real-time connectivity of social networks is called *status feeds*.

The top of your Facebook profile asks, "What are you doing right now?" On MySpace pages, your "Status" is front and center, too. And Twitter (a microblogging service discussed later in Chapter 13) leads every page with the question, "What are you doing?"

You should take advantage of these opportunities to share what you are doing with your friends on the social network.

These updates can be large milestone events in your life or career like, "Just quit my job for a new position as VP of Sales—moving to Dallas," or a constant stream of daily minutiae (e.g., "finished breakfast, taking the kids to school").

And, just as you can collect updates from your friends automatically, any updates in your own life or career can usually be automatically distributed back out to them. So whenever they check in to that social network, your most recent status updates will appear, with no work required from you or them. Depending on the social network you are using, there are usually additional settings that you can use to automatically alert all your friends via feed every time you make any other changes to your page, too.

As a marketer, you can profit from these status feeds by including promotional messages that help establish you, your products, and your brand in customers' minds.

For example, a car dealer might post, "Marking down our Toyota Prius inventory for big tent sale this weekend." Or a marketing executive might update her status to say, "Just finished Q4 planning—the launch of our new eco-friendly widgets is going to rock!"

While writing this book, whenever I updated my status to something like, "More writing and research for new (and hopefully bestselling) online marketing book," I got many positive e-mails and comments from my social network friends.

Here are some tips for updating your social network status:

▲ Your updates should be a mix of personal and business, so that people can get to know you.

▲ You can include pitches, too, but avoid the hard sell. It's true that the only people who see your status updates are those who have chosen to, but everyone already has enough spam.

▲ As with all the other publishing advice in this book, the key to attracting readers to your status feeds is to add value. No one will read your status updates (and therefore you've failed as a marketer) if they aren't fun to keep up with.

▲ Be consistent so that readers can decide if your style of updates is useful to them. (Then they will either unsubscribe or—hopefully—start inviting their friends.)

The use of feeds can be fun because it helps you keep in touch with your network, and it is also really helpful because it can save you a lot of time by reducing the need to post the same info on multiple platforms.

Dangers of Social Networks

Since social networks are free to use, their primary danger is the wasting of the time you invest in their use. Here are some details on that and other common pitfalls:

▲ *Time suck.* Many people who are active in social media spend a *lot* of time online. Many of them are young and/or single with apparently few obligations. With plenty of free time for socializing, social media is truly a part of their lifestyle. This may mean that they are willing to invest more time into social networks than you can afford (or want to afford), especially given the potentially inconsistent ROI from social media marketing.

▲ *Conduct unbecoming.* Mixing your business and social lives can also lead to difficulties. Do you really want your business contacts to automatically be alerted that you've posted your vacation photos online (especially those pics of you drunk on the beach in Cancún)?

▲ *Overdisclosure (TMI).* The Web's memory is long (and possibly permanent). You need to think twice about everything you post online, especially if it potentially crosses the line between social and business, as mentioned previously. There are more stories every day about job applicants losing out on jobs because of risqué or otherwise inappropriate materials that company reps found on their social network profile pages. And MySpace and Facebook party photos have been used by prosecutors to get longer jail sentences for drunk driving convictions, too.[5]

▲ *Friend overload.* This is a variation of the time suck issue. This is where you connect with so many people online that you can't keep up with all the updates. Your "real" relationships get lost in the noise. Often this leads people to log off entirely or quit and start over with a new account (thus losing much of the brand equity and network of contacts that they had worked so hard to build). This is why I advise getting started as soon as possible but taking it slowly once you're active on social networks.

▲ *Don't spam.* Although *spam* usually refers to unwanted e-mail promotions, all the new ways to communicate via social networks offer you many new ways to annoy people. Yes, you can use these tools for promotional outreach, but don't be evil—spam is still spam.

SOCIAL NETWORKS CAN HELP YOU "CONTROL THE MESSAGE"

Another reason why social networks are critical to modern marketers is that social network profile pages appear highly ranked in search engine results. Search engines like Google will pick up everything you post online *and* that others post about you there—whether you like it or not.

So, creating a profile on a social network *in addition* to your own web site gives you an additional point of product presence. It's another credible, public web site where you can control the message displayed in search engine results to potential customers who search for your company name or products online.

Social Networks I Use (and You Should, Too)

I have long been interested in social network marketing, but I made only enough time to pursue it intermittently until I became convinced of its value as a marketing platform.

LINKEDIN

Like many business-oriented (adult professional) users, I started with LinkedIn. I chose LinkedIn over MySpace or its predecessors because, as an e-commerce strategist and online marketing coach, my advisory work is mostly business-to-business (B2B). When I was not working on my own projects or businesses, I mostly wanted to meet (and be contacted by) other senior professionals in my industry. That's LinkedIn's strength.

Many social network users, including those on LinkedIn, actively recruit new connections. For example, my friend Carl Bressler has one of the largest networks on LinkedIn. His profile page showed links to more than 6,000 people (until LinkedIn changed the display rules to reduce competition among super networkers by limiting them to displaying "500+ connections.")

I first enrolled in 2004, but I've never actively pursued LinkedIn connections. I started by posting a simple résumé-type profile page and connecting with a few "friends." Over the last few years, simply remembering to offer connections to interesting people I've met (and accepting the same) has naturally grown my LinkedIn network to hundreds of people. This is a highly targeted, personally connected group of friends and colleagues that I value.

I have occasionally used LinkedIn's classic social networking "friends of friends of friends" connection tools to reach people I don't know. This has come in very handy for recruiting high-profile panelists for a conference, finding investors for startups I consult for, or checking out potential business partners.

I also asked (and answered) some questions using LinkedIn's Answers section as part of the research for this book.

As I have expanded my personal online marketing activities and become an author with a public persona, MySpace and Facebook have become larger parts of my marketing mix. They allow me (and you) to efficiently connect with large audiences of consumers (B2C), too.

COME JOIN ME!

To get started on social networks yourself, it helps to have friends who are well-connected there already. Guess what? You've got *me!*

Now that you've read my book, I consider us friends.

Please visit me on Facebook and join the Scott Fox fan page. You can also add me as a Facebook friend, we can connect on LinkedIn, on MySpace, and on ScottFox.com, too.

This will give your personal social network a jumpstart by connecting you to many other folks with shared interest in online marketing and Internet business ventures.

MYSPACE

I got started with MySpace as part of my work with a major entertainment corporation, a leader in the music industry. I knew that MySpace was rapidly emerging as a promotional platform for bands, and my own staff of young techies was all over it, too.

So I set up my first profile there in 2006, when MySpace was white hot. As an "adult," I was puzzled by the chaotic interface design of MySpace pages. Users can modify the layout, colors, and menus to suit their own preferences. This is great for creativity and personal expression, but it does make it more challenging to navigate or market products.

So, I invested some time in learning to customize my MySpace profile. As discussed in my earlier advice, I wanted to demonstrate that I "got it" at least well enough not to embarrass myself.

I did this and began attracting friends, but I have to admit that my enthusiasm for MySpace has never grown much. Although I have met some interesting and talented people through friend "adds," the difficulties of navigating the system, its constant outages, and the mostly superficial banter that seems to serve as content on the network don't do much for me or my business.

The system has improved significantly in the past year, however. MySpace is trying hard to grow its almost $1 billion in annual advertising sales to please its corporate parent, Rupert Murdoch's News Corp. But that growth has been seriously impacted by the rise of Facebook, so MySpace is looking more like Facebook all the time. This means that MySpace is becoming more organized, reliable, and friendly to corporate promotions—good news for you as a marketer. This includes easier-to-use design templates, standardized layouts, and more reliable e-mail and other in-system messaging.

For business purposes, my impression is that MySpace is best used to build word-of-mouth buzz. People on MySpace are generally killing time, having fun, and looking for distraction. So, as my earlier examples demonstrated, capturing attention is easiest to do if your products are the sorts of things that young people like to talk about or if you can be creative enough to spin them into interesting, chatter-worthy topics that can go viral. (Advertising is also a major opportunity on MySpace, but, as you know, this book is more about clever marketing than paid advertising.)

Many top users of MySpace have hundreds of thousands of friends. Obviously these are very weak ties. They do, however, represent an audience. Collecting an audience is a goal we agree upon, right?

FACEBOOK

As with all of the social media tools, I got started on Facebook because I was repeatedly told that I "had to be there." (This probably sounds familiar, right?)

As mentioned, it was much easier to get started on Facebook because its templates are standardized. Entering biographical information, uploading a photograph or two, and feeding in my blog's RSS feed created a regularly updated profile that exposes my brand to Facebook users.

I also followed the strategy I have outlined by inviting a few friends to get started and promoting both my new personal profile and my official fan page on my blog and in my noozles. This has resulted in lots of friends in the year that I've been active on Facebook. I started with a base network of people that I knew personally and directly, and this group has grown naturally as the friends of my friends saw my updates.

Facebook is my current social network recommendation for you to explore. The Scott Fox fan page on Facebook hosts a collection of interesting and talented people. I try to nurture that group with extra attention and special offers when I can. Please come join us on Facebook at www.ScottFoxFans.com.

THE SCOTTFOX.COM SOCIAL NETWORK

Putting my money where my mouth is, I have also started my own social network. The ability of social networks to connect people and facilitate the sharing of information around common interests is so powerful that I couldn't stay away.

Since my role these days is primarily as an educator and mentor, I have started the forums at ScottFox.com specifically to help readers like you grow their online marketing expertise.

By purchasing this book, you have automatically become eligible for a **free trial membership in this service.** I would love to get to know you, and so would the many other entrepreneurs, online marketers, and social media experts who are active on this site. Please visit ScottFox.com to join us today!

Social Networks Conclusions

Social networks link together many of the most active, affluent, and influential consumers in the world—the mavens of Malcolm Gladwell's book *The Tipping Point* (and some "connectors," too). More participants join them every day. The magic of social networks happens when all the individual profile pages are linked together into a network of social (and Internet) connections.

This makes it easier than ever before for you to reach lots of people, and to prequalify those new contacts based on shared, pre-existing interests. Whether you use the big, popular general social networks like Facebook, focus your efforts on professional networking on LinkedIn, or concentrate on a social network only open to members of your industry (like ActiveRain.com for real estate pros, SelfGrowth.com for self improvement experts, or ArtFairInsiders.com for artists), taking advantage of these tools can help you grow your business online by establishing new relationships and deepening preexisting ones, too. Both types of relationships can help amplify your marketing messages to sell more products and make more money.

Social networks are not going away. In fact, I see a lot of similarities to how the Internet was viewed in 1994. I remember showing friends and family how I could log in and access a library in Africa from my apartment in San Francisco. No one was impressed—they saw it as geeky and odd, a curiosity with no certain application for business.

Well, we all know how that turned out. . .

The Internet economy has had its ups and downs, but there's no question that there's a *lot* of money to be made from an effective online product presence. The sooner your brand establishes its own presence by marketing on social networks, the more likely it is that you'll profit from their continuing growth and commercialization.

Start today by setting up your own accounts on Facebook and the other networks I've discussed. Search for "Scott Fox" and contact me. I'd be happy to be your first social network friend.

10
. . .

BUILD YOUR OWN SOCIAL
NETWORK CUSTOMER COMMUNITY

According to a survey of organizations using online communities, their greatest value is that they increase word-of-mouth (35 percent), increase brand awareness (28 percent), bring new ideas into the organization faster (24 percent) and increase customer loyalty (24 percent).

—"The 2008 Tribalization of Business" study, conducted by Beeline Labs, Deloitte, and the Society for New Communications Research, July 29, 2008

IN ADDITION to becoming active on social networks as a user yourself, what if you could create *your own* community online?

E-mail lists, blogs, and Facebook groups are all steps in this direction. Creating your own Web-based community for your audience and potential customers gives your users an online gathering place to pursue whatever interests bind them together—and interests you as a marketer.

Rollerblading, parenting strategies, health issues, vacation travel, career advice, gardening, tax preparation, climate change, elevator maintenance, whatever. . .

You can offer such a community online as a way to attract attention and involvement from the targeted groups. Their self-selected participation in your community obviously makes them available for your marketing messages, too.

Today it is easier than ever to start your own online community. You can choose high-priced custom solutions that can be developed by expensive software teams or midpriced Web-based social network packages offered by companies like KickApps, YourMembership.com, and Sparta Social Networks. There are even free (ad-supported) social network services like Ning.com that you can use to start your own online social network for no cost at all.

I am a huge fan of targeted communities. They can be great for marketing products to any collected audience, and they also easily lend themselves to the establishment of membership programs that generate recurring subscription revenues.

Their functionality has also rapidly advanced from simple "message board" communities to embrace many of the innovations of the social networking revolution. This usually means enhanced profile pages, in-system communication tools like e-mail or instant messaging, and common areas to share photos, video, and comments.

There is a much longer list of successful examples of such targeted online communities available today than there was when I wrote *Internet Riches*. Moving deeper into demographic niches than iVillage (which generally targets women) or Facebook (which targeted all college students early on), today you can find online communities targeting tighter niches.

Just a few examples that you can visit for inspiration are:

▲ Ravelry.com (which targets knitters)

▲ Xfire.com (which serves online video gamers)

▲ LibraryThing.com (for bookworms)

▲ Shoutlife.com (for Christians)

▲ ClubMom.com (for mothers)

There's even an "Ask a Ninja" community for those of you looking for a ninja's point of view on life's questions. (I'm not kidding—this site, http://fans.askaninja.com, has over 10,000 members!) All of these services have successfully targeted niche groups to build interesting new businesses.

All of them would be happy to hear from you, especially if you are interested in advertising with them.

Even more interesting, however, is your opportunity to mimic their success by starting *your own* online community to build *your own* audience to talk about what *you* want to discuss. Of course, no one will come to your party if you are a pushy or boring host, but if you put some effort into it, an online community can be the beachhead of your word-of-mouth marketing effort—a great place to nurture your biggest fans, evangelists, and customers.

ONLINE COMMUNITY CASE STUDY: ARTFAIRINSIDERS.COM

As usual, I am speaking from personal experience when I recommend this strategy. While the multimillion-dollar success of my work with Bill O'Reilly of Fox News to establish BillOReilly.com (as detailed in my book *Internet Riches*) is probably not too surprising to you, I'd also like to point you to ArtFairInsiders.com. (Figure 10–1 shows my ArtFairInsiders.com badge.)

As I discussed in *Internet Riches*, ArtFairCalendar.com is a web site business run by my own mother. I helped her learn how to build and run it to see if I could train an Internet novice in the online business-building and marketing techniques that I have used successfully myself for years.

Happily, ArtFairCalendar.com has thrived since I handed off the operations of the site to my mother. She has learned a fair bit about technology, but, even more importantly, the Web continues to get easier to use every year. Today ArtFairCalendar.com has expanded from just covering the Midwest to listing art fairs nationwide. It has also succeeded in attracting a steady and profitable advertising business from the many art fairs that want to be listed on the web site and promoted in the tens of thousands of e-mails my mother now sends out each month.

Of course, that was not enough to satisfy me. In fact, as part of the research for this book, I set up a new online community for the art fair artists to whom her ArtFairCalendar.com web site appeals. ArtFairInsiders.com is a social network set up using the free Ning.com service that I mentioned previously. You can find this new online community at http://www.ArtFairInsiders.com.

While ArtFairInsiders.com is still new, early signs are positive: Hundreds of artists signed up for the service during its beta-testing period. All of them are interested in learning more about how to make more money by exhibiting at art fairs. This bodes well for the site's suc-

FIGURE 10–1.

cess as a business selling ads to companies that want to reach this niche industry, as well as offering great opportunities for my mother to promote her consulting services, art fair–related e-books, and other products.

By positioning her as an expert in art fair production, marketing, and operations, we are succeeding in expanding the ArtFair Calendar.com brand into the social networking arena.

If you represent a product or brand that can be positioned as a leader or expert, this same opportunity is available to you. You can create an online community based on people's need to learn your information and desire to mingle. Such a community will give you an excellent platform for promoting your expertise, services, or products to a presold audience of self-selected and like-minded customers.

ONLINE COMMUNITY CASE STUDY:
POOLCENTER.COM

A more established example of an online community built for marketing purposes is Poolcenter.com of Springfield, Virginia.

Poolcenter.com started as the web site for a local swimming pool services company serving the Washington, D.C., metropolitan area. It was one of the first web sites dedicated to providing technical support and customer service for swimming pool owners. The constant back-and-forth with customers who had swimming pool maintenance questions led to the creation of many pages of web site content addressing common swimming pool service issues. This also led to the collection of an audience that shared a common interest in improved swimming pool maintenance.

The helpful online customer support that the Poolcenter.com team offered attracted traffic. It also soon led the team members into selling swimming pool maintenance products in order to fulfill nationwide demand from customers whose questions they answered. The company's success online eventually led to the sale of its service division, the business that gave birth to the Internet strategy.

Today the success of the Poolcenter.com community has allowed it to grow into an online retailer of more than 15,000 ready-to-ship swimming pool parts, toys, and equipment and safety items. It offers an online discussion/forum giving past, present, and future pool owners a place to talk about their pools. They can ask and answer questions, post pictures of their pools, and swap stories about everything from their last pool party to how they fixed their Comfortzone Heat Exchanger.

Popular areas of the Pool Community include the original Pool Info pages, the Pool Talk discussion/forum, a new Pool Tube for users to view/post/edit pool-related videos (instructional, technical, safety, and just-for-fun videos), and Pool Groups where pool owners can get together and discuss topics that are specific to their swimming pool interests.

Rob Cox, who runs the online community for Poolcenter.com, says,

> Poolcenter.com recognizes the human need for connectedness in today's online world. We have tried to stay close to our customer by giving free advice—as though it came from across a counter at a pool store, from people they know and trust. And here's the kicker—it doesn't have to be a [paid] Poolcenter employee. We invite our site visitors to "Dive into the Community Pool" to share and learn through a variety of online tools and media.
>
> We did have to overcome some fear of what they might say about us. Or that our competitors will promote themselves. We have rules of conduct, of course, but the fact is—anybody can post—anything they like. This anarchy is scary at first, but we find that Mob Rule (and a little cynicism) keeps things in check. If an "uprising" happens, we step in—only if needed, to enforce the code of conduct. But the real beauty is that the pool community is self-governing and self-policing. Many "experts" in the field serve as our pool managers and lifeguards.
>
> Compared to the previous year, our launch of new community features has helped our online sales jump by as much 90 percent, and unique visits to some of our Pool Info pages (nonproduct pages) have tripled. We've also seen huge increases in all types of media interest—print, video, and radio—since our launch of the "community pool."

If you represent a brand or product that appeals to a niche audience, research online until you uncover an angle or subniche of that culture where you can play host. Establish an online community or social network, and invite other members of that neglected subculture to come hang out with you. Discussion and sale of your products will happen naturally if you get the right group of people to join and help you spread the word.

I recommend three ways to explore creating your own community online.

1. Sign up for Facebook and explore the free group tools it offers. (These are discussed in more detail in Chapter 9.)

2. Visit Ning.com to learn about its services. It will allow you to set up your own customers' social network for no cost.

3. Come to ScottFox.com. Membership site strategy and service providers are always an active discussion topic. Redeem the free trial membership in my online social network that you earned by purchasing this book. By signing up, you can learn by observing how we run this community and meet fellow entrepreneurs and online marketers to grow your own online marketing expertise, too.

11

. . .

THE VIRAL MARKETING POWER
OF SOCIAL BOOKMARKING
AND SOCIAL NEWS SITES

SOCIAL BOOKMARKING and social news web sites are online communities where users submit Web page links in order to share them with other users and the general public.

The point of these sites is to collect the referrals and opinions of users from across the Web to find the "best" content. By allowing users to submit their favorite web sites, web pages, news stories, articles, photos, videos, and blog posts, these services aggregate lists and summaries of Web content for easy reference. Some social bookmarking sites specialize in specific topics, like Sphinn, which focuses on search engine optimization and online marketing topics, while others, like Yahoo! Buzz or Propeller, offer more general categories ranging from news to politics or style.

There are three core features of social news sites:

1. Users submit links to blog posts, news stories, articles, photos, videos, and other content.

2. Users vote on the content submitted by other users.

3. The highest-ranked submissions are featured on the site's home page, driving traffic back to the source web site.

In addition to automatically counting votes from registered users, some social news sites also employ human editors to choose submissions to be featured (if the story is highly relevant and newsworthy) or removed (if it's objectionable or off-topic).

The reward if a popular social news site's user community likes your submission? Traffic—upwards of 50,000 page views in a day.

History of Social Bookmarking and News Sites

Social bookmarking sites are a reflection of the revolution in the production and distribution of news. As the Internet has enabled anyone with a keyboard and an Internet connection to broadcast her opinion worldwide, create original content of her own, and break real news stories, too, it has been increasingly difficult for all of us to find the best resources on any specific topic.

That's where social bookmarking sites come in. Users worldwide surf the Web, save their favorites electronically, and submit their nominations for useful web sites, blog posts, news items, entertainment, and other content. By collecting the recommendations of such users worldwide, social bookmarking sites are able to create rapidly updated directories of Web information recommendations that are based on real human intelligence instead of just search engine crawlers' collections of links.

Social bookmarking started with a web site called del.icio.us. This site's simple goal was to help users manage their favorite site "bookmark" listings. By helping users collect and share their favorite site listings easily, it quickly became possible for a social bookmarking site to explore its own database to calculate which sites were bookmarked most often and in which categories.

Allowing users to nominate and vote on the best sites in each category was a new way of measuring site popularity. Publicly posting which sites were most popular created a new type of business: a web site that displayed links to other Web content based on that content's popularity among its own users. (While search engines also create rankings, those are based on their own software calculations. Social bookmarking sites are driven directly by the submissions and votes from their own human user communities.)

This creates "social news" web sites, where users submit and rank (and therefore influence the display of) stories *instead of professional editors making those choices*, which has been the tradition in news publishing for centuries. By visiting Digg.com, for example, you'll see top news stories in many categories. These range from technology news (where many social bookmarking sites started) to business, lifestyle, sports, and even "offbeat." In each of these categories, the stories or links that receive the most votes from Digg.com users worldwide rise to the top and are most prominently displayed on the home page of that section.

Because users are in control instead of professional editors, this also enables broader coverage of topics that mainstream media may have neglected. For example, you can find lists of today's most popular Web design posts on del.icio.us, most popular science or video gaming news on Digg.com, travel or recipe articles on furl.net, "what's hot" or "controversial" according to reddit.com users, or the health, international politics, or sports-related web pages that matter most today to newsvine.com users.

Today the "crowd sourcing" and ranking of content from across the Web creates a business for these social news sites and (here's the punch line!) *a potential publicity outlet for you.*

Many online marketers spend lots of time crafting stories specifically to try to get them posted on the front page of Digg.com, for example. Such a posting can lead to enough sudden traffic to overwhelm the servers of most average-sized web sites.

The audiences of these sites are also often early adopters, so they are usually a desirable demographic for spreading the word about new products.

Social Bookmarking Niches

Most first-wave social bookmarking sites were technology news and humor-centric services that appeal to young, male, early adopters.

But today there are social bookmarking sites dedicated to collecting the best sites, posts, and other content in many different sub-niches, and also in different formats, such as web pages (the original), videos, images, and podcasts (audio).

Some examples:

- Autospies: automotive news, car reviews, and auto show photos and videos

- Ball Hype: sports blog content aggregator

- Dealigg: deals and coupons for bargain hunters

- DNHour: domain name industry news

- Hugg: environmental issues, plus some politics, science, fashion, and technology

- IndianPad: news from India

- I am bored: weird and offbeat news

- Lipstick: celebrity gossip

- Skirt: female-oriented opinion and fashion, plus entertainment, design, technology, and food

- SWiK: open-source software

- Winelifetoday: news and opinion articles related to wine

What all this has meant for the news business is that the audience suddenly has a voice. Publishing has traditionally been a one-way medium, with editors and reporters creating the priorities by selecting which stories appear on a newspaper's front page with big headlines.

Today, however, social bookmarking sites have broken that monopoly. Users worldwide decide among themselves what's important by clicking "Digg it" or similar buttons across the Web millions of times each day to submit and vote for stories that they find valuable.

You'll see how these sites are potentially useful to you as a marketer if you undertake the following exercise:

1. Visit Digg.com and sign up for an account of your own.

2. Submit a story of your own.

You'll see that others will get a chance to vote on it. If the users of that community like your submission, votes could quickly snowball to propel your submission to the top of the rankings and therefore the site's home page. This would attract large numbers of clicks and visitors to your site with no additional effort, greatly amplifying the reach of your story and its potential sales impact.

DIGG.COM SUCCESS CASE STUDY

10e20 is a marketing agency that was presented with a difficult challenge: Its client, a leading vacation packages company, wanted to promote its commercial web site on Digg.com. More specifically, it wanted to sell vacation packages—not a typical topic for popular Digg.com articles.

When the agency constructed a very deliberate content package designed to appeal to the Digg.com audience, the client was happy to receive more than 200 new e-mail list sign-ups, more than 1,000 new links to its web site, and even 12 direct vacation package bookings.

How did 10e20 do it?

The agency created a specifically targeted article to place on the client's site. Instead of talking about generic travel topics with a boring headline, it instead wrote an article titled "Top 11 Underground Transit Systems in the World." You can see the copywriting experts at work here: the use of the number 11 instead of 10 to catch your eye, the appeal to the global audience of Digg.com, and the tried-and-true tactic of creating a ranking list for people to discuss on a topic that almost anyone would be qualified to give an opinion on.

The link to the article was then submitted to an appropriate Digg category ("world news"), along with a review of the article that was personal and opinionated and that highlighted the key points that people were likely to debate. It also mentioned that the article contained "amazing pics and video," so it had visual appeal, too.

The submission to Digg.com caught the attention of the Digg user community. It was promoted to the Digg home page in approximately six hours. This quickly led to more than 20,000 unique visitors to the client's vacation packages web site in 24 hours. ∎

Of course, it's not always that easy because there is intense competition to get one's stories promoted in this way. This is because each social bookmarking site has its own community. That community has coalesced around shared interests that the social bookmarking site specializes in collecting content on. Each site's users therefore watch all submissions closely and often team up to drive stories that benefit each other to the top of each site's rankings.

Social Bookmarking Site Personalities

In most cases, the rise of a story to reach the home page depends on the support of the people and the community who collectively run that social bookmarking site.

It can be difficult to get traction with general-interest social bookmarking sites such as Digg, Propeller, or StumbleUpon or in broad categories like "news" unless you become an active community member. This means making friends on the site. Such friends often trade favors to help promote each other's stories up the rankings in order to gain more traffic.

Because of this, one of the chief recommendations for success in using a social bookmarking site for publicity is to become an active, contributing member of the community of that social bookmarking site before trying to submit your posts, and especially instead of trying independently to game its system to gain quick publicity.

Unless you have an exclusive scoop on something big, being a recognized member of the community is the best way to get others to vote your submissions into prominence. In addition to active users who are simply interested in the subject matter covered by a social bookmarking site, many such sites have community members who are active specifically because they have their own promotional goals. And, of course, many people just enjoy the challenge of trying to promote posts to the front pages as recreation.

I don't recommend this, but you can also try setting up a list of aliases to submit your stories multiple times and reinforce their rise with your own cloaked votes. Most sites have software in place to prevent simple versions of this, and community members are highly wary of it also. Discovery of such deceptive practices can get you banned from these sites. Bottom line: Either play the game as it's designed (by making friends to cross-promote) or don't bother.

E-RICHES TIP: SOCIALMARKER.COM

If you're serious about social bookmarking and news sites, you'll soon find yourself submitting posts numerous times to many different sites. This can be really time-consuming.

A free service called Social Marker, designed for active users of bookmarking sites, helps automate this process for you. You can enter your login credentials just once for each service where you have an account. Then Social Marker will help you quickly visit each site and log you in automatically. You can use it to submit your new articles, posts, or links to dozens of social news services, all from the same browser window.

STUMBLEUPON SUCCESS CASE STUDY: ALASKAFLYFISHINGGOODS.COM

StumbleUpon is another popular social bookmarking site. Its users often install a special toolbar into their Web browsers. This toolbar allows them to easily submit rankings and reviews of any site they visit to the StumbleUpon.com database.

Like the other social bookmarking communities we have discussed, regular StumbleUpon users ("stumblers") enjoy discovering new stories and being the first to "stumble" them by submitting them to the site. Then other users of the site contribute by voting the submission up or down in the rankings.

AlaskaFlyFishingGoods.com was lucky enough to attract the attention of the StumbleUpon community when it was launched.

Obviously the site offers detailed information about fly-fishing expeditions and tourism in Alaska. Although social bookmarking communities tend to react more strongly to current events or technology news than to the launch of a content and e-commerce site, Flyte New Media (the agency behind the site) submitted it to StumbleUpon.

Apparently there are more active fly-fishing enthusiasts on StumbleUpon than I would have expected, or else there was a distinct lack of previous fly-fishing entries in the StumbleUpon database. Either way, the results were good: Even before the site was receiving any traffic from the search engines, AlaskaFlyFishingGoods.com received more than 2,000 visits from StumbleUpon users alone. By the end of its first month, the site had received a total of 5,673 visits. Almost 60 percent of these came directly from StumbleUpon, while Google sent only 163 visitors.

Perhaps just as importantly, Rich Brooks at Flyte New Media was not a particularly active site user (stumbler) when he submitted the site—it just took off on its own as a result of the enthusiasm of the StumbleUpon user community. It certainly helped that the site is very attractive visually and also targets a narrow and specific niche. It's doubtful that a new site submitted to a more generic category like "news" or "shopping" would get as strong a positive reaction as this targeted submission to "fly-fishing" succeeded in attracting.

This is a surprising yet inspiring result. Social bookmarking traffic tends to be short-lived, but for this newly launched site, the traffic received from StumbleUpon was a big success. It helped establish the new site as a leader in its niche almost immediately.

My own blog at ScottFox.com has also benefited from friendly stumblers. For example, I conducted an interview with a Facebook marketing expert named Dan Byler for my online radio show/podcast. (Check out my free podcasts at www.ScottFoxRadio.com.) Not surprisingly, many StumbleUpon users are also active on Facebook. They found this podcast interesting and repeatedly stumbled it. This led to repeated traffic to the page on my blog that showcases the Facebook interview.

INTROVERTED?

Social media offer a major opportunity for anyone who is shy in face-to-face encounters. You can stay at home and even be anonymous or create a new persona, but still socialize for business. And you can do it on your own terms—when, where, and how you want to engage.

Online, it doesn't matter what you look like or how you're dressed.

Jump into MySpace or Digg or start your own online social network dedicated to products or topics that are interesting to you. Then you can socialize without needing to be the life of the party all the time.

Social Bookmarking and Social News Sites Conclusions

Social bookmarking services are as much a game, competition, and community as they are a real marketing tool. While the result of their members' rankings of web pages and articles from across the Web results in nicely graded home pages of ranked articles, the process that ranks those articles is often the result of favors being traded behind the scenes among influential Diggers or stumblers.

My recommendation: If you have extra time or staff to try to participate, social bookmarking sites can be useful for marketing purposes. They can send a load of traffic to your web site.

Unfortunately, the visitors that such rankings bring to your web site are often semi-professional Web surfers. Thus, they often have little interest in e-commerce conversion or in helping you reach your lead-generation or sales goals. This means that the traffic bumps from a Yahoo! Buzz or Reddit home page placement can be short-lived.

But if you can find a social bookmarking site that has a solid audience of people who are interested in your topics, that much more targeted audience can be well worth your time, and it can be educational and fun to become an active member of the community. Gaining good placement (and therefore traffic) from your posts will still require involvement. But because the community is more targeted, it should be easier to attract attention and friends, and it may even be fun for you.

Another benefit of submitting stories to social bookmarking sites can be that it creates a link from a highly-ranked site back to your site. In addition to the direct effect of attracting visitors to visit your web site by clicking on your stories when they are posted on the social bookmarking site, the search engines can also pick up those links and factor them into an improved search engine ranking for your site. This can obviously help attract other visitors to your site, because your site is listed more prominently in the results shown by Google, Yahoo!, or other search engines.

Appearance on a social news site may also lead to your site being indexed more quickly, because your web site is linked to by an authoritative social bookmarking site that the search engine trusts.

Take Advantage of Social Media and Marketing Tools

If you suck at networking to begin with, no amount of online social networking is going to help you.

—Peter Shankman, HelpaReporterOut.com

To succeed in social media, you need to take social networking *literally:* Be *social* and *network!* Share knowledge, offer to help, join in community activities, and so on—just as if you had moved to a new neighborhood and wanted to be invited to the next block party.

You have to "pay to play." Just as in the real world, communities revolve around the give-and-take of relationships. If you just blast out your marketing messages online, you'll be called a spammer and shunned (just as if you started telemarketing to your neighbors or planting uninvited yard signs around your real-world neighborhood).

All of these social media opportunities are like the Yellow Pages phone directories used to be. You didn't count on them for all of your business, but you always put an ad in there, didn't you? Not being listed in "the book" was almost like not having a business at all.

Today you should have a presence on the leading social media and networking sites. Anyone who is looking for business should invest the time to set up a basic profile on the LinkedIn and Facebook online networking sites, plus any other niche networks that are specific to your trade. Submitting your best content to Digg, Yahoo! Buzz, or more specialized social news sites is a good idea, too. Membership in all of these services is usually free and can attract new customers or business referrals.

The bottom line is that social media offer great ways to connect with potential customers. It's all opt-in, so if users do choose to sign up for your services, they are fulfilling a marketer's dream by *asking you to send them more information.* It's then up to you to close them. So you need to work on your soft sell and hope that it translates into revenues. That's a connection that has not yet been completely proven, but it's an opportunity that certainly has promise.

Are you overwhelmed?

In the quest for e-riches, it's easy to be overwhelmed by all the social media tools. My advice: Don't be an ostrich and stick your head in the sand. You need to pick a service or two and try it. It's not as complicated as you think, and it's often fun. Try a service where you have heard that your friends or colleagues are already active so that you will have some friendly support while you get your feet wet.

In particular, I've had good luck with the services that create feeds. Using feeds correctly means that you can create content once, post it online, and then let your feed automatically spread it across any place or platform where your new online friends and customers have requested it. (See Chapter 4 for more discussion of the magic of feeds.) This includes sending out your blog posts by e-mail and posting them on Facebook, sending status updates out by e-mail or text message, sharing photos automatically, and packaging audio or video into podcast feeds. (See Chapter 20 for more on podcasting.)

The more you can ease into social media marketing by integrating it into your existing work processes, the easier it will be to gradually learn a bit more about its power and utility every day.

Jeffrey Gitomer, a best-selling sales coach and author of the *Little Red Book of Selling: 12.5 Principles of Sales Greatness*, says, "The Internet is not going away."

I say: *You need to engage with social media marketing or you will be left behind.*

These tools can help you get the word out more efficiently—isn't that your job as a marketer?

Note: There is a constant "arms race" as social media sites keep adding new features. This competition for users won't abate any time soon, so please visit ScottFox.com for the latest tips, tricks, and recommendations on how to best use social networks and social news sites to grow your sales.

PART FOUR

ATTRACTING CUSTOMERS WITH BLOGS AND MICROBLOGS

12

. . .

WELCOME TO THE BLOGOSPHERE

I'M NOT A FAN of blogs. Most blogs are boring personal trivia, self-centered blathering, superficial marketing, or rarely updated with anything worth reading. And many are all four!

But I *am* a fan of tools that make spreading your marketing messages easier and more cost-effective, and that help you recruit new fans and customers. It turns out that blogs can actually help you to do all of those things, too.

If you separate the typical content and approach of most blogs from the tools underneath, you can see that the tools are valuable regardless of your impression of blogs and blogging in general.

When it is used for business, a blog is a promotional tool—a tool for developing a better relationship with your audience of customers. Publishing a blog is a key part of your online product presence that gives you the chance to present your company in a favorable light, promote your products or services, and, most importantly, make money by generating new sales or sales leads (either for yourself or for your advertisers).

My Magic Blog Formula

Here's my magic formula for blogging success:

If you have something to say that will grow your business, then start a blog.

Otherwise shut up.

More specifically, don't waste your time blogging unless your business will profit by positioning you as an expert and/or engaging your customers in conversation. There are millions of blogs online already today. The last thing anyone needs is your "me, too" blog with uninspired or self-promotional content.

Blogging Opportunities

So how can you use blogs to grow your business online?

A blog is essentially a publishing venture. Don't worry about the technology; think about blogging as publishing a magazine. Most blogs were originally personal (noncommercial), but with the revolution in publishing brought about by the Internet, now anyone can publish inexpensively to a mass audience. So today blogs are increasingly used as promotional vehicles.

If your blog is company-sponsored, work with your marketing department to find topics that reflect well on your firm's products, personnel, or strategies. You want to attract readers with a soft sell approach that provides useful information and gradually leads them toward purchases.

If you want to make money with your own blog, this is your opportunity to start a business covering the issues, expertise, or products that you personally find most interesting. You'll have the best chance at making money if you cover topics that lend themselves to online advertising (like financial services, cars, retail gadgets, or technology). If you're trying to make money purely by blogging, you can then implement advertising programs like Google's Adsense or sell sponsorships yourself to begin monetizing your readership. I recommend deciding up front whether you are promoting your own goods or those of advertisers—it's hard to do both well. See *Internet Riches* or my blog at ScottFox.com for more on the business models behind blogging.

Regardless of your motivations, the best approach, whether for your employer or for yourself, is to find a little-covered niche or angle where you have expertise. Then you can position your company (or yourself) as an authority by establishing the leading blog on that topic.

Even if you don't see yourself (or your company) as a blogger, you should publish a blog today if you are creating any kind of text, video, or pictorial content for your business.

Why?

Not because it's trendy or cool to have a blog, but because a blog can be the foundation for your marketing outreach. Blogs offer you instant participation in a worldwide network of easy-to-use, inexpensive, widely adopted, and getting-better-all-the-time infrastructure to spread your marketing messages.

Using a blog format is especially recommended for four simple reasons:

1. *Search engines love blogs.* Posting material on a blog automatically positions it to be found not just by customers, but by search engines. Each new blog post creates a new page in the search engine's index, which generates additional listings in the search engine's databases and can attract more traffic. The search engines also recognize the format of a blog as a regularly updated content source and therefore give high credibility in their search results calculations to content posted in blogs. The sooner you post content on a blog, the more likely it is that search engine spiders will find it, index it, and add it to their listings. Once your content is included in the search engines, it becomes more likely that customers will find it, too.

2. *Blogs are easy to update.* Setting up and running a blog should no longer be seen as an IT department exercise—the configuration, hosting, and serving details are minor these days, and daily posting of updates is even easier. Its heritage as personal diary software means that blog software has many years of development behind it. Much of that evolution has been directed toward making the software easier to use. Easy means that you are likely to update more often. That means increased communication with your customers—a good thing that can lead to more sales.

3. *Blogs are inexpensive.* Years of competition, and especially the introduction of free open-source software, have made starting a blog cheaper and often free. The increased ease of updating also means less reliance on expensive IT departments for routine operations. Easy and free is a great combination, right?

4. *Blogs create "feeds" for you automatically.* The regular updates that you post on your blog can be automatically syndicated across the Web to other web sites, into widgets that other sites display, into blog reading tools for users who read lots of blogs daily (highly desirable early adopters), into Facebook or LinkedIn or other social networks where you have an audience, and even into feed-based e-mail systems to automatically create and send out e-mail versions of your updates to subscribers! (Be sure to read Chapter 5 about how blog feeds can automatically produce e-mail newsletters for you for free.) This easy and automatic syndication of content across the Net and other platforms helps you offer your content to anyone who is interested, any time, anywhere, in any format. (See my explanation of feeds in Chapter 4 and my discussion of the Convenience Principle in Chapter 5 for more on these points.) Blogs help you create the feeds that make that redistribution of your info possible with no extra work.

Blogging Challenges

Starting a blog implies that you are committing to a long-term relationship with your audience. This relationship is based on a consistent publishing schedule that requires regular updating with high-quality material.

Creating posts that are both informative and useful can be challenging. The posts should not all be about your products or your company, either. (See the "What Should You Blog About?" section later in the chapter.) Coverage of industry trends, statistics, or even links to unrelated humorous web sites can all attract readers. Such third-party content is also quicker to produce, and therefore less expensive. These diverse posts can help establish your blog's "voice" as a useful read above and beyond just pitching your products. (They also help your more product-focused posts stand out better.)

Once a blog is established, there are two tendencies: to underpublish or to overpublish. You need to find a middle ground—one that supplies your readers with enough information to turn them into repeat readers, but not enough to turn them off.

You need to post often enough to keep readers hooked and to build a readership around topics that are informative and useful to your intended audience. Don't blog just to keep up with unproven demand or because you think you are "supposed to." Determine what your personal or company goals are, probably in terms of sales, lead generation, or press coverage, and publish to support the achievement of those goals.

Given the high traffic in the blogosphere online today, it's important that your blog clearly communicates your company's priorities, branding, and latest initiatives. So, your blog should be produced, or least supervised, by senior marketing and communications-focused executives. Their input can help your blog reinforce your public image and generate new sales. Not doing so can confuse customers, lead to bad press, and hurt sales.

Which would you choose?

WIDGETS

A widget is a graphic unit that displays small portions of your site or information on other sites. These can be spread virally by consumer self-adoption or placed on other sites as paid-for ad placements. Examples include feeding your latest blog posts, press release headlines, sale announcements, product pictures, or even local weather to display in branded graphic elements on other web sites.

Some widgets are merely promotional, such as those that syndicate your latest blog post headlines to display on other sites, while others are more functional and might allow a customer to purchase your products without needing to visit your site.

Please Don't Blog If . . .

If your product, industry, resources, or personal interests don't inspire you to blog, that's okay.

A blog is simply a format for regularly updating information and easily delivering it to your audience. Any business should have enough happening to create a blog post at least once a week if you have the desire to share that news with the blogosphere.

If you don't have either the staff or the personal desire to maintain a blog yourself, don't set yourself up for failure by starting one. Those are legitimate reasons not to do it.

There are many, many, many blogs online that started with a burst of enthusiasm, only to fade away after just days or weeks because of the ongoing time commitment required to meet the demand for constant blog updating.

After you read this section and give it some thought, if you still don't have a clear vision of how you're going to source your content, maybe blogging isn't the best tool for marketing your business.

In fact, you can probably get almost as much traffic benefit by writing comments on other blogs that serve your target audience. Although this usually won't bring you search engine ranking benefit (because most blogs use "no follow" code that causes the search engines to ignore the links that you might include in your comments), the visibility of such comments can attract the attention of the readers in your targeted markets, *and* you won't have to meet the constant demand that the blog be updated.

E-RICHES TIP: THE SECRET WEAPON THAT CAN KEEP YOU FROM HAVING TO BLOG

Part of the appeal of blogs is that they allow readers to post comments. You can use comments yourself as a marketing tool. In fact, by posting on other blogs, you can get much of the benefit of blogging (exposure to the audience that reads blogs) without having to commit to maintaining a blog yourself.

If you post comments on blogs whose readers are your target market (including competitors' blogs!), you can reach the same audience with a lot less work. Post something insightful, funny, or useful, and you'll soon see clicks arriving at your site from those other blogs—and with a lot less work than building your own blog and online audience.

Example: Although I'm a committed blogger myself at ScottFox.com, part of the fun of the blogosphere is participating in the conversations that take place in the comments sections after each post on the many other blogs I regularly read.

On BusinessWeek Online, I read a blog post about social networking by small business owners. I left a comment summarizing my recommended strategy for the use of social networks for online marketing.

Later that day, I received an e-mail from the community editor at BusinessWeek.com. She wanted not only to thank me for my comment but to ask me for a photo of myself to post with a link to the comment on the BusinessWeek.com home page!

That one comment post brought me more traffic than many other marketing initiatives that took a lot more work.

Even Your Company or Product Is Blog-Worthy

If you think that your business is too mundane or you just doubt that anyone will be interested in your product or industry, consider the following.

Becoming a blogger simply presumes that you want to write and become a publisher about your field in addition to being a practitioner—think of yourself as the publisher of a new magazine devoted to your niche. Even people with supposedly "uninteresting" jobs can blog successfully by expanding their daily activities to include posting industry commentary, providing news about trends, and creating an audience community around that field or niche target market.

For example, an assembly-line worker can blog about the challenges of life on the job, industry trends, health/benefits/union activity, or foreign outsourcing competition, and invite commentary from other assembly-line workers in the same or related industries.

A house painter can blog about the best paints and tools for different kinds of jobs, and can show a constant stream of photos of his latest projects, including "before," "in-progress," and "after" shots to demonstrate his expertise. (This business model can include both marketing the painter's own expertise and also accepting ads from paint and supply companies.)

A chiropractor can blog about the latest wellness or exercise trends, an auto mechanic can provide expert commentary on car parts and services, and a chef might make a lively online community by blogging about his adventures in the kitchen and with the patrons of his restaurant. Almost any kind of timely and valuable information, especially if it's delivered with a personal touch, can find an audience online.

"Nobody Demand"

In my first book, *Internet Riches*, one of the "Internet Millionaire Secrets" that I introduced was my theory of "nobody demand." Here it is again because it applies very well to your opportunity for marketing your products by blogging. (As you can see, I've changed some of the words to reflect our current discussion, but you can see that the logic still applies.)

> You may have a~~n interesting product or service~~ *concept for a blog* but doubt its marketability. More often, you are excited about its marketability, but friends or family, the people you trust,

doubt its potential! These naysayers will spend a lot of energy trying to convince you that "nobody will buy that." But is that really true?

. . .Luckily, the Internet offers ~~entrepreneurs~~ *marketers* a chance to reach more people than ever before, and that's a reason to have confidence in your new ~~product's~~ *blog's* potential: If you find your ~~product~~ *topics* interesting, the chances are that others out there in cyberspace may, too.

When your naysayers claim that "nobody" would ~~buy your product or service~~ *read your blog*, do they really mean absolutely zero customers would be interested? "Nobody" probably means "nobody I know" or "nobody in our town" because, in the past, that's as far as most ~~entrepreneurs~~ *marketers* could afford to market their goods. Most people's vision of customer markets is limited by geography because industrial-age businesses could not afford to reach a wide audience without a huge marketing budget.

. . . Because the Internet destroys the limitations of geography, it can help you reach millions of people inexpensively. If you can find interest from even one in 10,000 potential customers, you have an exciting ~~e-business possibility~~ *blog* on your hands because the cost-effective reach of the Internet is so broad.

GROWING BLOG READERSHIP USING MY "NUGGET THEORY"

I'm sure you are like me in that you would rather read one good post per month than a dozen or more filler posts, hoping for a nugget of insight or entertainment. With the latter situation, it's likely that I will unsubscribe before the next true nugget arrives.

So, don't make your blog readers "mine" for your nuggets. Differentiate your best blog posts with attention-grabbing graphics and catchy headlines.

> Even better is to minimize the "chatter" on your blog and post only when you really have something to say.
>
> Although once you have a blog, you feel a constant obligation to publish, readers really are not dying to hear from you. They're looking for information, entertainment, and solutions to their problems. Restrict your posts to the most valuable "nuggets" and people will value your blog posts (and read them) more.

What Should You Blog About?

Cover what you do best and link to the rest.

— Jeff Jarvis, author of *What Would Google Do?*

I recommend basing your blog on the expertise that underlies your company's products. Real-life examples from personal experience make much better reading than theory and conjecture. Current news and trends in your industry are also good subject matter. For a company blog, don't forget that you can draw on the combined expertise of your management team to find topics, too.

As with any writing exercise, you need to find something to say that's unique. Specialized information, industry insight, a contrarian perspective, or vision into trends or issues—all of these approaches are proven winners for blog content.

Five key techniques to rely on are:

1. *Solve problems.* If your blog can offer solutions to problems that your audience commonly faces, you will soon have a loyal audience. Solving their problems by promoting your company's products (or those of your advertisers) can be a profitable win-win approach.

2. *Encourage interaction.* You may find success by simply "broadcasting" one way on your blog, but the Internet revolution is interactive, remember? You'll attract more readership, both in quantity and in loyalty, by allowing audience members to contribute their perspective, too. (Most blog software is built to do this by simply turning on the comments feature. This

can require additional work to moderate the incoming discussion and ensure that it reflects appropriately on your brand, however.)

3. *Be provocative.* A great way to get people's attention is to surprise them. Challenge your readers with controversy or discussion-provoking posts (or at least post titles). This can help you develop a voice for your blog that engages readers and converts them into repeat visitors.

4. *Don't waste anyone's time.* Don't waste your time or give subscribers a poor impression of your blog's value by publishing "filler" content. Although it can feel like you are just talking to yourself when you are writing a blog (or publishing a noozle), you need to remember that the point is to get others to read it. This means putting your best foot forward at all times by providing nuggets that are of value to your readers. My rule of thumb for this when writing is to publish only those pieces that I am sure would interest a respected friend or colleague.

5. *Share the load.* Not everything on your blog has to be written by you. Lean on your colleagues for blog article contributions, ask your best customers to contribute, consult your industry trade associations or Chamber of Commerce for interesting statistics to share, get free content from online article banks (see Chapter 16), and welcome "guest posts" from other bloggers, too. In fact, even simple collections of links to other web sites can be valuable to readers if they offer carefully selected, useful information to your audience.

E-RICHES TIP: DON'T FORGET THE PICS!

If you look at producing a blog as being similar to publishing a magazine, you can immediately see the importance of photos and graphics.

Graphics such as your company logo should be easily available. And the easiest photos to obtain are those of your own products and colleagues, so don't be shy about putting your digital camera to use if you are a new blogger.

*If you don't have a steady source of visuals from your business, I rec-
ommend using stock photos and images to help ensure that your blog
looks attractive and professional.*

*There are many companies online today that offer photos and other
visual images for quick and inexpensive use online. Simply use your
favorite search engine to search for "stock photos"—or you can be
even more specific and search for exactly what you need to dress up
your latest blog post. Try "stock photo sunset" if your post could use a
sunset picture, for example.*

*You can also find many photos that you can use for free if you credit
the photographer. Try searching on Flickr or other photo-sharing sites for
images that you like. Then check their licensing details. Many photogra-
phers today post their work online using "Creative Commons" licenses
that will cost you nothing to take advantage of.*

*Pictures are eye-catching and "worth 1,000 words." Don't focus so
much on your writing that you forget the visual appeal.*

Winning Blog Content Strategies

You don't have to be a creative or copywriting genius to attract traffic to your web site or blog. You just have to write interesting content—content that your target audience finds valuable.

How can you do this if you're not Shakespeare? *By writing what
others want to read.*

An analysis of my own blog traffic, plus watching the comment
streams at other top blogs, has helped me develop a hierarchy of blog
content. (See Figure 12–1.) Based on its appeal to business readers,
here's how I grade my own blog posts. The more my posts climb this
scale, the better the audience traffic and links they attract.

A HIERARCHY OF BUSINESS BLOG CONTENT THEMES

Actionable. Readers' number one interest is in content that can help
them *do* something. They want specifics about what actions to take
to improve their lives and business. The world is full of vague advice
and strategies. You can differentiate your content by publishing
detailed, specific advice. This is why comparison-shopping sites succeed—they tell you where the best deal is, so that you can take action.

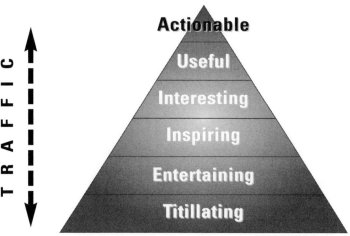

FIGURE 12–1. Blog Content Hierarchy

ScottFox.com

Specific opportunities for saving money are what powers Woot.com. Darren Rowse's Problogger blog teaches you how to make money as a blogger. Actionable details for starting an online business are what have attracted all the positive reviews for my book, *Internet Riches*, on Amazon.com, too.

Useful. Readers also appreciate advice that may not be immediately actionable, but that is useful and more general. Posting current news items or statistics relevant to your industry or target market is a great easy way to serve the audience here. You don't need to know what people will do with that news or those statistics, but if you've added value by filtering that info for them, they're likely to return for more.

That's why readers collect links and feeds from news sites, as well as subscribe to blogs and noozles like the Center for Media Research's Daily Brief, Michael Arrington's Techcrunch, or Search Engine Watch. Instruction is also appreciated, as demonstrated by the success of Brian Clark's Copyblogger copywriting blog or the many blogs that offer Photoshop or programming tutorials.

Interesting. Less actionable or useful are the "interesting" thoughts, factoids, or commentary that you can share. Readers file these away mentally and often use them for watercooler conversations. Celebrity gossip leader PerezHilton.com is a prime example here, as are Penelope Trunk's Brazen Careerist blog (and book), the political blog of Dick Morris (author of *Fleeced*), the "offbeat news" page on Digg.com, and Guy Kawasaki's "tweets" on Twitter (see Chapter 13 for more on Twitter).

Inspiring. Content that motivates or excites is both useful and interesting, but often vague. Helping people feel better about themselves is a valid goal, but if it is not actionable, it falls lower on the utility scale. Inspirational content can be a winner, however, because even when people forget what you *said*, they're likely to remember how you made them *feel*. If they felt good when reading your blog, they're likely to return for more.

Michael Masterson's Early to Rise, David Riklan's SelfGrowth.com, and Joyce Showalter's Heroic Stories make a business out of this category online. Print authors like Tony Robbins (*Awaken the Giant Within* and *Unlimited Power*), Deepak Chopra (*Creating Affluence, The Book of Secrets*), and Richard Bach (*Jonathan Livingston Seagull*) have sold millions of books here, too.

Entertaining. We all appreciate distraction from our daily chores. Humor and recreation are great attractors of traffic but are difficult to replicate every day. FARK.com's "news" (profiled in *Internet Riches*), YouTube's videos, and Kongregate's Web-based video games all entertain surfers with great success but less actionable result.

Titillating. Sex sells the best, of course. It's a great attention-getter, but it's difficult to use to build your business readership unless your business model tends toward porn.

Your goal as an online content producer is to attract repeat readers. I propose that the more your content climbs this scale toward actionable, the more useful business readers will find it.

BLOG CASE STUDY:
MARY WHITE, BNBFINDER.COM

Most businesses fail at blogging. This is often because they use the blog only as a platform for shilling their products. Who wants to read that? I don't.

As the hierarchy given previously suggests, helpful and actionable content is much more effective.

Mary White of BnBFinder.com gave me some great examples of actionable blog content. Her business is a directory of bed-and-breakfast inns. It helps vacation seekers find the perfect getaway with searchable worldwide listings of more than 3,000 B&Bs.

Two of the most popular recent entries on her company's blog are "What's the secret to making thick cookies?" and "How to make scrambled eggs fluffy." These questions were submitted by her customers, the B&B owners who advertise on the site.

In both cases, she posted the questions in her next noozle, with a link back to the BnBFinder.com blog. In the noozle, she asked other newsletter readers to leave any baking tips they had as responses in the blog's comments section. Both of these topics were great successes in terms of traffic and positive reader feedback. Mary says, "By combining interactive topics in our blog and newsletter, we have increased the readership of both, and brought more users and clients onto the site."

While cookie and egg recipes may sound like trivial issues to you, they are important business topics for the BnBFinder.com blog's audience of bed-and-breakfast inn owners. Keeping her audience's needs in mind helps BnBFinder.com's blog audience keep growing.

Throw a Blog Readership-Building Party

We see our customers as invited guests to a party, and we are the hosts. It's our job every day to make every important aspect of the customer experience a little bit better.

—Jeff Bezos, founder and CEO of Amazon.com

The foundation of attracting readers in any medium is producing good content. This brings positive word of mouth, more traffic, and better search engine rankings.

So I recommend thinking of blogging as if you are hosting a party. The "occasion" is your blog's content. It can be a birthday party, a circus, a convention mixer, a networking brunch—whatever metaphor suits your style. The point is that the party has to be interesting enough for people to want to attend (i.e., read your blog regularly).

Mingle and introduce and offer refreshments by using your blog to share anecdotes that are entertaining and educational and that help people connect with one another. This is the success formula for a successful party in real life and for a successful blog online.

Beyond writing your own insanely informative, actionable, and entertaining blog posts, you don't need to be the center of attention; everybody knows that he is at your house. If people have chosen to visit (i.e., read your blog), then you have their attention and the benefit of the doubt—it's up to you to entertain them and keep them coming back.

You can "invite" others to attend your party by covering them and discussing how clever they are in your blog (and linking to their blogs and web sites, too). Try blogging about your best customers or clever uses of your products to make others look good instead of only promoting your own products. This makes for entertaining reading because it contains specific examples. It also encourages the viral spread of your content as the people you cover link back to your blog and forward links to your blog to friends, too.

Six Blog Success Stories

While it is easy to put up a blog that simply covers your own products or company, that usually makes for boring reading. In fact, 99 percent of blogs are like that—worthless.

The blog success stories that make up the remaining 1 percent generally fall into one of three categories:

1. *Personal blogs.* Despite our business-focused discussion, it's still true that most blogs are personal ones. These can be fun, but they aren't relevant for this book.

2. *Information product blogs.* The most active business blog sector is that of information marketers, most of whom are busy selling online marketing advice to each other. I'm not going to focus on these either because it's pretty obvious what their products are and how they promote themselves. (They also get plenty of coverage in the blogosphere anyway.)

3. *Company blogs that market a brand or product.* Here is the new wave of opportunity that I recommend you pursue to grow your business online now. The best way to prove that your company, too, has the potential to blog successfully is to show you. So, I looked hard to find blogs run by real companies that are promoting real products.

Here, in their own words, is a bunch of short examples of real companies that have successfully expanded their product presence with product marketing blogs. Not surprisingly, most of them hit the "actionable" level on my hierarchy of valuable blog content.

```
Dear Scott,

My company is 28 years old, and I, Rob Packard,
have unique experience in the commercial skylight
repair/replacement field. I have sold about $2
million worth of business through my blog in the
last three years.

My story is that I always wanted to share my
knowledge with the rest of the nation (or world)
but did not have an efficient or cost-effective
way of doing so. Now, because of the findability
of our blog, people can find our company and are
happy to use our services. The blog builds cred-
ibility because they can look to see our knowl-
edge base and what projects we have worked on,
etc. It also provides a link to our web site,
where we keep more specific data that is more like
marketing-type material.

Therefore, when a future client calls, the per-
fect match has already been made (kind of like
these matching couples sites). Our credibility
has already been established, so I spend very
little time "selling." We get down to what are
their needs and how can we help them. Our sales
area has expanded to the nation and I assume some-
day the world.
```

Also, we do sell products from the blog that get shipped directly from the manufacturer to the customer's home. That is an easy way to make profit.

Rob Packard, President/CEO
Skylight Specialists, Inc.
Englewood, Colorado
http://blog.skyspec.com/

Hi Scott,

During a brainstorming session in 2008, Moishe's Moving and Storage decided to create a handful of company blogs as a more direct way to interact with our customers. Shortly after the meeting, we began posting daily, with information focused on the many industries Moishe's has a hand in, providing tips and industry news, and pinpointing the different services offered by the company.

Since the blogs were created, Moishe's Moving executives have kept readers in the know about a wide range of topics, including self-storage, document storage, international moving, mobile storage, wine culture, and NYC-based art. As the CEO of Moishe's, I think it's especially important to stay in touch with our customers. I've joined in the blogging efforts as well, keeping a weekly "Thoughts from the CEO" blog that discusses goings-on at the company and in the moving industry as a whole.

Our blogs have made a noticeable impact on both our web site traffic, which has increased by roughly 15 percent, and the direct response we routinely receive from our customers. Although it's difficult to correlate the exact increase in business with the introduction of the blogs, we can say anecdotally that many of our customers have mentioned them when inquiring about a price quote for moving or storage space.

Eugene Lemay
CEO, Moishe's Moving and Storage
New York, New York
http://www.moishes.com/

Hi Scott,

I only started blogging about six months ago. I'm mainly a property and casualty insurance agent. I don't update my http://InsuranceRenegade.com blog as often as I probably should, but I've experienced fantastic results.

I can't imagine people sitting around waiting for the next insurance article, but I have a couple of goals that my blog is helping me achieve:

* Establish myself as the "go to" expert in Arizona for insurance.

* Educate consumers that insurance is more than just price (and we don't sell just on price).

* Educate consumers that a quality insurance agent is an advisor and it won't cost more.

* Generate business for my agency for auto, home, business, and other lines of insurance.

We've gone from zero Internet business to about one quote request per day and growing. To get traffic, I use pay-per-click advertising and put the site URLs on all our marketing materials. I've also started posting comments on related blogs, especially those written by people in related businesses like Realtors (since I sell home insurance).

When clients or prospects have a question, I will often e-mail a link to a blog post with the answer, and it helps solidify the relationship. They then also read the articles and ask questions about other products.

Matt Fox
Fox Insurance Services, LLC
Mesa, Arizona
www.InsuranceRenegade.com

E-RICHES TIP

Use the free services from AddThis or ShareThis to make it easy for your readers to add your content to their favorite social bookmarking sites. These free services offer easy-to-install buttons and widgets for your blog. Once these are installed on your blog, your readers can simply click on their buttons to be offered a menu with quick submission buttons for most of the major content-sharing services and social networks, including Digg, MySpace, Furl, Technorati, and Facebook. By making it easy for your users to promote your content on these popular services, you can benefit from increased traffic, too.

(See Chapter 11 for more on how social bookmarking sites can help your promotional efforts online.)

Scott,

My company, StaffScapes, Inc., is a Professional Employer Organization that outsources HR, payroll, and other employee-related problems. Blogging about HR and payroll issues has helped grow my business.

We have been blogging for almost two years. During that time, we have had increased web page views and, more importantly, we have had many new sales opportunities and closed new clients because of our blogs.

Many of the new requests for proposal that come in are from small business owners who are doing research at night or on Sunday while at home. It seems that many business owners want to implement new programs such as HR outsourcing but can't find the time to work on it at the office. This leads to new work for my sales team every Monday morning.

The hidden value of blogging is employee education. I have a small office, and I encourage all staff to blog weekly. Just like in school, when you had to write a paper for class, you had to research that paper. That research has expanded the education level of my staff, and with the increase in education, they are better able to service clients, resulting in better retention rates and happier clients.

Good luck on your new book.

Jim Thibodeau
StaffScapes, Inc.
Westminster, Colorado
http://www.staffscapes.com

Dear Mr. Fox,

Our blog, PhoenixMarketTrends.com, is an online outlet for our offline services business. We, Artur & Joanna Real Estate Team, in Phoenix, AZ, are agents who work in residential and commercial real estate. Since we started our blog in April 2007, our page views, unique visitors, and return visitors have been increasing quickly and steadily on a monthly basis. We receive e-mails and calls from potential clients on a daily basis as a reaction to what we cover in the blog. The most successful posts have been those covering either specific real estate market happenings or specific communities.

The PhoenixMarketTrends.com blog has helped us generate new business. We ask each client where they found us so we can track our success rate with any advertising.

This year we have had a good portion of clients from the blog buy properties while our database of active clients has been growing. The clients we have found have come from places like Canada, Hawaii, and locally in Greater Phoenix. Several

have mentioned that they had been reading
PhoenixMarketTrends.com for up to a year before
they contacted us.

In addition, the blog has reduced our printing
costs and enabled us to keep in touch with former
clients more efficiently.

Artur Ciesielski, CCIM
Premier Marketing Group of Realty Executives
Phoenix, Arizona
http://www.PhoenixMarketTrends.com

Hi Scott,

My client, Lake Tahoe's Heavenly Mountain Ski
Resort, started with a few thousand visitors per
day to its blog, and traffic has steadily climbed;
60 percent of these are new visitors, bringing a
333 percent increase in traffic from the blog to
the main web site.

Heavenly's blog has given them another channel to
communicate the personality of the brand. Instead
of carefully scripted press releases (which their
customer base is not apt to respond well to),
Heavenly staff is able to discuss other aspects
of the mountain in a real voice. They talk about
snowmaking, ski school, team riders, and environmental initiatives that extend the conversation
not only in comments but also in linking and
linkbacks from other web sites.

We have also seen several blog posts get picked
up by other bloggers. Examples are when they
installed storm drain filters to prevent runoff
into Lake Tahoe, and another when they were recognized as a leader in ski resort marketing for
their use of various online marketing tools.

Sincerely,

Robert Payne, Marketing Director, Twelve Horses
Reno, Nevada
http://blog.skiheavenly.com

What Blogging System or Software Should You Use?

Starting a blog today is no longer the technical exercise that it used to be. A blog can be cheap or even free and easily administered by anyone who can point and click her way around a Web browser window.

The software that powers most blogs today is usually offered in conjunction with its hosting. Even many very highly trafficked and profitable blogs use popular hosted services such as Wordpress.org, Wordpress.com, Blogger.com, or TypePad instead of installing, maintaining, and serving their own blogs in-house.

These tools are quite affordable, too. They range from free (Wordpress and Blogger) to cheap (TypePad starts at just $4.95 a month), and many other services today include free blogging platforms inside them (Facebook and Amazon.com, among others).

Of course, you can pay more for custom hosting and configuration and design if you'd like to!

Criteria for selecting the best blog hosting/software solution for your marketing needs include:

- ▲ Easy posting and editing

- ▲ Clean, useful layout templates that don't require custom implementation

- ▲ The ability to organize posts into searchable categories and mark them with searchable tags

- ▲ Photo hosting

- ▲ Post scheduling

- ▲ Multiauthor multilevel permissions

- ▲ Access to the underlying HTML page for customization of the design if necessary

- ▲ Control over meta tags for SEO

- ▲ Domain mapping to replace the provider's URL with your own

- ▲ Detailed traffic reporting

▲ Automatic generation of RSS feeds of the content you post
   and the comments received

▲ Easy comments moderation

▲ Import/export to/from other blog platforms

▲ Technical support

▲ Price

▲ Comment spam blocking

Luckily for you, the blog software market has really matured in
the last couple of years. Today there are just a few players left, and
they all offer pretty good tools at low prices.

My favorites are:

TypePad. This paid service is my current favorite. I moved all
of my own web sites over to TypePad in 2008, in fact. The new
platform the company recently launched continues to have
bugs that make blog post editing a bit balky, but the ability to
host multiple blogs in one account makes it a great (and very
cost-effective) web site hosting service. Visit www.TypePad
Review.com for updates to this recommendation.

Wordpress.com. This open-source software-based service is
free. I've had trouble with its reliability and support, but it
seems to be rapidly improving. It is increasingly the top choice
for startup bloggers.

Visit ScottFox.com and search on "blogs" or "web site hosting" to
find my latest recommendations.

THE #1 OBJECTION TO STARTING A CORPORATE BLOG

Not every company or product deserves its own blog, but there
are millions of them that do that have not yet started.

Why is that?

Today the technical hurdles of starting a blog have fallen completely. Anyone (including you) can visit Wordpress.com,

TypePad, or Blogger.com and set up a blog in just minutes for almost nothing.

So what's keeping marketers out of the blogosphere?

Fear.

Fear of embarrassing themselves or their brand (or their clients or partners), *fear* of hearing what their customers really think, *fear* that the time invested will be wasted, and especially *fear* of losing control over the traditional one-way marketing message and instead confront the public directly. Yikes!

I agree with and understand all of those concerns about blogging and other social marketing strategies. The problem is that they are not sufficient excuse to delay playing a more active role online. The bottom line is this: *If you are not managing your product presence by talking about, promoting, and defending your products online, others will be doing it for you instead.*

It would be great if all those who decided to write about your products were happy fans. But the odds are that at least some of them will be unhappy customers or even competitors. If your team is not online to present your side of any discussion and protect your reputation cloud, you are losing the battle for customer mind share right now. (And this trend is only accelerating.)

Combining your expertise with the inexpensive, worldwide reach of the Internet as a publishing platform can be a winning combination to expand your product presence. Properly executed blogs can generate sales and publicity to benefit both your employer and your career. Startup costs are minimal, and the upside is real.

The sooner you get started, the sooner your blog can grow into a valuable marketing tool and become a strong part of your product presence.

What are you waiting for? Get your blog party started!

13

. . .

MICROBLOGGING
WITH TWITTER

*All this twiddling of your thumbs online with Twitter sounds like "business
haiku" to me.*

—Bob "Sully" Sullivan, Business Talk Radio Network's *Big Biz Radio Show*

SULLY IS RIGHT: Short-form "microblogging" is a new communications wave that brings with it its own style.

Microblogging tools are the latest trend in digital communications.
As the terms *micro* and *blog* imply, these services specialize in helping
you send very short, bloglike updates to anyone who signs up to "follow" the posts you make to a microblogging service like Twitter.

To use Twitter you post a message either by sending a text message from your mobile phone or by typing it into your account page
on the Twitter web site. Your short messages are then displayed
online on Twitter.com in a publicly visible "timeline," and can also be

sent to your friends' phones as text messages and to their Twitter.com account pages for online viewing.

Twitter users subscribe to follow the posts that individual users like you may send out each day. These subscribers are called "followers." The result is a service similar to the subscriber distribution and management functionality of an e-mail service like Constant Contact but delivered to the Twitter web site and your friends' phones.

Unlike e-mail, however, a microblogging service limits you to writing very short messages that it posts to its own web site and sends to your friends' mobile phones as SMS (simple message service) text messages. These messages can also be received by your friends online using various software tools and feeds. (It's up to each of your followers whether they read your messages online, on their phones, or using other software that we'll discuss.)

Twitter is the current leader in microblogging. Other similar services include FriendFeed, Jaiku, Yammer, and identi.ca—each of which has its own slightly different set of features, delivery strategy, and helpful plug-ins.

I'm going to focus on Twitter. It's the leader in the space; the company has raised more than $55 million in venture capital, and it seems positioned to dominate this new form of digital communications. (Of course, it may also be overtaken by competitors and turn into a Friendster, Netscape, Napster, or Pets.com, but we have to start somewhere, right?)

Twitter uses SMS, which is more commonly known as text messaging, as its basic communications tool. The protocols of SMS text messages limit Twitter messages to just 140 characters. Messages also include no formatting (e.g., colors, font sizes, bold, or highlighting) or pictures. This is because SMS was designed for "simple" use on the limited display screens of previous generations of mobile phones.

What Is It Good For?

Twitter is good for sending out short bursts of information ("tweets") to anyone who is interested in your topics. If you choose to use it for personal communications, it's great for "tweeting" your status or activities throughout the day to friends or family (who must also be regular SMS users or Twitter web site visitors to retrieve your messages).

Short messages like "I'll be there soon," "Just had a great lunch with Fred," or "Anybody want to see the new Harry Potter movie tonight?" can be a great way to keep in touch.

As these examples suggest, your tweets can go privately to selected friends, like a private e-mail, or they can be broadcast to wider public audiences composed of anyone who wants to sign up to follow you on Twitter.com. All tweets are publicly viewable and archived at Twitter.com, too, although private direct text messages are also available.

While most activity on Twitter is either entirely personal or personal updates by people to their business contacts, major news organizations such as CNN, the BBC, and the *Los Angeles Times* now tweet breaking news and news headlines daily, too.

This is an interesting new platform for marketers because it offers an additional way to reach customers who express interest in hearing from you. If a person signs up to follow you on Twitter, she is interested in hearing your messages, so it's incumbent on you to send her something interesting.

Many large companies, including Dell, Whole Foods, Comcast, Dunkin' Donuts, and JetBlue, have set up accounts on Twitter to take advantage of this. These corporate Twitterers have attracted thousands of followers by using Twitter to answer customers' questions and to let customers know about special offers.

For example, Dell is using more than 10 different accounts promoting offers from its different sales divisions to Twitter users. A typical tweet might read:

```
20% off refurb Latitude XT tablet or XFR fully
ruggedized  Laptop.  Enter  code  @  checkout:
J?$P12345678
```

While repeated promotional messages like this might be seen as spam in other contexts, the company's Twitter followers have specifically requested to hear from Dell with 140-character-long messages of this type, so it's a win-win marketing strategy.

Because Twitter is still relatively new, its audiences are very targeted. This means that it also can offer surprising access to people you may not encounter otherwise.

My fellow blogger Jonathan Fields (author of *Career Renegade: How to Make a Great Living Doing What You Love*) shared a good example of how he met and benefited from tweeting with Steve Baker, a *Business Week* writer (and author of *The Numerati*):

Knock, Knock, It's *BusinessWeek* Calling!

A few weeks ago, writer and blogger Steve Baker wrote the cover story for *BusinessWeek* magazine about blogging and social media. Not too long before that, I'd never heard of Steve, and I am fairly confident he'd never heard of me. But I started following him on Twitter because I enjoyed his "tweets."

While writing his story, Steve asked his Twitter followers to share their feelings about the role of blogs, social media, and Twitter. I tweeted back something like, "Blogs are the big show, IM/social media is the backstage pass and Twitter/microblogging is the afterparty. It's about layers of access."

Steve dug the quote and a few months later I was quoted in the cover story in *BusinessWeek*. Pretty cool, right?[1]

Using Twitter for Business

You can see the similarity of this tool to both blogging and e-mail: As often as you have something worth saying, you can say it inexpensively to people who have chosen to listen. For marketing your business, this means another opportunity to promote yourself or your products.

So, I recommend creative and judicious use of Twitter. Just as with the other digital community tools we are discussing, you want to "publish" consistently to share relevant information with your followers. Just like blog and noozle readers, Twitter followers will unsubscribe if you spam them. (And remember, some people pay for text messages, so your tweets had better be good!)

Joel Comm (author of *The Adsense Code* and *Twitter Power*) calls microblogging a "virtual watercooler." He says, "Instead of relying on an occasional blog post [to keep in touch], [Twitter users] get brief updates that, because they only take a second to write, come in on a regular basis. Now I'm not a distant friend who sends occasional letters. I'm the guy in the next office whom they pass in the corridor."

I think this is a helpful metaphor. It expresses that microblogging, like the office watercooler, is not key to the functioning of your business, but it's where people (especially self-employed, tech-oriented people) drop by a few times each day to socialize. Valuable business information is often exchanged at the watercooler, too.

The most popular Twitterers update regularly with short bits of info. For example, noted entrepreneur Guy Kawasaki (author of *Reality Check*, *The Art of the Start*, and *Rules for Revolutionaries*) often posts dozens of tweets daily.

Like both Guy and me, you can add Twitter (or competitors identi.ca, FriendFeed, Plurk, or others) to your marketing mix at no cost. If you offer value or entertainment to your Twitter followers, they will reward you with attention and word-of-mouth promotion. The most appropriate content is usually clustered around common interests shared by that group—whether it's social, business, research, sports, or whatever other niche interests may apply.

More importantly for a marketer, the whole point of microblogging is that it makes it easy to share content. Your Twitter followers are all self-selected to share similar interests (or they would opt-out). This means that any content you tweet is likely to get attention from that self-selected audience because all the people who receive it have similar interests *and* are restricting their intakes to similar preselected sources. So, microblogging often actually has less competition for attention and more likelihood that people will forward it ("re-tweet"). This can help your content spread virally and gain popularity as interested users publicly reply to it, post and comment on it on their blogs, amplify it with Digg or StumbleUpon social news site votes, and so on.

Can you imagine the customer attention you could attract if you simply tweeted a 20 percent off coupon code to your followers every week, for example? You would rapidly grow an appreciative audience of followers, and see your discount offers heavily re-tweeted, too. Not bad for free, right?

What Twitter Is Not Good For

I should also warn you of the dangers of microblogging. The primary issue is that any of these services can be terribly *distracting*. Once you sign up and follow a few people, you'll start receiving a constant stream of messages from them to your phone or Web browser. I've found that being an active Twitterer requires discipline to avoid constantly scanning Twitter's timeline of user posts for interesting links, trivia, info, and updates from friends. Microblogging can be as disruptive to work as Instant Messenger often is when used indiscriminately.

Using specialized (also free) software like Tweetdeck, Twhirl, or other organizational tools can help you manage this flow by grouping your most important contacts into prioritized groups. But being active in the Twitter community requires involvement, just like being active in the social networks or social news sites discussed previously does. So it's up to you to test microblogging for yourself and evaluate its potential impact on your marketing plans and workday.

Other tools that can be helpful in extending your product presence using Twitter include:

- ▲ Twitterfeed: This service takes the RSS feed from your blog and sends out the first 140 characters of each post as a tweet to your followers.

- ▲ Tweetlater: This service helps you by allowing you to schedule tweet postings at specific future times. Very handy for scheduling promotional campaigns.

- ▲ Twellow: A directory of Twitter users that's useful for finding interesting new people to follow.

- ▲ Tweetbeep: A Google Alerts–type service that will e-mail you when keywords you select are included in tweets by others.

Twitter is another example of new tools that you can use to build an audience among highly connected and often influential people. Like e-mail newsletters or blogs or the friend groups on Facebook, Twitter is another way for you to reach friends and potential customers with your marketing messages. In this case, the messages are quite short, but that format is what some customers prefer. And your job as a marketer is to entice customers into profitable interactions by giving them what they want.

If this introduction to microblogging intrigues you, there are several competing services for you to explore. Twitter is currently the leader, but there are other companies that offer their own variations of short-form messaging and related services that may be helpful in your marketing:

- ▲ FriendFeed
- ▲ identi.ca
- ▲ Plurk
- ▲ Yammer
- ▲ Jaiku

Visit Twitter.com to get started. Once you set up your free account, please follow me by visiting www.Twitter.com/scott_fox. And you can visit ScottFox.com for my latest recommendations on how to use microblogging to boost your marketing strategy, too.

PART FIVE

NEW ONLINE PUBLIC RELATIONS
AND PROMOTIONS TOOLS

14

. . .

THE TRUTH ABOUT
PUBLIC RELATIONS

PUBLIC RELATIONS is the art of gaining free press coverage for your products. Appearing in a credible publication automatically positions you and your products as credible. This implied endorsement leads to much better audience reaction than traditional advertising because it positions your message as authoritative, with the reporter and the publication standing behind you as references.

Even though you can't control the final output, this is very cost-effective because through successful press placements you can gain exposure to audiences that you would not be able to afford to reach yourself.

Unfortunately public relations is mysterious and even intimidating to many online marketers. Online marketers often neglect publicity efforts because by nature they prefer to tweak technology rather than engage in the personal contact traditionally required to sell their stories to the media. That means that PR is an underused technique for e-businesses and therefore has the potential to help you grow your online audience.

Public relations is often seen as similar to sales because you need to pitch a story repeatedly and well to tough customers (reporters) who are professional skeptics. This is not easy or fun to do—I get it.

But that's because most people are doing it *wrong*. They're still working the hard end of the public relations process based on twentieth-century principles. As with most of the strategies I discuss here, in *Internet Riches*, and in the forums at ScottFox.com, the twenty-first century offers much more effective, Internet-based tools for publicity.

Today your goal in using public relations and publicity techniques is not just to get traditional press coverage that hopefully attracts sales, but to use press coverage to attract potential customers into long-term relationships directly with you through your web site and other online tools.

The key to attracting press coverage today?

If you focus on helping reporters do their jobs, you can use cost-effective new online techniques to turn PR from an intimidating chore into a win-win strategy.

The Goal of Modern PR:
Capture Your Own Audience

The traditional purpose of public relations and publicity was to reach readers by getting your products covered in major press outlets like the *New York Times* or on the *Today Show*. A successful PR campaign used to be measured simply by the number of such "media hits" your products received. This coverage of your products was then extrapolated into an estimate of the number of customers reached and influenced toward purchase.

Today, however, just getting prestigious press coverage is no longer enough. The massive expansion of your ability to reach and build relationships with customers through digital media has changed the PR game. *Newspapers, radio, television, and magazines are no longer necessary for you to reach customers yourself.*

Anyone can now afford to keep in touch with mass audiences directly and inexpensively via web sites and e-mail. This is why you need your own blog, your own Facebook page, your own online Press Room, and so on, as discussed throughout this book.

I see PR as the wide end of a funnel. When a press placement attracts attention, it can introduce your products and marketing messages to mass audiences that you might not have reached yourself. It's then your job to capitalize on the attention that PR has brought to your products and your web site to engage the potential customers into profitable longer-term relationships. This can eliminate the press as the middleman in your relationship with customers.

PUBLIC RELATIONS IS NOT ADVERTISING

Public relations is the opposite of advertising. Advertising is controlled by you—you get to dictate the headlines, the graphics, your descriptive copy, and the overall message that your ad conveys. With public relations, however, it's your job to supply journalists with information that will help them construct a credible and informative story for their audience. You can share information, opinions, photographs, and referrals in an effort to obtain positive press mention or even feature coverage.

But the key thing to remember is this: *Reporters don't work for you.*

They are doing you a favor by covering your products from among the many, many others that are offered to them daily. If you can get over the presumption that your products somehow "deserve" coverage and work instead to help reporters develop good stories to tell their audiences, public relations is much more likely to be a successful marketing strategy for your brand.

You're Probably Wrong About Public Relations

The explosion of media outlets brought about by the World Wide Web and digital technology has greatly increased the number of places where your product can be covered: blogs, e-mail newsletters, podcasts, online video, and so on. Adding all these new outlets to the twentieth century's newspapers, radio, TV, and magazines creates a dizzying array of publicity choices.

This means that a significant investment of time may be needed to even scratch the surface of public relations success.

Additionally, most people have it wrong. They misunderstand the opportunities offered by PR. Somehow, because we all read newspapers and watch TV, we think we understand how the media work. As marketers, we try to put this to work. Unfortunately, our uneducated impression of how news stories are generated and distributed is not only largely inaccurate *but backwards.*

The media are businesses. That means that they have their own complexities, business challenges, resource constraints, competitive pressures, and operating procedures known only to those who are on the "inside."

If you're going to gain free press for your product to attract more customers, you need to understand how the PR game is played today. Here are some insights to help get you up to speed on the *business* of public relations.

Publicity Myths (Why Your Press Release Won't Work)

PUBLICITY MYTH 1: JOURNALISTS LIKE PRESS RELEASES

As the media have grown, journalists of all sorts have increasingly become targets for publicity seekers. The crush of pitches was already huge in the twentieth century, with most reporters' inboxes groaning under the weight of postal mail and faxes. With the arrival of digital media, much of the traffic has transferred itself to e-mail (although the snail mail and faxes still keep coming).

This deluge has forced most press outlets into a reactive posture when interacting with the public. They get pitched so hard, so often, and without breaks that many journalists just shut down and stop reading press releases at all.

But carefully writing press releases is the path you will pursue if you follow the (usually expensive) guidance of many public relations "experts" and public relations firms. They will advise you endlessly on the proper form for a press release and how they will distribute it to hundreds or even thousands of media outlets for you.

Unfortunately, that advice is way out of date.

The bottom line is that the Internet has created such a tidal wave of products and pitches that nobody at a major media outlet is likely to pay attention to your press release—no matter how well written it is—unless you have a preexisting relationship, a top brand name, or an expensive publicist on retainer to open doors for you.

Publicity Fact. *Press releases can be useful as supporting material if a reporter is looking for past info about your products, or they can be useful in helping your site's search engine rankings (if they are published on other sites that then link back to yours), but the mass "blasting" of e-mail press releases in hopes of major press coverage is not effective anymore.*

PUBLICITY MYTH 2: REPORTERS ARE LOOKING FOR STORIES

If you have not worked in the media, your impression of newsroom operations has probably been shaped by movies and TV shows about investigative reporters. These intrepid news sleuths uncover hidden truths and make the world a better place by informing the public of important issues.

As a marketer, however, it's not the investigative reporters that you want to attract. You are most likely interested in coverage in a feature story, meaning flattering coverage of your product relating to human interest or current events topics.

Today, most feature stories you see in the press or on TV are not generated by reporters responding to news releases. In fact, most stories are generated from the opposite direction: a editor has an idea, then a reporter is assigned to research that idea, find sources, and write and publish the story. (This is why you need to know the editors and reporters yourself, hire a PR firm that does, or reach them directly, as discussed later.)

This means that it is rare for new stories to be developed by reporters reading press releases, then deciding which are the most interesting bits of news to cover. This is backward.

Publicity Fact. Feature story ideas are usually initiated not by reporters but by editors (or producers in broadcasting). Then it's the reporter's job to find examples that support the argument that she has been assigned to prove.

PUBLICITY MYTH 3: THE MERITS
OF YOUR STORY ARE ENOUGH

I know that you are in love with your product, but the fact is that no one in the media is. If anything, it's their job to be skeptical, and the crush of pitches by publicity seekers that confronts them daily forces them to be suspicious of any pitch you make. Unless you have a medical breakthrough or a really entertaining stunt to offer, most reporters are too jaded to be interested in your product, no matter how cool you think it is.

Many marketers think that their product deserves coverage because it's so interesting or so valuable. Unless their product is a cure for cancer, they are usually wrong—in fact, this assumption can lead to much frustration and wasted effort.

Publicity Fact. If you are frustrated because reporters won't give your product the coverage you think it deserves, there's a simple solution: Buy advertising instead.

PUBLICITY MYTH 4: REPORTERS ARE OBJECTIVE

As newspapers and magazines shrink their news holes and lay off employees, PR people are reporting an increase in the number of times their clients are buying ads in exchange for publicity.

　　　　　Joan Stewart, *The Publicity Hound,* www.publicityhound.com

Of course reporters try to be impartial, but the media business is under tremendous pressure. The increased competition from the Internet, with its millions of amateur journalists and 24-hour coverage of anything and everything, threatens the very business model of traditional media. It also compresses the time available for reporters to do real research or provide in-depth coverage.

Instead, there's a whole world of information brokering that you need to understand if you are interested in publicity for your business.

Reporters are under constant pressure to produce new material. Since they are human beings like the rest of us, it's only natural that they try to do their jobs as efficiently as possible. They, too, want to go home and play with their kids.

Unfortunately for you, this means that whenever you see a product mentioned in the news, it is likely that somebody helped the reporter to locate sources to inform the story. At least outside of hard news, reporters rarely do much completely independent research these days. Just as you would do, reporters naturally turn to friends and colleagues who have been helpful to them before. This means that quite often a PR firm helped get that coverage for a client. PR firms are paid to find press exposure opportunities for their clients, so they specialize in building relationships and trading favors with the reporters and editors and producers who control the stories you see in the press and on TV.

This can be tough competition because PR firms make a business out of facilitating the press coverage that you may be trying to get as an afterthought.

Publicity Fact. *The best way to get press coverage is by building relationships and helping reporters do their jobs—or hiring a PR firm to do that for you.*

Typical "Expert" PR Advice—Ignore It!

Here's what most books, PR firms, and publicity "experts" will advise you to do in your quest for publicity. They offer three categories of outreach—usually taught in the following order. (Notice that the things you can do well yourself are last, while the things that they specialize in getting paid for are first.)

1. Create news—write press releases, send them out, and pitch reporters.

2. Respond to reporter inquiries.

3. Offer resources to support reporters—including an online Press Room.

I reverse this order.

There is a time and place for PR firms, but, as I always recommend, I'd like to see you try these marketing strategies yourself first.

It's more cost-effective to do it yourself, it's more likely to come out sounding authentic, and it positions you to be a smarter client for a PR firm later.

You can pay a PR firm lots of money to use its relationships with editors and producers to get you coverage (although few will guarantee any results), but I would still start with the following plan.

So What Can You Do to Get Free Press Coverage?

My e-riches recommendation: "Get in where you fit in."

Sending out press releases to reporters in the hope that they will magically latch onto your pitch and cover it is not a very effective use of your time.

Why?

Because it's going to be tough for you to convince the existing newsroom team to cover your story instead of pursuing the ones that they have already been assigned. And the editors and producers who have the authority to initiate new stories pride themselves on having that authority—meaning that they're not likely to share it easily.

It is easier to succeed at publicity by helping reporters find the right expert sources to validate their preexisting arguments than by trying to bring them new ideas, stories, issues, or products for promotion.

The more that you help reporters create the stories that they have been assigned, the more likely they'll cover your business. That coverage will attract visitors to your web site. You then have the opportunity to recruit the visitors into long-term relationships. Doing so will create a private audience of fans whom you can then reach inexpensively using e-mail, blogging, and the many other digital marketing tools discussed throughout this book. Just as importantly, you'll no longer have to rely on the media for publicity to reach those customers for repeat sales.

In other words, it's easier for you to just help reporters do their jobs. Now let's talk about tools that can help you do that.

15

. . .

THE PUBLIC RELATIONS OPPORTUNITY MATRIX (PROM) SYSTEM

SO WHERE should you start in trying to promote your business through public relations?

There are many ways to approach the pursuit of press coverage for your business. I see them as depending on how *proactive* versus *reactive* your press effort is.

Depending on your time, budget, and resources, any of the strategies discussed here can be implemented by you personally, implemented by an in-house team, or outsourced to a public relations agency. As usual, my emphasis is on strategies that you can start with yourself (to save money) and then upgrade later once you've found the tactics that bring you the best return on investment.

To evaluate the opportunities available to you, let me introduce you to my E-Riches Public Relations Opportunity Matrix (PROM).

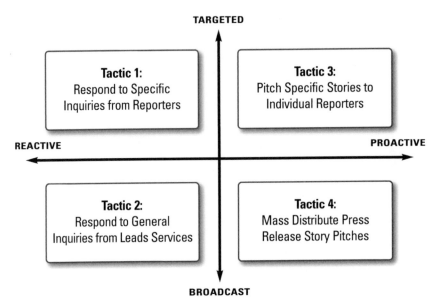

FIGURE 15–1.

It shows how I think about public relations.

As you can see in Figure 15–1, I divide your opportunities for press publicity using two scales. They are:

▲ Targeted vs. Broadcast

▲ Reactive vs. Proactive

Displaying these graphically creates four quadrants of press opportunities for you to consider.

I recommend that you pursue these strategies as they are numbered—from easy/general to harder (targeted/custom)—by starting in the upper left corner with Tactic 1. This approach is Targeted (and thus in the upper half of the matrix) and also Reactive (by which I mean that the press leads come to you—so it is displayed in the left half of the matrix).

PROM Tactic 1: Set Up a Press Room on Your Web Site

Start by setting up a "Press Room" on your web site to catch and service press inquiries. This page simply makes information about your company easily available to reporters. Of course this assumes that your web site has any traffic or press appeal, but posting this content creates an evergreen publicity resource, so get it done as an investment in your future.

Your new web site Press Room can be started simply with a short history of the company, pictures of your top products, and your management team's bios and photos. It does not have to be fancy.

What's most important is accurate and complete contact information that reporters can use to easily reach you. You have to find a balance between giving out your personal cell phone number and being as available as possible if a reporter wants to reach you immediately because of a deadline. (I split the difference on my sites by posting a phone number for a voice mailbox that immediately forwards the message to my mobile phone.)

Then build out the Press Room web site page by posting short articles (or press releases if you are issuing them) that document your products or your latest company achievements. If you add items occasionally, over time this archive will grow to display your company's evolution to any interested reporter (or potential customer) who visits your web site.

Journalists also love tidbits and factoids that they can use to add color to their stories (and make it sound like they interviewed you when they did not!). So post news on any awards, notable financial results, upcoming events, speeches, and even links to related web sites. Downloadable PDF documents that summarize your corporate history and talking points are often appreciated, too. Especially useful are clippings or links to previous media coverage and print-ready images of your top products and senior management team.

Their business runs based on deadlines, so journalists are almost always in a hurry. If you make these resources easily available so that they can add additional detail to their stories *without having to schedule time to talk to you*, they are more likely to cover your product.

A Press Room or media page by itself is unlikely to generate any news coverage for you, but setting up your web site's Press Room page once can help you for years. It can also be very helpful in ensuring that reporters cover your company correctly (and without additional work from you) once you succeed in attracting them.

PROM Tactic 2: Sign Up for News Leads Services

The second of my recommended Public Relations Opportunity Matrix strategies is to sign up for a "leads service."

These e-mail–based services use the Internet to connect reporters with the sources they are looking for. The result is an efficient match-making of publicity wants and needs. They can help you grow your business with very little expense.

Leads services turn the traditional public relations paradigm on its head. They are what allowed me to state earlier that I think traditional public relations advice is backward. If you use news leads services like these, instead of you chasing stories and reporters, you can have reporters querying you about stories they are already working on!

You will still have to compete to be the best choice for reporters to feature in their work, but when you are responding to "hot leads" that are targeted to your specific topic areas, you are way, way ahead of the game compared to blindly sending out press releases and hoping for a press hit.

Services like this can help you get the publicity coverage that is usually offered to the clients of big PR firms. They level the playing field by helping you avoid the need to cold-call reporters—in fact, instead of you having to contact reporters, they contact you!

Here are profiles of the three leading publicity leads services.

PROFNET

ProfNet is an online service that is part of PR Newswire (which itself is a subsidiary of United Business Media). ProfNet was founded in 1992 to help reporters connect with expert sources. The service has grown to become a major player in the media business because it helps to facilitate the research that underlies many major news stories every day.

By signing up for this service, PR professionals can post profiles of the companies that they represent and make their clients available to journalists who are looking for such expertise as sources for their stories.

The service includes a searchable online database that journalists can use to quickly identify and contact expert sources for their research.

As cool and revolutionary as that service was, what's even better is that ProfNet automates the sourcing of experts for the journalists via e-mail.

If you are a ProfNet client, you can select the specialized areas of interest to which your or your clients' expertise best applies. There are hundreds to choose from (see Figure 15–2). Then, whenever a reporter posts a request for expert sources in that category, you will be notified both on the ProfNet web site and by e-mail directly into your inbox.

For PR professionals, this means that they can connect dozens of their expert sources and corporate clients with possible article coverage

FIGURE 15–2.

every day. If you are a small company represented by a PR firm, or even a solo entrepreneur, you can use the service to monitor for journalists looking for expertise like yours.

When you see a journalist's query asking for input on a topic that is relevant to your expertise, you then simply reply by e-mail to the system or by e-mail directly to that journalist offering to help.

Typical ProfNet inquiries look like this:

```
Brokerage Services—Freelancer

For a national trade magazine, I am looking for
experts to comment on brokerage firms investing
client funds in commercial real estate properties.
Potential sources include registered representa-
tives, investment managers, consultants, real
estate developers and individual investors,
attorneys, etc.

Contact: Max Jones, mjjones97@yahoo.com
Submitted by: Max Jones
Organization: Freelancer
Deadline: Sep 12, 2009 02:00 PM
PST(America/Los_Angeles)
```

```
Beverage Industry Analyst for Comment
on New Sodas—Major Daily Paper

I am profiling a start-up soda pop brand and
wanted to talk specifically about the company, as
well as the prospects of being an upstart in a
business that seems to have peaked. I prefer con-
tacts from the Midwest and with familiarity with
the beverage business in Illinois. I'm a free-
lancer pitching to a major metro daily paper.

Contact: Jane Carter, jjanec789@domain.com
Submitted by: Jane Carter
Organization: Major Daily Paper
Deadline: Nov 05, 2009 12:00 PM
PST(America/Los_Angeles)
```

You can see how reviewing dozens of inquiries like these each day is likely to offer you an opportunity that's appropriate to your product, right? These are live story leads from real reporters, and they are delivered directly to your e-mail inbox.

The problem with ProfNet is that it is designed for public relations firms—this means that most users pay at least $3,000 per year.

PR LEADS

PR Leads is a Web-based service run by Dan Janal. (See the interview with Dan later in this chapter.)

PR Leads is a major breakthrough for individuals and small companies because it allows them to "play with the big boys" by positioning themselves as the "experts" that the media loves to quote.

It repackages ProfNet for smaller companies and individuals to use cost-effectively. Where a corporate-level membership in ProfNet can cost thousands of dollars per year, PR Leads is just $99 per month. This puts the preestablished reporter relationships of the ProfNet network in the hands of small companies and entrepreneurs who may not be able to afford a public relations firm.

On top of the ProfNet service, Dan and team offer coaching for clients new to the publicity game. By offering teleseminars and even personal "pitch coaching" by e-mail, Dan helps introduce hundreds of new publicity seekers to the world of publicity every year.

I worked with Dan myself to learn the quick, concise, on-point format he recommends when responding to ProfNet inquiries. During the promotional push for my first book, *Internet Riches*, working with Dan helped get me coverage in several media outlets, including the *Los Angeles Business Journal*, a placement that easily could have cost thousands of dollars if it had been facilitated by a PR firm. Visit www.PRLeadsReview.com for more information and my latest updates on this service.

HELP A REPORTER OUT (HARO)

HARO is the new kid on the publicity block. I introduced this company as an example of Facebook marketing success in the Facebook section of Chapter 9 because its founder, Peter Shankman, started the service through clever use of Facebook.

As a potential user of the HARO service, however, here's what you need to know.

Help A Reporter Out is a leads service like ProfNet and PR Leads, but it's free. If you sign up for the service as a "source," you'll receive daily e-mails with dozens of queries from journalists looking for expert sources to quote in their stories.

And the service is ad-supported, so receiving the daily e-mails full of journalist queries costs you nothing.

The queries themselves are similar to the ones shown in the ProfNet discussion. The topics range from business to health to style to psychology to retailing to sports to culture to technology and so on.

I recommend signing up for these services ASAP so that you can start receiving publicity leads that can help you get press coverage for your business.

HOW TO USE PRESS LEADS SERVICES

Because they are e-mail–based, press leads services are quite easy to use. Here are the basic steps:

1. Sign up for whichever services interest you.

2. Review the e-mails that then begin arriving in your inbox to identify publicity leads that are appropriate to your products and expertise.

3. Respond quickly—these services make it easy to receive targeted inquiries from journalists, but there is plenty of competition to be the response the journalists choose to cover.

4. Your response needs to be concise. That means short. The posting journalists will get lots of responses, and you'll lose their attention quickly if your response doesn't quickly come to the point.

5. Be helpful, on target, and specific. Respond only to queries where you really have relevant expertise. Offer two or three specific quotes or examples that answer the questions posed by the reporter. Don't waste your time and the reporter's by pitching off-topic.

6. Don't be too self-promotional. Reporters understand why you are responding. They are not paid to promote you and your products, however. Their business is writing a good story. Help them do that and they'll pay you back with appropriate coverage.

7. Include a short summary of your credentials so that they understand who you are and why your opinions on the topic are worth trusting and reporting.

8. Additional resources such as relevant web site links or referrals are helpful and therefore appreciated, too. (Offering relevant assistance is a great way to build a relationship with reporters, even if you are not covered in the story at hand.)

LEADS SERVICES WORK FOR ME!

I used these news leads services myself for several months before writing about them. They are more than worth the money if you want to find press coverage for your business or products.

Between PR Leads and HARO, I received multiple placements, including in the *Los Angeles Business Journal*, on About.com (as a recurring contributor), and even in the e-zine for Lowe's Home Improvement Stores.

I also used both PR Leads and HARO from the other side as a "journalist." I had success in attracting submissions each time I posted asking for referrals and success stories (several of which are even included in this book).

PROM Tactic 3: Send Out "Some" Press Releases

But not for the reasons you probably think. . .

WHEN PRESS RELEASES DO WORK

Press releases are not totally dead. However, there is so much competition for attention from reporters today that it's fairly rare for a one-shot press release to suddenly get picked up and blossom into a story.

Instead, today the production and distribution of press releases is a good way to help manage the distribution of your marketing message in a rather unexpected way: search engines love them.

A properly written press release is full of the good headlines, keywords, and links that search engines use to calculate their results rankings. When you send out a press release online, it can be picked up by other web sites worldwide. Often those receiving web sites will use the content from your press release on their own sites. This leads to valuable links back to your site—just the sort of thing that search engines use to improve your rankings in their results.

So, although sending out a press release is not likely to gain you a lot of short-term media attention the way it used to, it can be helpful in the medium term to help attract reporters to your site through improved search engine rankings.

PRESS RELEASE DISTRIBUTION SERVICES

If you do decide to write and issue a press release, the first place to post it is in the press section of your own web site. Once you have done that, there are many Internet-based press release distribution services that can help you distribute it. The higher-quality services charge $40 to $500 or more per release (depending on the distribution options you select), but many others are free.

Online Press Release Distribution Services

PR Newswire: http://www.prnewswire.com

PR Web: http://www.prweb.com

PR.com: http://www.pr.com

Click Press: http://www.clickpress.com/releases/index.shtml

PR Leap: http://www.prleap.com

1888 Press Release: http://www.1888pressrelease.com

EcommWire: http://www.ecommwire.com

PR Zoom: http://www.przoom.com

24-7 Press Release: http://www.24-7pressrelease.com

PR Log: http://www.prlog.org

In my experience, you get what you pay for with these services.

If you are just looking to syndicate your press release in hopes of attracting some random blog attention, the free ones are probably adequate.

But if you are hoping for links back to your web site and the accompanying SEO benefits (as I recommend, and as opposed to expecting the *Wall Street Journal* to call you), you should be sure that whatever service level you select includes live links for any URLs that you include in your release's text.

Most of the press release services offer upgraded services, too. For a fee, the upgrades generally allow additional files, logos, or images to be attached to or included in your release; the release to remain in the database (and therefore searchable) permanently; live web site links to be displayed within the press release; and other such options. (Of course, you can visit ScottFox.com for updates on these providers and strategies anytime.)

The key to getting a press release picked up for coverage by the media is your *story*. You can't presume that reporters are interested in your product or service. The way to get their attention (and therefore coverage) is to help them do their jobs. If you make it easier for them to write a story, they'll often reward you with a quote or other coverage.

That leads us to our next topic: *how to pitch a news story*.

PROM Tactic 4: How to Pitch a News Story

As you now know, my least preferred PR strategy is for you to pitch a story yourself. Given all the competition for media attention and the many opportunities you have to reach the audience directly yourself online, personal pitches are usually the least effective use of your valuable time.

Dealing with the press can be intimidating at first, and the pressure of knowing that your statements may be broadcast to the world and archived forever can be daunting. You will always need to be careful in what you say and how you say it, but once you understand how the media industry works, you'll see that reporters are just people, too.

They are trying to do a good job covering a story while laboring under difficult deadlines, a constant barrage of inquiries from publicists and press seekers, and constant demands from their own bosses.

If you take the time to understand how the public relations industry works, you can succeed in attracting publicity, too. The key (as with most things) is to help make the other guy's job easier. The easier it is for a reporter to cover your product, web site, or news item, the more likely it is that she will.

And, if your pitch is picked up, it can be a game-changing experience for your product or web site. So, here's how I recommend pursuing the fourth quadrant of my PR Opportunity Matrix.

EIGHT STEPS TO MEDIA PITCHING SUCCESS

Since I know specifics are more helpful to you than theory, here are the specific steps that I recommend you take to pitch a news story:

1. You need to identify your niche and find the media that customers in that niche consume.

2. Then start reading/watching/listening to those outlets that reach your target market to note the reporters' names and specialties as well as the kinds of stories and formats they prefer.

3. Tie your pitch to the interests of the reporter or publication you are pitching. Nothing frustrates journalists more than having to deal with time-wasting pitches that are not appropriate for their outlets.

4. Think in terms of stories, not your products. It's no one's job but yours to promote your product. No media outlet has an obligation to cover you or book you. The media's job is to create interesting stories that offer information to their audiences.

5. Make sure that your "news" is newsworthy. News is about current events—that's why they call it "news." Your local paper or radio station isn't interested in hearing about topics that its audiences will ignore. It is looking for *new* topics to cover or, more often, interesting angles on current events. For you, this means that you need to keep your pitches fresh and timely.

I know that it's unlikely that your product changes daily, but the news must. *So instead of trying repeatedly to get press coverage of your product itself, try instead tying its benefits or features to a current event that is already hot in the news.*

Even more helpful to reporters can be creating a story package. This is a group of sources or examples that doesn't focus only on your products but helps reporters develop a theme or tell a broader story that you know appeals to a particular magazine, blog, show, or paper.

6. Be concise. You need to make a strong case in a very short space. Because they are deluged with pitches and are always working under tight deadlines, media people cannot afford the time to wade through overly long pitches. Liberal use of bullet points, bold, and highlights is recommended to help the journalist quickly understand what you are offering them (refer to my copywriting tips earlier in the book).

7. Follow up. Given all the submissions that they receive, even an interested reporter may not get around to contacting you because of competing distractions. It's your job to spoon-feed the story to the reporters and convince them that it's worth covering. Polite, pleasant, and persistent reminders, whether by e-mail, phone, or letter, are a part of doing business in the world of public relations. Additionally, if a reporter says no, you must believe her and back off. Wait until you have a new angle on the story or a different story entirely to contact her again.

8. Pitch formulas can be very helpful. Watch your evening television news to quickly learn the easiest way to attract the attention of reporters. If you note the way that the news anchors tease the stories for upcoming segments, you'll quickly get the idea of how to both summarize your story idea and make it as attractive as possible. Common examples include pitch formulas like "the secrets of X that Y don't want you to know," "how to do X faster or cheaper than you ever thought possible,"

"three simple steps to X," "the dangerous fact about X that you need to know to protect your kids," "how to save money by doing X," "the surprising truth about X," and so forth.

E-RICHES TIP: GOOGLE ALERTS'
FREE "CLIPPING SERVICE"

Another great way to use Google Alerts is to track your press mentions. You can use this free service to have the Google search engine sweep the Web daily for all new mentions of your product, company, or name. It will then e-mail you links to any web pages it finds that contain your keywords.

This is a very efficient and cost-effective way to:

▲ *Find customers, blogs, sites, or publications that are talking about you or your products.*

▲ *Track "breaking news" related to your product or your industry.*

▲ *Find reporters who cover your topics so that you can start building relationships with them.*

▲ *Find blogs, web sites, and online communities interested in your products.*

▲ *Be alerted when your topic is hot in local markets so that you can contact the local press.*

Once you're "alerted" to mentions of your topics, you can reinforce the exposure by visiting and contributing to the discussion, as appropriate. If the pickup was from press coverage, you can also e-mail the writer personally to thank her and start building a relationship.

This service is so effective (and cheap) that many marketers have dropped their subscriptions to old-style article clipping services!

Bonus Tip: Set up Google Alerts to track your competitors' names and products, too. Being alerted whenever they get attention online gives you the chance to find what pitches are working for them and add your pitch to the discussion, too. (They'll think you're psychic!)

EVERGREEN NEWS STORY IDEAS

If you want to try to develop professional-style targeted PR pitches yourself, here are some story ideas that you can prepare in advance. These topics are covered repeatedly, worldwide, every year, so you'll have a better chance of press coverage if you can provide an interesting new angle on recurring topics like these.

Ask yourself, how does my product tie in with:

▲ Major holidays. (What's your Christmas angle? How about Valentine's Day or the Fourth of July?)

▲ Natural disasters. (Sadly, every year brings more hurricanes, earthquakes, and floods. How can you pitch your product as complementing a story on these topics?)

▲ Elections.

▲ Olympics/Super Bowl/World Cup/ World Series.

▲ Graduating classes. Every year produces a new crop of graduates with the same needs for jobs, apparel, housing, financial planning, and so on.

▲ Surveys. Create one and publish the results.

▲ Consumer protection issues or money-saving tips.

▲ Celebrity weddings or divorces.

Media outlets are always covering these types of stories but looking for new ways to make them fresh and interesting to their audiences. Help them do their jobs and you'll be rewarded with coverage.

- -
E-RICHES TIP: "IF IT BLEEDS, IT LEADS"
Audiovisual aids make all the difference when you're pitching television reporters. They need compelling video, and if you can provide interesting visuals, your story has a much *better chance of being covered on TV.*
- -

INTERVIEW: DAN JANAL,
PUBLICITY EXPERT, PR LEADS

Dan is a veteran of the public relations world—he started as a daily newspaper reporter himself, and over the years he has worked in almost all aspects of public relations. He's written six books on PR and is an expert in online publicity.

Scott: Hi, Dan—can you give my readers an introduction to publicity?

Dan: Publicity is not advertising. Advertising is that stuff you see in the newspaper that is carefully crafted by advertising agencies to mold public opinion about their products. They get to choose which messages, pictures, and headlines you see.

But the problem with that is that most people don't believe ads. People are naturally suspicious of a company promoting its own products.

Publicity, on the other hand, is a lot more credible. If a reporter from a recognized newspaper or magazine reviews your book, your software, your new dental procedure, or your new product or service, there's an implied endorsement in that review. Who is going to argue if credible third-party media say something positive about your products?

That's the difference between advertising and publicity—publicity's implied endorsement will help you build credibility, attract more clients, and get new business.

Scott: Why should marketers care about PR?

Dan: The credibility that being quoted in the press can bring you is tremendous. In today's competitive world, it can be the differentiating factor between two products or two candidates for a job or between two movies.

Would you see a movie that's not endorsed by a newspaper or magazine? If the *Los Angeles Times* or the *New York Times* says so, it must be good.

That's what we're hoping for. And that's how, whether you're a brick-and-mortar store or online, it can help you sell more stuff.

Scott: Where do the stories come from that you see in the media?

Dan: A reporter or editor comes up with a story idea. If he can sell the story idea to his editor, he will begin writing a story on that topic. The next step then is to find sources for the story. He'll want a variety of sources to include "experts" plus some "real people," advertisers, or other qualified opinions to include in the article. Finding all those people conveniently and quickly is his challenge.

Scott: So the reporter or editor picks the story, then proceeds to find the sources that back up that story? That's the opposite of what most beginning marketers want to do, which is to say "I am the story" and try to force the reporters to cooperate.

Dan: I am so glad that you brought that up. I did not say write a press release or write a pitch letter, send it to reporters, and then make 500 phone calls to try to follow it up. You know why? Because it doesn't work.

Reporters get all the spam that you and I get, plus hundreds or even thousands of press releases from people they've never heard of. But they can write only so many stories each day.

Even before e-mail, when I was a daily reporter myself, we got more press releases by postal mail than we could possibly use. At best, we would sometimes just look at the envelope and open the ones that had interesting return addresses. We already had our assignments for the day, and press releases rarely match up to the needs that a reporter has on a specific day.

If you think you're going to write a press release and successfully get the attention of reporters today, it's just about a one in a million shot.

Scott: OK, so no press releases. How does a newsroom work?

Dan: Reporters are the men and women who write the stories. They have to get approval for the stories they write from their editors. Depending on how big a newspaper is, for example, they might report to a city editor, or an assignment editor, or a section editor, or a bureau editor. The newsroom is full of checks and balances before any story gets approved, much less printed. So the reporters need to sell their story ideas to editors, just the way you have to sell your story ideas to reporters because there's so much competition for the space.

A big paper like the *Wall Street Journal* might put a story through six or seven layers of approval before it reaches the public in print. And even when it does, the headlines are often written by a different team from the articles themselves. Business-to-business publications have a different structure, as do broadcast outlets like TV and radio.

Scott: How can press coverage help increase your search engine ranking and site traffic?

Dan: A lot of articles that appear in print publications appear online these days, too. So if you're interviewed in your local paper, and then Google indexes that article, when people type in keywords related to your subject, your web site can pop up.

The more links coming into your web site, the more that will help your search engine ranking.

And not all links are created equal. A link from the *New York Times* is very valuable. So if you can get these media web sites to link back to your web site, it will help your name appear when people search on "chiropractor" or whatever your specialty is. It may link back to your site directly, but even if it links back to the *New York Times* article, it's there. So if your name pops up there when a customer searches that topic, who do you think they're going to want to go see? You, because you were mentioned in a *New York Times* article!

Scott: What should my readers look for in a PR firm, if they decide to hire one?

Dan: If you ever think about hiring a PR firm, the one rule I would highly recommend is that the firm you hire has a first-name-basis relationship with the editors of the publication you want to reach. These should be people whom they go out to lunch with, who answer their phone calls, and who will respond to their inquiries. Make sure they know the people you need to reach before you start spending money with them.

What I think is more important today is that you can create your own sensation, almost overnight, because the Web is breaking down so many barriers for people to reach the public.

As important as media relations or public relations is, today you can bypass the media and reach readers directly. That's the purpose of getting into the *New York Times* anyway.

Warning: You'd Better Be Ready to Convert Visitors When PR Works

In the increasingly crowded media landscape, a better investment than traditional public relations tactics is in using PR to build your own relationships directly with customers. The tools for this are easier to use and cheaper than ever before, but their use does require a change in your mindset. More specifically, building fan relationships requires a willingness to "get your hands dirty" dealing directly with customers and accommodating their feedback.

This means that the best way to get results from PR today is to use it as just one part of your distributed engagement marketing strategy. You'll want to spread your product presence through articles in the *New York Times*, on Yahoo! News, on CBS News, on popular blogs, or anywhere you can get coverage. But that is only one step toward your goal of attracting new potential fans of your products to your web site or other contact information collection points.

Once these new visitors arrive, you need to be ready to capture their e-mail addresses on your web site, recruit them as new Facebook and MySpace friends, get their blogs to review your products and link to your site, follow you on Twitter, and all the other hallmarks of Web 2.0 marketing success.

As discussed throughout this book, getting a long-term relationship started with these new fans is your mission. If you are ready to do that, nurturing your own audience is by far a better use of your funds and time than relying on traditional publicity strategies for more press coverage.

But if your web site is not ready to handle the traffic from successful PR or has no mechanism in place to capture the contact info of site visitors, how do you expect to benefit from media coverage? All those visitors are not going to buy on their first visit to your site!

Example: I was interviewed on WJR last spring, a major radio station that broadcasts across the Midwest and Canada out of my hometown of Detroit. The hosts of the show were interviewing me and the CEO of a local startup company. The young CEO was talking about all the press coverage his new company had received from a recent appearance at the Consumer Electronics Show in Las Vegas.

I innocently asked him how many e-mail addresses he had collected as a result of all the great press. Dead air was the result. He stammered back that his company hadn't gotten around to installing an e-mail collector on its web site yet. Ouch! All that positive press and no customer contact information for his sales team to follow up on. . .

Press Pickup Success Examples

Most of the stories you see in the press and on TV today are the result of at least some pitching. Even when you use the leads services as I recommend, you still need to make the best response that a reporter receives before your product will be covered.

I'm not going to bother trying to prove to you that if a reporter visits your web site looking for your Press Room, it's likely that she is going to write a story about your products. That's obvious.

I think it's also obvious that if you have a specific product or announcement that you need to promote, you can't sit back and hope for a leads service to send you the perfect reporter query—there are times you need to go out and pitch directly. When you do that correctly and your info matches the needs of a journalist, you'll obviously get good coverage, too.

You may, however, be skeptical about these leads services I'm recommending.

Here are some examples of how using leads services can bring you very cost-effective "bang for your buck," whether your products or your company is large or small:

Hello Scott!

I've landed several top-tier media placements for Jobing.com by responding to press leads received by e-mail. One of the best resulted from an "anonymous" reporter query asking for "ways gas costs have affected your work." I responded with a brief description of Jobing.com's vehicle wrap program, where employees are reimbursed for gas and get a monthly stipend for branding our personal vehicles with company signage. I was thrilled (as was our CEO) to see the program covered in four full paragraphs in the *New York Times* and quoting me personally.

Joe Cockrell
Director of Public Relations
Jobing.com
Phoenix, Arizona

Hi Scott,

I am the wife and Creative Director for internationally recognized artist Pablo Solomon. While trying to build name recognition for Pablo, I enjoy giving tips on the artist lifestyle and exposing the reader to the intimate world of the working artist. It's not easy for an artist to get publicity, but thanks to the HARO leads service, I was recently featured in *Woman's Day* magazine (with a readership of 23 million). I got a huge response to my good news and rekindled interest in Pablo's art.

Thanks,

Beverly Solomon, Creative Director
musee-solomon
Lampasas, Texas
http://www.pablosolomon.com

Hi Scott,

I use HARO to identify opportunities for my business, AllegroMedical.com, as well as for my network of customers willing to share their medical stories. Recently, I responded to a freelance reporter's query on behalf of one of my customers, a plastic surgeon in San Francisco. It turned out that the reporter was writing an article for the *New York Times* about surgeons who refuse to operate on patients who smoke. The two connected, and Dr. Friedenthal was subsequently quoted in the *New York Times.* I gained a very valuable press contact and helped my customer, too.

Valerie Paxton, Co-Owner/EVP
AllegroMedical.com
Mesa, Arizona

Dear Scott:

I received an e-mail lead from ABCNews.com for an "Online Job Hunt Do's & Don'ts" article. My client, Decision Toolbox (www.dtoolbox.com), is a national recruitment process outsourcing firm headquartered in Irvine, California. As requested, I submitted a "do's and don'ts" list to the journalist that was put together by Nicole Cox, director of recruitment for Decision Toolbox.

The reporter e-mailed me back right away and said she was going to use some of Nicole's list for her article. It ran the following week on the ABC News web site and is still live there as part of its archives. The client was thrilled, and we now have a link to the article on Decision Toolbox's online press room, too.

Jennifer Heinly
J & J Consulting
Foothill Ranch, California

How to Start Your Own Press/Publicity Campaign

Not surprisingly, my recommendations for helping you start your own PR efforts follow the topics discussed throughout this book, with special emphasis on the Public Relations Opportunity Matrix outline given earlier in this chapter.

So, I suggest:

1. Develop web site press resources—like setting up a Press Room on your web site to service journalist inquiries.

2. Use leads services. Visit www.PRLeadsReview.com, Help A Reporter Out, and RadioGuestList.com (discussed in Chapter 20, on Internet radio) for updated info or to sign up to start receiving publicity inquiries directly into your e-mail inbox. Read these e-mails daily and respond as appropriate.

3. Send out some press releases, but only if you understand why you're doing it and have appropriate expectations. Be sure to post them in your Press Room and/or on your blog, too.

4. Pitch reporters individually, but only if you really have a good story that's appropriate for their audiences.

5. Hire a PR firm. You can see that this is the last of my several recommendations. But it may be necessary and worth the expense if you have a really critical story that you need to get into specific editorial hands. Try to ensure that any PR firm you hire has good relations with the specific editors, producers, reporters, and bookers that you most need to have cover your story.

E-RICHES TIP: SOCIAL NEWS CREATES PRESS COVERAGE

The piece I haven't discussed in this chapter is the potential importance of social bookmarking and social news sites to your PR effort.

Today, hot news stories are just as likely to "bubble up" from the Web as they are to be mandated by an editor or producer. This means that often your best bet for getting coverage is to get your topic or article attention on Digg.com, Yahoo! Buzz, StumbleUpon, Twitter, and other such sites. Journalists watch the trends emerging on these sites closely for story ideas.

So an alternative strategy is to try taking the effort you were going to put into writing and distributing a press release into making friends on a top social news site instead. Then, when you have a really good, interesting, or helpful story, you'll have friends to help you promote it on the social media web sites. This can help you attract the press attention you need for your products. Review the social news and social bookmarking discussion in Chapter 11 for more details on social bookmarking sites and social news publicity strategies.

Resources

Help A Reporter Out: http://www.HelpaReporter.com

Joan Stewart's Publicity Hound: http://www.Publicity HoundReview.com

PR Leads: http://www.PRLeadsReview.com

RadioGuestList.com: http://www.RadioGuestList.com

16

. . .

Attracting Customers (and Search Engines) with Online Article Syndication

WRITING INFORMATIVE articles about your field of expertise is a good strategy for positioning yourself as an authority, both in the eyes of customers and in the search engine rankings. By authoring pieces that demonstrate your expertise on the facts, figures, trends, or strategies that are of interest to your target market, you can introduce your brand and spread the word about your products across the Web.

Publish these articles on your own web site or blog, or you can syndicate them to other web sites and blogs. This syndication can be accomplished either manually, by direct submission to the receiving blogs or web sites, or through article submission and distribution services, often called "article banks."

The best promotional articles are useful, evergreen content that is helpful or interesting to online audiences. The more helpful or interesting the article, the more likely that it will be selected for reposting ("syndication") by other web sites and blogs worldwide. Such syndication then attracts to your web site potential customers who read the articles you syndicate and click on the links they contain. It also helps your search engine ranking by attracting search engine bots to the links in your articles (an important factor in determining search engine results rankings).

You should check the guidelines of any site or service that interests you, but articles are typically 500 to 700 words. Your promotional appeal is generally limited to whatever small product mentions may fit appropriately within the context of the piece itself, plus a brief bio at the end of the article. (Of course, these promotional mentions can and should include links back to your web site.)

While writing and distributing articles may sound like a lot of work for a limited return, the worldwide reach of the Internet, the importance of third-party links to your web site's search engine ranking, and the Web's long-term memory combine to make this a more effective strategy then you may realize.

There are two major benefits of a successful article syndication marketing strategy:

1. By sharing your articles with other sites and blogs that appeal to similar target markets, you can attract some of their readership for your material.

2. Perhaps just as importantly, once these articles are published online, they last pretty much forever. This means that the search engine optimization benefits of the links they contain can accrue over the long term to attract both visitors and search engine ranking points to your site.

For example, imagine writing just one informative, short article on your company's industry or your personal area of expertise each month for one year. Setting up submission accounts with three article syndication services would then yield 36 new placements of your promotional content across the Web after one year.

Since you would include links back to your web site or featured product pages in each article, this simple strategy would create long-term, highly ranked links to your web sites from the article banks. This will help your site's search engine ranking and therefore attract more visitor traffic.

And these helpful results are attainable even if no other web sites pick up and republish your articles. If they do (which is likely because that's the whole point of these article bank services), you could receive many more links and additional visitor traffic, too.

ARTICLE MARKETING CASE STUDY:
CHRISTIANWORKATHOMEMOMS.COM

ChristianWorkatHomeMoms.com is a blog targeting (not too surprisingly) Christian moms who want to work at home. Jill Hart, the founder of the site, has built a successful six-figure-a-year business in this triple niche (Christian + work-at-home + moms) online content market.

Jill started her business in 2000 as a result of her own search for work. She was looking for opportunities that would allow her to generate an income while staying home with her two children. Researching online from her Omaha, Nebraska, home, she found plenty of interesting information. When she posted these notes on her own blog, it quickly began attracting visitors as a result of the demand for information from other moms who were interested in similar part-time employment opportunities. She soon realized that her ideal work-at-home opportunity had been revealed to her right there: Collecting, filtering, and hosting information to help other moms interested in work-at-home opportunities was a business in itself. Of course she was right—soon after her audience began growing, advertisers contacted her to try to reach her readers.

Today CWAHM.com content revolves around information on how to start a home-based business, telecommuting jobs, interviews with work-at-home success stories and industry vendors, and Jill's own podcast online radio show, which helps spread information about home-based businesses. Jill had "absolutely no" technical background, but her husband, Alan, an Air Force systems administrator, has helped her with the more technical aspects of growing her web site business.

CWAHM.com's business model is based on advertising sales. Jill offers text ads from Google, display banner ads, and custom placements, and sells leads generated from the site as well.

Of the many marketing tactics that Jill has used over the years, she is the most excited about article syndication marketing. She has written articles with titles like "Telecommuting: Five Ways to Find Your Next Job," "Four Work-at-Home Perspectives: Summer Months versus School Days When Running a Business," "Four Ways to Save Time When Working from Home," and "Practical Parenting for Weary WAHMs."

Once they are submitted to the online article bank services that collect and redistribute such articles, the articles are then accessed by other web site owners looking for fresh content to post on their own web sites. Through these services, Jill's articles appear across the Web on many small blogs, especially those targeting moms, working women, or readers interested in telecommuting or work-at-home employment. Some of her bigger placements have been on the highly targeted and trafficked DrLaura.com and ClubMom.com sites.

The result of this syndication of her articles across the Web is a small but steady stream of traffic from each one. Because the articles are placed in highly targeted sites that attract demographics similar to those that CWAHM.com wants, many readers naturally click on the biographical information that Jill includes in the footer of each article.

These visitors are valuable because they have self-selected by visiting a "mom" or "work at home" or "Christian" or telecommuting-related web site to start with. When they encounter Jill's articles there, they automatically see her as a credible authority on the topic that they are researching. It's not surprising then that they click on her biographical information and links to CWAHM.com.

Jill says, "The results from these articles are so amazing for just a few hours work. Just a byline at the bottom of each of them is enough to attract readers." The many links back to her web site also attract the search engines. The search engines catalog these additional links to CWAHM.com and further boost its ranking in their search results.

Jill's tips for success using an article syndication strategy include finding the intersection between your expertise and the needs of your audience.

"The best way to get a popular site to post your articles is to write about things that will be useful to their audience. Try to tailor your writing to fit the web site—check their writer's guidelines to find topics that they are specifically looking for," she says. "Stick to what you know. Then write 'How-to's,' 'Top Five or Top Ten Ways to Do Something'—these types of articles are eye-catching and seem to get the best response. The more you write about a topic, the more quickly you'll establish yourself as an expert in that field."

Article Syndication Services

As Jill from CWAHM.com does, you can also use article collection and submission services to automate the distribution of any articles you write.

Each of these services requires a login account and then also has its own article entry requirements. You don't need to use all the services available to successfully get your articles spread across the Web, however—many of the smaller services simply source and distribute content from the larger sites without a direct submission needed from you. (There is also constant debate in the online marketing community about the perils of "duplicate content." Some SEO experts insist that Google will penalize your site for placing the same content in too many places. Others deny that this is an issue at all.)

Currently popular online article syndication services include:

- EzineArticles.com

- 1stArticles.com

- ArticleAlley.com

- iSnare.com

- Articlesbase.com

▲ Goarticles.com

▲ Buzzle.com

▲ SearchWarp.com

▲ WebProNews.com

▲ ArticleDashboard.com

▲ ArticlesFactory.com

There are dozens of these services, so you should check ScottFox.com for the latest recommendations in this area before you launch your own article syndication campaign.

E-RICHES TIP: GUEST BLOG POSTS

A variation on the article syndication strategy just detailed is a blog "guest post." You can gain exposure for your products by writing blog posts that are similar to the articles just discussed, but posting them as a "guest author" on popular blogs instead of syndicating them as articles. To do this, you need to contact blogs that are appropriate for your proposed material and develop a relationship with the blogger. Often a swap of guest blog posts can be arranged. This helps each writer to introduce her content to the other blog's audience.

For more on marketing your products using blogs, see Chapter 12.

HOW "FREEMIUMS" GIVEAWAY PROMOTIONS MAKE MONEY ONLINE

In February 2008, Oprah Winfrey announced on her TV show that a year-old book written by a frequent guest, financial self-help author Suze Orman, was available for free download. More than 1 million copies of Women & Money *were downloaded in the next 33 hours. Almost two years after its original publication, the book was still a best seller.[1]*

SURPRISINGLY, in the new Internet economy, you can make a lot of money by giving your products away. In fact, "free" is a top business model in a world where the cost of distributing a digital product is essentially zero.

This allows clever marketers to give away far more than anyone would have been comfortable with 10 years ago. The trick is to give away enough to attract visitors whom you can then upsell into purchasing something profitable later.

As competition among online marketers continues to increase, incentives are becoming a key to attracting customers online. Especially if you are in a business that enables you to offer something downloadable as an "information product," you should be giving away copies (or at least teasers) of the products online as an incentive to get customers to give you their e-mail addresses.

Giveaway strategies are familiar, but they are more powerful than you may realize. King Gillette's razors and the "free prize" inside a cereal box are traditional examples. The article syndication marketing strategy outlined in the previous chapter is another variation.

The giveaway game has gone "on steroids" on the Internet, however. Because it is so easy and cheap to distribute e-books, MP3s, teleseminar invitations, or "special web site access," the conversion rates necessary for profitability have dropped significantly.

When King Gillette pioneered this "loss leader" model more than 100 years ago, he probably still needed at least three or four customers out of every ten to buy the razor blades he was hoping to sell after he gave you the "free" razor.

Today you can give away 80, 90, or even 99 percent of your product and still make money if you do it right. That's right, converting less than 1 percent of your "window-shoppers" into paying customers can be profitable because on the Internet, it costs you basically nothing to serve the other 99 percent! The Internet has helped this marketing approach graduate from a loss leader strategy to what we today call "freemiums." These giveaways are not loss leaders because they cost nothing to manufacture and therefore cause no loss.

This flips traditional giveaway promotion metrics on their head. It is why I recommend highly that you consider adding freemium incentives to your marketing tactics.

You may give away the goods yourself directly to visitors, or you may partner with other web sites to spread your promotional materials. You often see this "joint venture" approach when new products are launched or new books are published. Online marketers will cross-promote each other's products by offering free giveaways such as downloads, CD sets, conference passes, or other products to encourage people to buy the partner's product. For example, "If you buy my new book today from Amazon.com, you'll also receive this CD set from expert A, a free teleseminar download from expert B, and a six-month free subscription to this magazine, too. Act now!"

Such joint venture partnership strategies are particularly useful for building buzz or growing an e-mail list. By partnering with others who have similarly targeted audiences, you can upgrade your reach by piggybacking on their promotional effort and the combined buzz generated by the several contributors to their "bonus packages."

FREEMIUMS CASE STUDY:

MREXCEL.COM

Bill Jelen is known online as "Mr.Excel." He has earned that title as a result of his expertise in helping accountants and financial analysts advance their skills in using Microsoft Office's ubiquitous spreadsheet program, Excel.

Bill has built his after-hours hobby into a full-time operation employing six people based primarily on giving away copies of his Microsoft Excel training books.

He started with a consulting-style business that helped advanced Excel users with their spreadsheet use problems. While that was a nice small business, he quintupled his business when he started packaging his advice in books and related products. The development of his first book was a bit of an accident: He started by writing one simple Excel user tip each week. Soon he had dozens of tips that he could easily compile to create his first book.

Surprisingly, the marketing breakthrough that has built Bill's business is to *give away for free* as many chapters from his books as he can. By giving away chapters of his books, Bill has seen the books' sales skyrocket.

He stumbled into this approach almost accidentally. He was scheduled to appear on an episode of *Tech TV* with Leo Laporte, but he had no book ready to promote. So when the interview was finished, he made an offer to the viewers: They could download his latest book for free, one chapter at a time.

He soon found that each week he was e-mailing installments of *Learn Excel from Mr.Excel* to more than 15,000 new readers who were interested in perfecting their Excel skills.

While this sounds like a recipe for financial disaster, Bill found that once the full book became available, it sold more than twice as fast as his previous book had. He attributes this to the huge reader community he had built along the road to its publication. The many new friends he has made and the fellow experts he has met have been a bonus, in addition to all the valuable feedback he received on the book as it advanced toward publication date.

Mr.Excel's giveaway model looks like this:

▲ Sign up today and get the first chapter.

▲ Then receive a subsequent chapter every week.

▲ At the end of this delivery cycle, receive the final chapter plus an offer to purchase a downloadable file of the full book.

Bill is often surprised at how many people purchase the final downloadable file, given that the recipients have already received the full collection of chapters. The benefits of purchasing the complete file include having all the chapters in one document and making the document more easily searchable.

Although the market for technical books is not as big as that for popular fiction or "how to" best sellers, Bill's promotional efforts greatly increase the velocity of his sales—meaning more profits sooner even without a great increase in the overall number of copies sold. His previous book sold around 10,000 copies in three years. Once he started his giveaway strategy, however, his next book, *Learn Excel from Mr.Excel*, sold about 10,000 copies in just one year. He also applied his weekly giveaway strategy to *Excel 2007 Miracles Made Easy*. Sales were strong, despite the slow adoption of Office 2007 software.

Since the books have price points of $19.95 to $39.95, you can see that selling thousands of copies of multiple titles each year quickly becomes a nice business for Bill, especially when the purchases are for "bundles" that include his self-published works, which carry high margins. The business gets even more profitable given the low overhead of online distribution and the low living costs in Akron, Ohio.

The most surprising fact about the success of MrExcel.com is its success despite a very low conversion rate. In fact, the company is a great demonstration of my "Law of Large Numbers." Discussed extensively in *Internet Riches*, this law states that a little number multiplied by a big number can still yield a big (and profitable) number. To be more specific, MrExcel.com attracts about 500,000 visitors per year and Bill estimates that he converts less than 0.2 percent of site visitors into purchasers.

But, because it is so inexpensive to give away his products (e.g., there are no printing, shipping, or extra marketing expenses), MrExcel.com can be quite profitable even with such a low purchase rate because the web site can service the hundreds of thousands of non-purchasers for almost nothing.

Interestingly, sales stumbled for Bill's latest book, *Learn Excel 97–2007 From Mr.Excel.* He switched from weekly installments to instant free download of the entire text for this book. He tried this because although he says his "come-on was 'HEY—GET THIS BOOK FOR F R E E,' I felt like a jerk for making people wait 40 or 52 weeks to get the whole book." But it turned out that fewer people purchased that one, so he'll probably be switching back to installments soon.

Bill thinks the "dribble it out strategy" is superior for several reasons:

1. It allows extended engagement with the customer through weekly e-mails. "I get to maintain a conversation with the reader for months instead of a single communication. This keeps me front and center for them every Tuesday."

2. He often polls the readers. "Hey, everyone . . . I need an idea for a new book in the *Excel for Professionals* series. What profession do you work in that you would like a book targeted toward your profession?" Or, "Hey, everyone, I need to find a real-life use for the Excel function =FACTDOUBLE. If

you are using this function, let me know and I will send you a print copy of the next book."

3. And lastly, "I am asking them to spend 5 or 10 minutes to read 10 pages. I think everyone can stay engaged and people can read every page. When I send them 900 pages at once, it is too much and nothing gets read."

Bill attributes much of MrExcel.com's success to "karma." He says, "Give useful stuff away and karma takes care of the rest. I don't really have a better explanation. Since I started giving stuff away, more people started buying my books. I think of the free e-book as a great calling card. Sure, 99 percent of the people will just take the free download and use it, but if 0.01 percent of the 500 million people in my target audience buy the book, I have a best seller on my hands." It may be karma, but I also call it smart "modern marketing."

MrExcel.com is a good example of my thesis that modern marketers need to pay more attention to the quality than the quantity of customers. Mr.Excel's emphasis is more on developing long-term, loyal relationships with good customers than on trying to make money off every visit or visitor.

The fact is that today you often must offer incentives to get the attention of new customers. The cost of distributing information is so low that you'd better be ready to share your wisdom. Everybody, including your competitors and unqualified random idiots, is in the marketplace trying to attract the same customers' attention and dollars that you are. (This is also putting price pressure on information products of all sorts—but that's a topic for another day.)

My recommendation: Put together a short PDF e-book with a clever title today. Promote it on your site as a free gift for subscribing to your noozles. That will help you build your list much faster than asking for sign-ups alone. This can be set up in just a couple of hours and can greatly increase the reach of your marketing messages for very little cost.

Whether you do this or not, everyone else is.

PROFITABLE B2B MARKETING

Another reason for the success of MrExcel.com is Bill's successful targeting of a lucrative business-to-business niche. Financial analysts, accountants, and other spreadsheet users are a great market because:

1. They have specific needs that are business-related.

2. This means that their purchases are easily justified and are also usually reimbursed by their employers and/or tax deductible.

3. They often control the budgets for such purchases personally and therefore don't need approvals to buy his products.

Such professionals are also often subject to "continuing education" requirements. This has given Bill the opportunity to build another lucrative promotional angle by offering free continuing education seminar presentations to any audience that will buy copies of his books for all of the attendees.

The proven success of freemium promotions suggests a simple new marketing maxim that you may be able to use to grow your business: *The more people who try your product, the more people are likely to buy it.*

ScottFox.com offers many freemiums. Visit today to check out my latest giveaways for new free e-mail subscribers!

PART SIX

PROFITING FROM
ONLINE BROADCASTING

18

. . .

CUSTOMERS LOVE
ONLINE VIDEO

Fifty-seven percent of online adults have used the Internet to watch or download video, and 19% do so on a typical day.[1]

Per capita time spent with PC, web and mobile video will increase from just under 1 hour per day currently to nearly 2.9 hours by early 2013. . . . While daily time with TV will remain close to 4 hours, traditional TV's share of the total video entertainment pie is projected to shrink from 63.9% today to 47.1% by 2013, given the overall increase in consumers' total video-based entertainment consumption.[2]

THE WORLD OF online video has exploded in recent years. It even seems poised to finally overtake television, at least for some genres. The rapid emergence of online video capabilities has led to the proliferation of video content of all sorts. There are major aggregators of videos online like YouTube.com, most television networks have their own video-powered web sites, thousands of smaller sites offer video around different targeted interests, and retailers like Netflix and iTunes offer video online, too.

Perhaps most importantly, both the production and the distribution of video content have left the control of professionals and been given to millions of amateurs worldwide. These days anyone can capture video on a digital camera or even a cell phone and easily upload that video online for worldwide viewing. Additionally, it is easy for those same folks to "borrow" professionally produced video by ripping their own clips from TV broadcasts, DVDs, or other sources.

Any and all of this content can then be spread across the Web by downloading or simply by embedding a small piece of code in a web site. These "embed" codes are a real breakthrough because they allow any web site to offer video inexpensively and with little technical support required.

Although the dominance of broadcast television networks has long been declining as a result of competition from cable and satellite television, this proliferation of distribution points for video is battering down the walls of the previously closed worlds of broadcast television and Hollywood movies.

Online Video Advertising

Ad agencies, media buyers, and advertisers are trying desperately to squeeze the new world of online video into the traditional ad-buying paradigms that worked so well for them in the twentieth century. So, for an advertiser, the basic approach for participating in online video is much the same as that for television. You can produce a short piece of video and pay to have it run before, during, or after someone else's video.

While there is a lot of opportunity here, our focus is not on advertising, but rather on low-cost, marketing-driven strategies.

Webcasting Live Video

Webcasting has come a long way since the 1990s, when jerky, postage-stamp–sized videos first hit the Net. Lots of companies, including big names like the House of Blues chain of concert halls and venture capital–backed wunderkinder like DEN (the short-lived Digital Entertainment Network), tried hard to overcome the limits of low bandwidth to deliver compelling live video online.

Today, bandwidth, PC processor speeds, and video compression technologies have all finally combined to make live Webcasting a reality. It's not yet HD quality, but today you can visit many sites for examples of live video streams 24/7.

For a marketer, the challenge with Webcasting is that you need to create truly interesting video if you expect people to watch it. This means that you are truly in the entertainment business if you want to attract eyeballs with a real-time production that allows for no editing. Live video is difficult to do well—that's why the nightly news and sports are almost the only live video you'll find on TV.

Live video can be very compelling if your topic is urgent or otherwise appropriate to the medium, but in most cases you'll have a much better chance of being entertaining if you prerecord your video. This gives you a chance to edit it, add music, add graphics, and create a more polished production.

If you want to stream video in real time for a public stunt, a conference, or a presentation that will benefit from live presentation, here are some services to use:

Ustream.com: http://www.ustream.com

LiveVideo.com: http://www.livevideo.com

Justin.tv: http://www.justin.tv

Online Video Promotions

The number of Americans watching video on their computers has doubled over the past year. The study found that the number of American consumers watching video streamed through a browser had soared over the past year, from 32 percent a year ago to 63 percent today.[3]

More interesting and revolutionary is the opportunity for any company to produce and distribute its own preproduced video. When video distribution was limited primarily to the television and film industries, most promotional videos were of high quality. A lot of money was spent on creating "perfect" car commercials, movie trailers, and entertainment programming to attract eyeballs.

Online video has empowered legions of amateur producers creating video for less selective audiences. In other words, with just a cheap Webcam and an Internet connection, you can now create and distribute video worldwide almost as well as the BBC, NBC, or Sony Pictures.

To capitalize on this collapse of the "must-see TV" paradigm, many smart marketers (especially for smaller companies and entrepreneurs who have less of an existing brand image to protect) have ventured online, creating videos to promote themselves and their products.

YouTube.com showcases thousands of low-budget product pitches for products, industries, services, and "experts" of all sorts. (This includes me, of course! Visit YouTube.com and search on "scott fox" to see video of some of my speeches free.)

Creating your own video for online distribution can be money well spent. If a picture is worth a thousand words, even an amateur video can obviously convey that much more information, emotion, and inspiration to purchase.

E-RICHES TIP: DYSLEXIC?
HATE WRITING OR TYPING?

Video promotions are also a great opportunity for you if you prefer talking to writing. Blogs, e-mail publishing, and even social networks may all be more writing-focused than you like.

If you are a poor speller or a bad typist, or if you just don't have the patience for all the written marketing communications that most online tools require, marketing by online video may be for you.

Fire up that Webcam or camcorder and get it started!

Web Site Video Strategy

FindLaw research indicates that when choosing a lawyer online, consumers visit an average 4.8 websites before making a decision. That drops to 1.8 sites when the site contains a video.[4]

Adding video to your own web site can be a great way to impress visitors and encourage sales. The motion, emotion, and immediacy of video are much more attention-grabbing than the prettiest still images or the best-written copy.

Video on your web site communicates that you are up to date technologically, and also appeals to many visitors, who may prefer to watch or listen instead of reading your site's content.

Once you have video produced, there are two ways you can offer it from your web site: You can host it yourself on your own servers, or you can post it to a popular video-sharing site like YouTube.com and let that site do the heavy lifting.

I recommend the latter. You can host it yourself, but why bother? YouTube.com will do most of the hard work, and also provide you with free tools that allow people to comment on and share your video—thus enhancing its potential for going viral.

E-RICHES TIP: SEARCH ENGINES ALSO LOVE VIDEO

Posting a video on a top video sharing site like YouTube can help you attract a top ranking in Google's search results, even if you don't have a web site!

Video is more challenging to produce than simple text or photos, so fewer people do it. This obviously reduces the competition for you if you want to promote your products using video. The many, many video-hosting and video-sharing sites now online make it easy to spread your video worldwide. So the trick is to create a video that people want to watch. Even better (but harder) is to create a video that people want to share with their friends.

As online video continues to grow in popularity, it's easier every day to see that it represents a real threat to the television industry. You can gain some of the viewership and engagement that are normally reserved for television by creating and posting your own videos online. This is easier to do than you might suspect.

How to Create Online Video

The standard for online video today is the use of a program called Flash.

Flash has been a revolution for online video because it allows almost any Web browser program to play full-motion video without any additional software. This breakthrough has allowed the delivery of online video to desktops worldwide and fueled the rise of YouTube.com and other online video sites.

Flash allows for small file sizes, high-quality frame rate, and compatibility with more than 90 percent of the Web browsers commonly used. This combination has brought online video to the masses and enabled the rise of "citizen video."

To promote your brand or products online using video, the production steps are fairly straightforward:

1. *Shoot a video.* Shooting a video today can be as easy as turning on your Webcam or clicking "record" on your mobile phone. Of course, the more you invest in the recording and visual presentation, the better your video will look to viewers.

2. *Download the video to your PC.* If you are using a Webcam, the video you recorded is probably already on your hard drive. If you are using a phone, camcorder, digital camera, or other device, plug it into your PC and transfer the video to the PC hard drive.

3. *Save the video file in one of the popular digital video file formats* to ensure compatibility with most online services. These formats include the .WMV, .AVI, .MOV, MPEG, and .MP4 formats (all of which are accepted by YouTube.com, for example).

4. *Sign in to your favorite online video service.* After logging in, you'll want to visit the account settings or the "upload" section of YouTube.com, Blip.tv, Google Video, or whatever service you have chosen. Using a standard point-and-click "browse" tool, you can upload your video file to the web site. Keep in mind any restrictions that may apply. For example, YouTube limits uploaded video files to 10 minutes in length and 1 GB in size. (See Figure 18–1 for You Tube's video upload page.)

You Tube   Broadcast Yourself ™
            Worldwide | English   (0) ✉ 📺

| Home | Videos | Channels | Community |

Video File Upload

✓ **scottfoxvideo**   **Success**

Add Video Name, Description, and Edit Privacy Settings   Embed and Sharing Options

Title

Scott Fox Video

Description

Tags

Category

Please select a category: ▼

Privacy

◉ Share your video with the world (Recommended)

○ Private (Viewable by you and up to 25 people)

[Save Changes]

Select a video to upload.

[Browse...]

[Upload Video]

Total videos uploaded: 1   [Go to My Videos]

About Uploading

- Upload up to 10 videos at a time
- **Best video formats** for YouTube
- Up to 1 GB in size.

Need more help? Visit the YouTube Handbook
Want to upload large numbers of videos in the background? Try our Bulk Upload Plugin

FIGURE 18–1.

5. *Customize your video presentation.* Complete the upload form by adding the video title, summary, and descriptive keyword tags. (This information is collectively called metadata because it is data about your data.) Completing these form fields is very important so that your video is easily searchable by that site's users.

6. *That's pretty much it.*

These simple steps will help you create a free page showcasing your video online. You can then link to the video from your own web site so that your site's visitors can see it.

Once your video has been submitted (assuming that it is approved by any moderators that are part of that site's posting process), the service will likely convert it into the Flash format discussed earlier. You will soon be able to click and play it in full motion and full color on the service's web site. Even better, anyone that you invite to view your video will also be able to watch it. Even "better better" (but depending on the specifics of the service you use), you'll be offered a host of tools that you can use to promote the video. These free tools include "forward to friend" e-mail tools, social network sharing tools, "embed codes" that allow others to easily insert your video onto their own web pages, comments and discussion posting, playlists, and more—all designed to help spread your promotional video across the Web for free.

Video "Embed" Codes

The most important functionality of video-sharing sites (after their ability to host and play your video, of course) is that they generally offer "embed" codes. An embed code is a short bit of web page code that you can copy and use on other web pages. By copying an embed code and inserting it into the HTML of a web page of your own, you can show the video you upload anywhere on any web page that you control. It will show a still frame of the video that users can click on to play the video without leaving your site, like this:

You can also grab the embed codes from other people's videos to use on your own web pages. This can make it very easy to piggyback on any video that you find online.

For example, a very popular post on my blog was one of the easiest for me to create: On YouTube, I ran across an educational video by my friend Robert Kiyosaki (of *Rich Dad, Poor Dad* fame) about his book *Cash Flow Quadrant.* In it, Robert made some good points, and his presentation was entertaining, too. So I simply copied the embed code offered by YouTube and pasted it into the HTML of my blog. Voilà—I have a cool Robert Kiyosaki video on my blog. My readers liked this video, too, and the post continues to attract a lot of traffic to my blog at ScottFox.com.

Conversely, if you can produce a video that others find interesting enough to want to share, people you don't even know are likely to grab your video and embed it on their own pages to share it with their own audiences. That's called viral video.

Here's an example of the embed code for one of my more popular videos on OneMinuteU.com:

```
<script
type="text/javascript">oneminuteu_param_flv_url =
"http%3A%2F%2Fwww%2Eoneminuteu%2Ecom%2Fcontent%2F
353DBEDC%2DD0BA%2D44C1%2DBD8F%2D4759C290970D%2F33
1132%5Fembed%2Eflv"; oneminuteu_param_video_title
=
"SEO%3A%20How%20Can%20I%20Get%20A%20Top%20Search%
20Engine%20Ranking%20For%20My%20Website%3F"; one-
minuteu_param_video_link =
"http%3A%2F%2Fwww%2Eoneminuteu%2Ecom%2Fbranch%5Fc
ontent%2Etaf%3Fpage%3Dcontent%26id%3D1114"; one-
minuteu_param_video_author = "ScottFox%2Ecom";
oneminuteu_param_video_author_link =
"http%3A%2F%2Fwww%2Eoneminuteu%2Ecom%2Fdefault%2E
taf%3Fpage%3Dprofile%26profile%5Fid%3D10662";</sc
ript><script type="text/javascript"
src="http://www.oneminuteu.com/inject_embed_playe
r.js"></script>
```

If you're clever (or can read code), you'll see in this code that the title of the video is "SEO: How Can I Get a Top Search Engine Ranking for My Website?" that it was authored by me, and that it links back to ScottFox.com.

I know the code itself is not very sexy-looking, but simply copying this code from OneMinuteU.com (or YouTube or whatever video site you're using) to your own web or blog page will enable you to play that video on your own site.

These embed codes are a truly amazing free service that can help you install video on your web site at very little expense and with almost none of the technical complexity that was associated with streaming video just a few years ago. You don't have to invest in video-hosting and video-serving technology at all these days. Free video hosting is provided by YouTube.com (or whatever other provider you choose) as part of its business. The use of embed codes can save you money and time and help you spread your marketing messages at the same time.

Now that's sexy!

ONLINE VIRAL VIDEO SUCCESS STORY:
GARY VAYNERCHUK, WINELIBRARY.COM

An entertaining and creative use of online video is the video series produced by Gary Vaynerchuk of WineLibrary.com. Gary's videos are simply a series of clips that show him tasting wine and giving his opinions. They are a great example of the use of online video to simultaneously encourage retail sales both online at WineLibrary.com and at his family's liquor store in New Jersey, while also building a brand around Gary V. himself as a business personality.

The publicity platform that Gary has constructed online is driven primarily by his consistent and entertaining production and syndication of wine-tasting video clips.

Gary's Russian immigrant parents, Alexander and Tamara, opened Shopper's Discount Liquors in Springfield, New Jersey, in 1983. Gary rebranded the store as Wine Library and helped them build their first web site in 1997.

In 2005, he began producing the short wine-tasting videos that have made him famous. Today, video clips syndicated from Wine Library.com are seen by upwards of 80,000 viewers each day. Gary says this worldwide promotional platform has helped drive Wine Library sales to $50 million annually, roughly half of which is attributable to online sales.

Although today Wine Library has more than 100 employees, WineLibrary.com's video production team is mostly just Gary and his cameraman/editor/producer, Chris. They bought a pretty good digital videocamera to shoot the episodes, but other than that, they don't worry too much about production value. In fact, the "shows" are completely unrehearsed and unscripted.

Gary thinks that authenticity is more important than polish. He says, "It's okay not to be George Clooney. Your online video should be more about your story and your personal connection with the audience than expensive props, sets, and lighting."

Gary says that his key to success with online video is to "Embrace your DNA. Share with the audience who you are and your expertise will be even more appreciated."

In addition to driving major sales growth at WineLibrary.com, Gary's success at using online video as a marketing tool has also helped establish him as a bit of a celebrity in his own right. He has been quoted in *Time, Forbes,* the *Wall Street Journal,* and *Wired,* and he has appeared on television with Conan O'Brien, Ellen DeGeneres, and Jim Cramer, and on *Nightline.* And he got a book deal to publish *Gary Vaynerchuk's 101 Wines.*

When they started producing their promotional videos of the wine tastings, Gary and Chris just posted them on YouTube.com. Since 2005, however, the online video marketplace has exploded. For a while they tried posting on a whole range of different video-hosting services. This became a time-consuming and repetitive effort, though.

Today a site called TubeMogul.com has come to the rescue because it allows you to upload your video once; it then automatically posts your video to whichever other video-sharing sites you designate.

Gary measures the success of Wine Library's video wine tastings in two ways: sales and reaction from the online audience. Both are strongly in favor of more "Gary V. TV"!

ONLINE VIRAL VIDEO CASE STUDY:
VERMONT TEDDY BEAR

Another way to use online video's viral power is to get others to create videos for you. For example, The Vermont Teddy Bear Company (VTB) took advantage of YouTube's huge audience for a successful Valentine's Day promotion when it launched an outreach effort specifically targeting vloggers.

(A vlog is a video blog, and its publisher is called a vlogger. Vlogs are simply blogs produced in video instead of text. The most common approach is for the vlogger to turn on her Webcam each day and speak to the camera. She then uploads the recording to YouTube or another online video service to share her latest thoughts with the world online, just as a blogger does with text copy.)

VTB's challenge was to reach men in the critical days leading up to Valentine's Day. Its goal was to convince them that a customized

Vermont Teddy Bear would make a great gift for the woman in their life.

To do this, VTB e-mailed vloggers who were active on YouTube, especially females with a primarily male viewership. The company offered to send each vlogger a teddy bear customized to reflect his or her on-air personality. Vloggers who accepted were asked to feature the teddy bear in an episode ramping up to Valentine's Day. One vlogger in particular, TokenBlackChic, produced an entire episode telling a love story by animating Vermont Teddy Bears! (This funny three-minute video is still available on YouTube and has racked up 62,565 views.)

The targeted male audience on YouTube responded strongly to the online video promotions: 82 percent of the video viewers who clicked through the video to visit the customized "Show Her You Know Her" Vermont Teddy Bear micro site submitted the "teddy bear customization quiz" offered there, boosting awareness of the company among its target audience right before its most important holiday, Valentines's Day.

Video-Sharing Sites

Popular video-sharing sites as of this writing include:

- ▲ YouTube.com

- ▲ Blip.tv

- ▲ DailyMotion.com

- ▲ Google video

- ▲ Viddler.com

- ▲ Veoh.com

- ▲ Metacafe.com

▲ OneMinuteU.com

▲ TubeMogul.com

Any of these sites may have changed its focus or its business model by the time you read this. Come join the discussion at ScottFox.com to help you master the marketing potential of online video for your business.

19
. . .

THE NEW MARKETING POWER
OF FREE TELESEMINARS
AND WEBINARS

OFFERING FREE teleseminars is an increasingly popular strategy for publicizing any business that is based on expertise. The Internet has enabled this new promotional medium because it has driven down the cost of telephone calls to almost nothing. In fact, there are now many free services that offer you the ability to host your own conference call for 100 or even 1,000 people at a time for no cost.

With this ability to reach large groups of people inexpensively comes the opportunity for you to market your business. If you have expertise that you can share, have insights into current events or industry trends, or can simply host guest speakers who do, teleseminars may be a viable marketing tool for you. By hosting a teleseminar or appearing on one hosted by someone else, you automatically position yourself as an expert. This is great both for your credibility and to attract sales.

As with most of the techniques we've discussed in this book, the audiences for online teleseminars are self-selected. Thus, teleseminars can be very targeted toward the specific topics that promote your products most effectively. And, like online video, podcasts, and online radio shows, teleseminars can be archived for future listening. This can attract ongoing attention from additional potential customers who may not have caught your original call.

Even if you have only a few people listening, if those folks are interested in the specifics of what you have to say, then they make great customer prospects for your business.

How to Produce Your Own Teleseminars

You can set up a free conference call using services like freeconferencecall.com or simpleevent.com. These services allow you to invite 100 or 1,000 guests to join you on a telephone conference call. The service costs you nothing, although it will cost callers regular long-distance charges to the number provided by the service.

Depending on which service you use and how you want to position the opportunity, callers can call in live during your real-time broadcast, listen on the Web through their PCs, or listen to recorded versions either by phone or on the Web after the teleseminar has been completed. Each of these strategies reflects different promotional approaches and business models for revenue generation.

Once you have this ability to reach an audience, you simply need to develop your content and promote the event to attract listeners.

You can also either take questions live or just respond to presubmitted e-mails to make the program more interactive.

Recent teleseminars that I have given have been based on my own expertise and on requests from readers like you. They have included "Search Engine Optimization Critical Basics," "Web Site Design for E-Commerce Businesses," and "Making Money with Affiliate Programs," as well as "open mic" sessions where I take questions live from listeners.

**E-RICHES TIP: TELESEMINARS =
ONLINE RADIO = PODCASTS**

*If you like giving teleseminars, turn this into a habit and call it an online
radio show. You can offer your own online radio show and syndicate the
recordings as podcasts, too. Visit any of the sites mentioned in the online
radio section of Chapter 20 for details.*

What's a Webinar?

A webinar is like a teleseminar, but with the addition of a visual component on the attendees' computer screens. An attendee may listen to the hosts either by phone or via PC speakers, but also sees the visual aids that the host uses (usually PowerPoint presentations or web sites) during a webinar to amplify the points made and aid the discussion.

Today, services like WebEx, GoToMeeting, Dimdim, and many others offer this capability at a wide range of price points. A teleseminar is often restructured into a webinar when an audio-only discussion isn't quite enough to get the points across fully.

WEBINAR MARKETING CASE STUDY: TAYLOR BUSBY, AGILITYRECOVERY.COM

An example of a company that successfully uses webinars as a marketing tool is Agility Recovery, a business continuity and disaster recovery company headquartered in Charlotte, North Carolina.

The company targets small to medium-sized businesses that need disaster planning and replacement office space, especially for their IT operations. It has experienced significant growth over the past few years, and online marketing has played a significant role. In addition to its work with SEO, e-mail newsletters, and an online user community, Agility Recovery's webinar series has been particularly useful in attracting new customers.

The company conducts educational webinars through its www.PrepareMyBusiness.com web site using GoToWebinar.com. It offers an average of at least one webinar every week. Each program attracts dozens of attendees who are interested in learning how to manage business operations in case of flood, fire, or other business interruptions. The webinars have titles like "Effective Emergency Communications," "The Human Side of Crisis Management," and "Business as Usual, No Matter What." The company varies the content, format, and hosts of the webinars in order to keep attracting new attendees.

These attendees are all highly targeted business-to-business potential sales prospects for Agility Recovery's sales force to follow up with. In the first half of 2008, for example, more than 2,000 individuals registered to attend the programs—the 1,161 attendees generated $24,150 in monthly recurring revenues through sales of the company's ReadySuite membership product.

Taylor Busby, the company's Vice President of Marketing, told me that Agility Recovery loves online marketing because it's so trackable and provides such "warm" leads. The webinars are particularly effective because every webinar attendee provides contact information when he registers. The company's sales force knows whether the registrant has attended the webinar or whether he was a no-show. Then the salespeople can customize follow-up tactics accordingly.

Taylor recommends webinars as an effective marketing tactic for two reasons: They support the sales force, and they build credibility for the company's brand before, during, and after the sale.

How to Attract Listeners for
Your Teleseminars and Webinars

Attracting listeners to your teleseminar or webinar is a fairly standard marketing exercise. If you have an e-mail list, send out an e-mail. If you have a web site, post a notice or ad banner there. If you want to advertise the event online, you can buy ads wherever it is appropriate for your target market and your budget.

You can also submit your free teleseminar or webinar events to FreeTeleseminarList.com, a directory of such events that I started as part of the research for this book. That site accepts listings from any educationally oriented teleseminar-type program. Event listings that are approved for posting are then publicized both on the web site itself and by e-mailing the subscribers on the FreeTeleseminarList.com free e-mail list. Free events listed recently on FreeTeleseminarList.com come from marketers worldwide. They cover topics like "Larger Profit Yields Through Client Follow-up," "Learn PR Secrets from a Master," "Upgrade Your Clients," "Closing Middle Market Deals," and "Developing a Prosperity Mindset."

Webinars listed on this free service have recently included "Business Continuity in the Face of IT Problems," "Coaching Excellence," "Environmentally Friendly Logos," "Inbox-Worthy E-mails," and even a webinar titled "Promoting Your Webinar."

Visit FreeTeleseminarList.com to submit your events.

Resources

Free Conference Call: http://www.freeconferencecall.com

Simple Event: http://www.simpleevent.com

FreeTeleseminarList.com: http://www.freeteleseminarlist.com

20

. . .

ONLINE RADIO
AND PODCASTS
GUEST INTERVIEWS
OR HOST YOUR OWN

THE INTERNET revolution's virtually free worldwide live telecommunications have also brought us a wave of new online radio shows hosted by nonprofessional broadcasters.

More than 80 million Americans now listen to Internet radio each month.[1] Millions more people are listening from all over the world right now as you read this.

Online radio shows are the audio equivalent of blogs—they showcase the personal interests, lives, and business pursuits of their amateur online radio hosts. Just as with blogs, anyone can host such a show today. So, also as with blogs, this means that there are a few really good radio shows online and thousands of smaller ones that may have little or no audience.

However, because most online radio shows have small audiences, they are often looking for guests who are willing to appear. If you choose to appear on online radio shows that have a specific target audience that meets your publicity needs, even a very small audience can offer you a great marketing opportunity.

A quick review of leading Internet radio sites offers thousands of shows that may be useful to you. Traditional talk radio topics like politics, business, sports, and health are popular, as are thousands of shows that are targeted to different niches, like Let's Talk Nutrition, Saving Dinner, The Common Sense Psychic, Wild About Pets, American GunRadio, Shutterbug Radio, the Las Vegas Comedy Show, Craft Radio Network, Empowerment Hour, and thousands more.

Getting interviewed by online radio shows and podcast broadcasters offers many benefits:

▲ They are easier to get booked on than bigger radio shows.

▲ They generally have smaller but highly targeted audiences.

▲ Shows are usually archived publicly to create podcasts. This means that people can continue to find and listen to your interview for months or years after the initial broadcast.

▲ Online radio show hosts will usually promote your appearance online, creating links back to your web site that can help your search engine rankings.

Appearing on Internet radio programs may seem like a small opportunity compared to getting booked on Rush Limbaugh's radio program or Oprah's TV show, but how likely is that for your product anyway?

I think online radio is a great promotional outlet because its audiences are so targeted that you are sure to have an interested audience if you pick your appearances wisely. Online radio is also a rapidly growing industry—if you develop good contacts now, they could pay off with free publicity for your company for years.

Online Radio Resources

To find online radio shows that match your marketing objectives, you can visit any of these leading online radio web sites:

▲ BlogTalkRadio.com

▲ Talkzone.com

▲ Alltalkradio.net

▲ Voiceamerica.com

▲ WSradio.com

▲ RadioGuestList.com

GET RADIO BOOKINGS USING RADIOGUESTLIST.COM—FREE!

For marketers, the most targeted site of those listed is RadioGuestList.com. This is a free resource that I created as part of the research for this book. This free service helps match guest experts with online and small-market radio shows that are looking for guests.

Visit the site to sign up for the free e-mails full of queries from online radio hosts, terrestrial radio bookers, podcasters, satellite radio programs, and even the occasional TV show that's looking for experts to interview: www.RadioGuestList.com. Subscribe and you'll receive daily e-mails full of guest booking requests from radio show producers looking to interview experts like you!

Hosting Your Own Online Radio Show

Creating an online radio show of your own can create an additional publicity outlet for your promotions, as well as enhancing your credibility.

As discussed earlier, the explosion of cheap communications technologies has helped online radio programs proliferate—so instead of just looking to be booked on one as a guest, why not host your own?

Online radio shows are yet another potential way to reach your target customers. You can do this live by broadcasting online at a regularly scheduled time, or you can record your shows and offer them as podcasts for others to download and listen to at their convenience.

SCOTTFOXRADIO.COM

I have a great time producing my weekly *E-Commerce Success Radio Show*. (Please visit www.ScottFoxRadio.com to join the audience, too.) It gives me an opportunity to share with an additional audience my message of e-business empowerment and the specific tactics that I recommend for online success. I do some of this by simply talking into the microphone to share my opinions, but what is even more fun (and often more interesting to listen to) is conducting interviews "on the air" with experts in online marketing, authors, and entrepreneurs. More importantly, my show has been finding an increasing audience of listeners who are interested in the same topics I am.

So far I have been using the free online radio show service provided by BlogTalkRadio.com. This easy-to-use service has helped me start, record, publicize, and syndicate my show across the Web for free. The site provides plenty of tools to help you get started, too. Most importantly, hosting the show itself is easy—you just call a dedicated phone number and start talking. The system automatically broadcasts the show to anyone who is interested in listening online and records it in an archive, too. You can then offer the recordings as downloads or syndicate them as podcasts through iTunes.

As with all the strategies we discuss in this book, I'd suggest exploring online radio as a marketing vehicle for your company. Whether you appear as a guest on others' shows, host your own show, or both, online radio is a great way to reach highly targeted audiences. Once you've tried it yourself, you can then decide where to prioritize this marketing strategy among the many we're discussing together.

If you'd like help finding interesting guests for your new online radio show, please visit RadioGuestList.com. This free service will allow you to post your guest interview needs and e-mail them to a worldwide audience of interested expert subscribers.

What Is a Podcast?

A podcast is simply a recording that is distributed online. So a radio show, an interview, a book reading, a musical performance, a lecture, or any other type of audio that can be recorded can be distributed as a digital file and called a podcast. (Since video can be handled similarly, TV shows and other recorded video can also be packed into podcasts, too, FYI.) I offer free audio and video podcasts about online marketing at ScottFox.com.

Why do podcasts matter?

The podcasting revolution is about both improved access to content and improved flexibility of scheduling and format for listeners. The production of content is no longer controlled by major media companies—podcasting makes anyone with a recording device into a worldwide, 24/7 broadcaster.

And instead of waiting for a certain time to listen to a broadcast on the radio, listeners can use their PCs to pick up recordings from the Web at any time. Then they can listen to their favorite shows anytime, anywhere—on their iPod, on their PC, on their phone, and so on. Today, 19 percent of all Internet users say that they have downloaded a podcast so that they could listen to it or view it later.[2]

Wow . . . sorry, old media companies. My Convenience Principle applies here, too. You have insisted for too long that people accommodate your broadcast schedules, even when it was inconvenient for them. Well, today the flexibility of podcasting allows the audience to take control and listen or watch where, when, and how it wants (and also increasingly to enjoy programs *not* produced by the big networks!).

Visit ScottFoxRadio.com, iTunes.com, Podcast.com, or Podcast Alley.com to find free podcasts that interest you and learn more about podcasts.

PART SEVEN—BONUS!
PAY-PER-CLICK KEYWORD AND AFFILIATE PROGRAM ADVERTISING STRATEGIES

INCREASE YOUR SALES
WITH SEARCH ENGINE
KEYWORD ADVERTISING

Half the money I spend on advertising is wasted; the trouble is, I don't know which half.

—Attributed to John Wanamaker, department store pioneer

THERE IS A lot about online advertising that is similar to offline advertising. The need to develop attractive graphics, compelling copy, and the media buys to deploy them are similar. These techniques continue to be used in online advertising just as they have been for decades in print and TV. Online, these graphic "display ads" are usually referred to generically as "banners" or "buttons," depending on their size.

What is newer because of the Internet is the rise of different billing mechanisms for ads. These include cost-per-click (CPC) and cost-per-action (CPA) advertising, as well as different distribution methods, such as search engine marketing (SEM) and affiliate programs.

These forms of online advertising technically fall outside the scope of this book, which is focused on marketing techniques rather than on paid advertising. However, because they are such important tools in the modern marketer's arsenal, I have added this "bonus"section with a discussion of pay-per-click (PPC) search engine marketing and affiliate advertising strategies anyway.

(Another reason I'm including a discussion of online advertising in this marketing book is that in corporate environments, online advertising is likely to be managed by the Internet team simply because it's a technology-driven discipline. Senior management that doesn't understand online marketing is likely to lump online advertising in with web site production and operation, e-mail marketing, and other such techniques and expect you to know about it. And if your operation is smaller, or perhaps even just yourself, the distinction between marketing and advertising doesn't matter anyway—it's up to you to get the job done as an entrepreneur.)

Once again, my goal here is to help you. I'd like to help remove the "fear of the unknown" that you may have if you are new to online advertising. Like the other technologies discussed in this book, search engine marketing, pay-per-click, and affiliate programs are strategies that you can learn and implement successfully yourself. This can save you lots of money and help you grow your business very cost-effectively.

Why Search Engine Marketing (SEM)?

The percentage of Internet users who use search engines on a typical day has been steadily rising from about one-third of all users in 2002 to a new high of 49 percent. The number of those using a search engine on a typical day is pulling ever closer to the 60 percent of Internet users who use e-mail on a typical day. Search engine use is also growing more than four times faster than e-mail adoption.[1]

Conclusion: Search engines are not just for online research. They are also major marketing tools.

Search engine marketing is simply the use of search engines to attract customer traffic to your web site. SEM includes search engine optimization (SEO), which is designing your web site so that it attracts a high "organic" ranking in search engine results, and pay-per-click keyword advertising, too.

Although optimizing your web site to attract high search engine rankings is an important skill, SEO is outside the scope of this book. Please see my first book, *Internet Riches*, or visit ScottFox.com for an updated discussion of SEO strategies and products that can help attract traffic to your web sites.

Here we're going to focus only on the PPC keyword advertising tools offered by the search engines.

Pay-per-Click Keyword Advertising

59 percent of small businesses with web sites don't currently use paid search marketing. And of those, 90 percent never even attempted it. What's more, 73 percent of small business owners say they are so intimidated by search marketing that they would rather do their taxes than create a search marketing campaign. Among the participants' chief concerns, most cited common misconceptions of cost, time, and complexity as major hurdles to conducting search marketing campaigns for their businesses.[2]

I'd like to be sure that you don't fall prey to the misconceptions quoted above. Not understanding and using paid search keyword marketing strategies is likely hurting your business.

What am I talking about? Let's start with the basics and I'll add why I think this deserves your attention.

Pay-per-click keyword advertising is a form of online advertising that shows your ads on the Web when customers search on topics related to your advertised services. Also known as *keyword advertising*, these ads are displayed only when a search engine user types in a search request using your chosen keywords. Then you pay for the ad only if a customer clicks on the ad to visit your web site. You pay only for the click; thus, this kind of ad is called pay-per-click or cost-per-click.

PPC strategies are more cost-effective than traditional advertising methods because you pay *only when a Web surfer clicks on your ad*. This almost guarantees that your ad money is wisely spent because the ad costs you something only when it delivers an interested customer to your site.

PPC ads are easy to place, too. There are step-by-step tutorials available online that make it easy for you to learn. (Google "pay-per-click advertising tutorial" or visit ScottFox.com for help.) Best of all, there are usually no up-front agency or program fees to participate in these PPC search engine marketing programs—you pay only "per click" at prices you can determine (and limit) up front.

Popular pay-per-click ad networks include:

- ▲ Google's Adwords

- ▲ Yahoo! Search Marketing

- ▲ Adbrite

I'm a big fan of keyword advertising.

This is because as a PPC advertiser, you are much more in control than you ever were with traditional advertising. You can limit the display of your ads to Web surfers who type in specific search terms that you choose, and you can precisely control how much you spend each day, the number of visitors you attract, the web pages to which those visitors are delivered, the geographical area in which your ads are displayed, the general demographics of the Internet users who will see the ads, and even the time of day you want your campaigns to run.

And while this targeting is of great benefit to any marketer, the real revolution in advertising brought about by keyword advertising involves pricing. With pay-per-click advertising, you pay only for visitors to your web site who are brought there by clicking on one of your ads. Because they actually clicked before you pay anything, this means that you are paying only for already interested leads, instead of paying for everyone who walks past your storefront or drives by your billboard on the freeway. Excellent!

PPC/CPC strategies are a revolution from the traditional method of charging for ads, which was CPM. CPM stands for "cost per thousand" (where the M is the Roman numeral for 1,000).

CPM was the "state of the art" audience measurement metric in the twentieth century for TV, radio, and print ads. It simply estimated the number of people who would see an ad (usually based on a newspaper's circulation or a broadcast program's estimated audience or the amount of traffic that passed a billboard each day). The advertiser then paid a certain number of dollars per thousand based on the estimated value of those viewers of the ads.

Obviously this was pretty crude—closer to buying potatoes by the bushel than today's CPC or CPA (cost per action) pricing. Online, one can track audience behavior far more precisely than in such traditional media. This allows you as an online advertiser to pay only for customers who actually take action by clicking to visit your web site (CPC or PPC) or even making a purchase (CPA).

PPC keyword ads also have no long-term contract requirements, and you can quickly and easily change the campaign targeting, the ad copy, or where the ads link to at any time.

This targeting, cost-effectiveness, and flexibility, as well as the instant and worldwide reach of the Internet, have led to tremendous growth in pay-per-click advertising strategies. For example, the Adsense and Adwords programs run by Google are the only significant revenue stream that Google has, believe it or not.

**AVOID THE BIGGEST MISTAKES
IN SEM/PPC KEYWORD ADVERTISING**

Please pay attention here! This section can save you a lot of money.

In my seminars and radio call-in show appearances, I regularly am confronted by people who claim to have tried pay-per-click and given up because "it doesn't work for my business." The biggest mistake that I see novice keyword advertisers make is to *give up* on keyword advertising because their first attempts were not implemented correctly and they lost money.

Nine times out of ten, I have found that these folks actually had done a poor job of implementing their PPC strategies. Usually this is because they bought very generic keywords that both were expensive and generated poorly targeted (and therefore poorly converting) visitor traffic.

The days of buying the keyword "car" or "book" and expecting to attract traffic to your car or book web site cost-effectively are gone. You need to drill down instead and pay for keywords that more specifically reflect the unique services offered by your site. This will help you attract visitors who are more likely to be interested in those unique services. So, paying to have your ads show up when people search on "used Cadillac mufflers" or "cheap medical school textbooks" is more likely to attract appropriate visitors cost-effectively. And those ads will also be cheaper because there is much less competition in these niches than there is for the general keywords that are desired by so many competitors.

How to Get Started with
PPC/SEM Keyword Advertising

Here's what you should be doing to attract customers online using pay-per-click advertising.

As soon as you have a domain name and a basic web site posted, you should set aside a small budget to buy keyword ads associated with your new venture.

Set up an online account with a pay-per-click advertising service like Google's Adwords (http://adwords.google.com). You will need to enter your work name, address, contact information, and payment information (usually a credit card).

Start by entering keywords that you expect people to use to search for products like yours online. The advertising system will help you brainstorm appropriate choices and also give you estimates of how much traffic each keyword combination is likely to attract and at what cost per click.

I recommend thinking broadly about what keywords are applicable to find the best ones and include all potential categories, but then also narrowing the specifics of the keywords that you actually buy ads against. This is because more narrowly targeted, specific keywords are less competitive and therefore cheaper. You can use the free online tools offered by the search engines' advertising services to estimate the cost and traffic for different keyword ad buys before committing to spend any money. (See Figure 21–1 for Google Adword's keyword cost tool.)

Enter $50 as your campaign limit for the month (or whatever is appropriate for your budget). This is probably not enough to attract a huge audience, but that's okay—you're not trying to maximize your audience until your site has its sales conversion strategy clearly developed.

Following these steps to get started with pay-per-click keyword advertising can help make a new web site visible to potential customers weeks before the search engines find it and begin including it in their search results. The point is that because of the huge volume of traffic that search engines process, you want to be sure that your site is at least minimally visible to any customers who may be

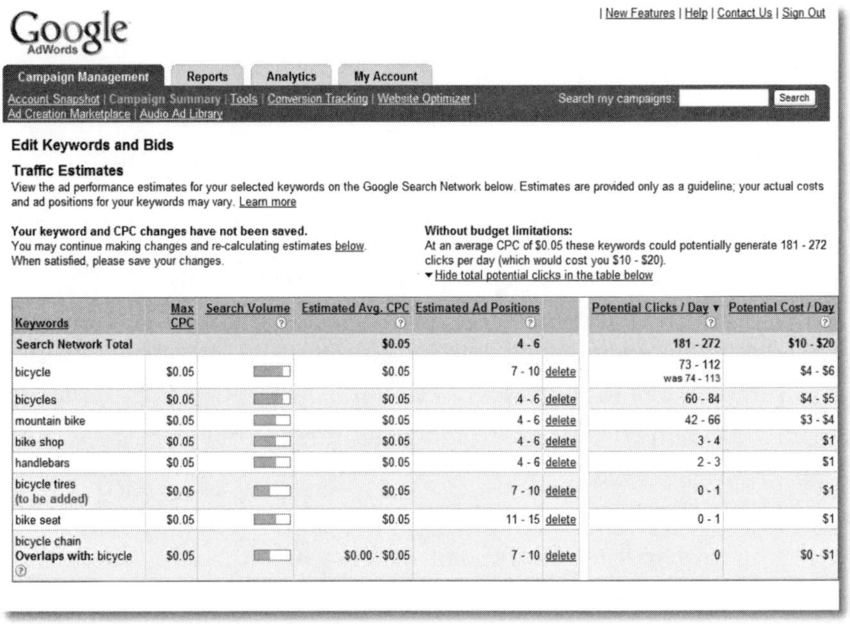

Keywords	Max CPC	Search Volume	Estimated Avg. CPC	Estimated Ad Positions	Potential Clicks / Day	Potential Cost / Day
Search Network Total			$0.05	4 - 6	181 - 272	$10 - $20
bicycle	$0.05		$0.05	7 - 10 delete	73 - 112 was 74 - 113	$4 - $6
bicycles	$0.05		$0.05	4 - 6 delete	60 - 84	$4 - $5
mountain bike	$0.05		$0.05	4 - 6 delete	42 - 66	$3 - $4
bike shop	$0.05		$0.05	4 - 6 delete	3 - 4	$1
handlebars	$0.05		$0.05	4 - 6 delete	2 - 3	$1
bicycle tires (to be added)	$0.05		$0.05	7 - 10 delete	0 - 1	$1
bike seat	$0.05		$0.05	11 - 15 delete	0 - 1	$1
bicycle chain Overlaps with: bicycle	$0.05		$0.00 - $0.05	7 - 10 delete	0	$0 - $1

FIGURE 21–1.

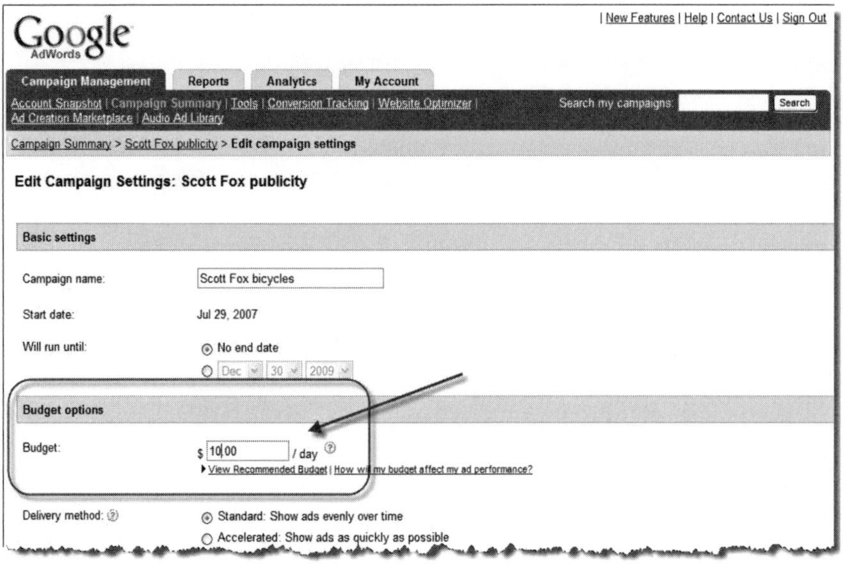

FIGURE 21–2.

interested in your topics as soon as possible while you develop your strategy further.

You don't have to spend any money to set up a PPC account like this, but be careful, because you are working with "live ammunition." As soon as the ads start getting clicked on—which can be just minutes after you activate them—you will be billed for any clicks delivered to your site. So, you want to set a low limit on your expenditures to start. (See Figure 21–2 for Google Adword's budget controller.)

Then develop and activate your keyword ads focusing on specific niches rather than on more expensive general terms. Failing to take these two basic steps when you get started can easily lead to hundreds or thousands of dollars on your credit card bill because poorly targeted ads delivered lots of expensive visitors to your web site with little or no sales conversion.

You'll then want to write several ads. (See my tips for successful text ad copywriting at the end of this chapter.) I say several ads because you want to try posting variations to see which ad copy attracts the most clicks at the lowest prices.

You can also limit your ad display by geography, or even time of day, to lower your costs further. (See Figure 21–3 for Google Adword's Daily Scheduler.)

Maximizing Your Online Advertising Cost-Effectiveness

Keyword advertising is a busier marketplace than it was just a few years ago when I wrote my first book, *Internet Riches*, but it still offers excellent marketing opportunities if you know how to use it correctly.

The prices of keyword ads have risen significantly in recent years. Although you used to be able to attract pay-per-click web site visitors for as little as 5 cents each, today the minimums are more often 10 cents or 20 cents—and keywords in lucrative, competitive categories often sell for several dollars per click.

This means that to put PPC keyword advertising strategies to work effectively for your business, you need to understand how to

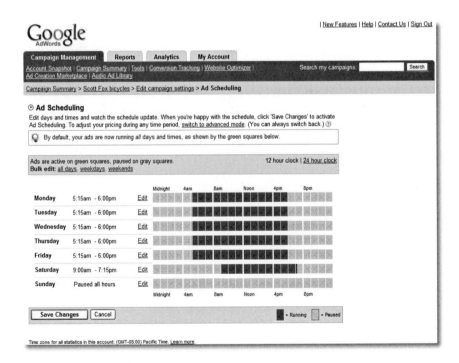

FIGURE 21–3.

pick the right keywords in order to minimize competition and maximize your ROI.

An attractive feature of PPC advertising is that you can set up tightly targeted ads and limit their expense up front to analyze the effectiveness of such campaigns and control their costs. For example, you could run ads specifically targeting health insurance buyers in Dayton, Ohio. You can further limit your outlay to $10 per day until you're certain that the strategy meets your needs.

This targeting is also key to keeping your costs manageable. Just buying the keyword "insurance" could easily cost you $15 for each visitor it delivers to your web site. It may also deliver life or automobile insurance customers when you were really trying to attract customers for health and medical coverage.

But if you more specifically target "health insurance," the cost per click drops to around $9 per visitor, and the visitors are more likely to be interested in what you're selling, too. The even more specific keyword phrase "dental insurance" averages only $4.50 per visitor. The more specific you are, the less expensive the keywords should be because there will be less competition for them from other advertisers.

You can also limit the geographical area in which your ad is shown to users. If you limit your display to searchers from the greater Dayton, Ohio, metropolitan area, your budget can be even lower because you're ensuring that you don't get customers from faraway states, thereby helping every dollar count.

This geographical targeting is a big improvement over the Internet advertising of a few years ago, which was based merely on user views nationally, and a massive change compared to the scattershot broadcast and print ads of the twentieth century.

PPC also allows you to get started with a much smaller budget than in traditional media. You can literally get started for $1 on Google's Adsense, for example. Inexpensively testing different ad copy, localization, and keyword combinations to determine the optimal mix for attracting new business can be a great way to grow your web site traffic.

These may sound like new or experimental advertising strategies to you, but they are well established online. In fact, the majority of Google's $20 billion in annual revenue comes from its Adsense and Adwords pay-per-click advertising services.

Some businesses spend $100,000 per month or more on SEM advertising to generate $110,000 of sales, making a slim profit, while other companies use tiny budgets to target narrowly targeted niche keyword markets for specific products or customers. Most PPC advertisers have budgets that are in between, like Carolina Rustica.com.

PAY-PER-CLICK ADVERTISING
PROFILE: CAROLINARUSTICA.COM

Richard Sexton runs a high-end furniture store in Concord, North Carolina. It specializes in iron beds and iron furniture, as well as butcher blocks, chandeliers, ceiling fans, and baker's racks. CarolinaRustica.com is his web site.

Richard has had great success using online pay-per-click keyword advertising to market his business. In fact, he attributes more than 85 percent of his sales to online advertising. Since his small company has grown from nothing to over $4 million in annual sales since 1997, it's clear that his PPC strategy is working. In fact, he is now working to expand his real-world store and warehouse facilities to keep up with the growth of his business online.

Here's how he does it.

CarolinaRustica.com receives about 5,000 unique visitors each day. Richard and his team attract most of these visitors through search engines. They have optimized their web site to obtain good organic (meaning free) rankings for most of their popular products.

They also are heavy users of pay-per-click advertising, especially for products or web pages where they don't rank as well organically. In fact, CarolinaRustica.com spends as much as 10 percent of its revenues on search engine keyword advertising.

Richard and his team use more than 3,000 different keyword terms to trigger the display of pay-per-click ads on the Google,

Yahoo!, and MSN search engines, as well as on the associated "content network" web sites that those search engine advertising programs reach. They spread their PPC ad budget across these three main search engines proportionally to the market share of the general Internet user population that search engine represents.

They buy "clicks" for the keywords at an average price of $0.80 each. While $0.80 per visitor may sound expensive, CarolinaRustica.com sells high-end handcrafted furniture, lighting, and kitchen accents, many from top designers. This means that its average order size is $300 to $400, so it can afford this per-visitor cost given the high average transaction value.

Richard helps manage the costs of the company's online advertising campaigns with these helpful strategies:

▲ *Avoid generic keywords; use more specific terms instead.* Richard says that generic keywords like "bed" are too expensive: "You want to stay away from them as much as possible." Their price is driven up by a combination of major corporation competitors who are not as price-sensitive and many smaller, more amateur competitors who don't know better than to overpay for the generic term.

Additionally, he says, "'Bed' can mean different things to different people," so being more specific by using keyword phrases like "antique iron bed" greatly increases the chance of attracting the right kind of visitor to the site.

▲ *Balance free organic search traffic against more expensive PPC visitors.* A well-designed, content-rich web site should rank decently in search engine results for your keywords and phrases without your having to pay for SEM advertising. For example, in response to a search for "iron bed," CarolinaRustica.com displays as number seven on Google. You can save a lot of money by not paying for advertising if you're getting a good ranking anyway.

▲ *Use negative keywords.* As mentioned previously, you have a lot of control over when, where, and how your PPC ads are displayed. Another valuable strategy is to use "negative keywords" to limit the times when your ads are displayed. For example, CarolinaRustica.com uses this strategy to prevent its ads from being displayed if a search engine user types "discount iron beds" or "iron beds rebate." Richard doesn't want to attract bargain hunters, so configuring his keyword advertising accounts to ignore queries that include his negative keywords saves him from paying for clicks and visits from customers he doesn't want anyway. He calls this an "important tool in managing costs."

▲ *Never bid for the #1 spot.* Surprisingly, Richard never pays up to gain the top advertising slot in his keyword ad buys. He says that studies have shown that the second, third, and even fourth placements actually yield a better ROI. Plus, he doesn't see any need to compete in the "ego game." "If another advertiser wants to pay more to be ranked first when that doesn't necessarily make them any more money, go ahead," he says.

▲ *Create customized landing pages.* Creating a landing page for each product or keyword topic area or product type can greatly improve your conversion. Richard says, "Make sure your landing page conveys what people expect to see when they click on your ad. Don't just link to your home page because they are likely to be responding to a more specific pitch in your ad. If you give them what they expect, they are much more likely to convert."

CarolinaRustica.com uses a variety of tools to manage its large collection of keywords across the Google, Yahoo!, and MSN search advertising networks. Richard recommends the free keyword brainstorming, performance tracking, and campaign management tools that Google and these other companies provide. "It's not too surprising that they provide great tools for you to use to manage your ads with them—they're happy to help you spend more money." His advice: "Don't be intimidated by the complexity of SEM PPC advertising. Logging in for the first time to Google's Adwords dashboard can be overwhelming, but it can also be a lot of fun. If you need help, their representatives are more than happy to help you out, and there are lots of educational tutorials available online, too."

Copywriting for Text Ads

A major challenge for the successful use of text ads is their limited length. Because a text ad is generally limited to just a few dozen characters, space is at a premium. You need to make not just every word but every single character and space that you are allowed count.

Text ad example: In Google's Adwords program, text ads are limited to 130 characters, including spaces. For me, that resulted in one ad that looks like this:

Scott Fox Internet Riches
Official Scott Fox e-Business Blog
Internet Riches book, free noozle
www.ScottFox.com

I set this basic ad up to display through Google's Adwords service whenever users type in the title of my first book, *Internet Riches.*

Writing a good keyword text ad follows a combination of copywriting and keyword targeting principles. Of course, the headline is your most important asset. You want to write something eye-catching that also ideally includes your target keywords. The rest of the ad should also follow the copywriting principles I outlined earlier in the book. These include catching the reader's attention, demonstrating a benefit for them, and providing a compelling call to action. Here's an example:

Hand-Forged Iron Beds
Solid Iron Beds Hand-Forged in the USA.
Low Prices Online or In-Store!
CarolinaRustica.com/Iron_Beds

Richard Sexton, owner of CarolinaRustica.com, says that copywriting for text ads may be the hardest part of keyword advertising. "There's extremely limited space, especially if you want to include a manufacturer's name along with 'buy' or 'sale' or other obvious words."

He writes the obvious ads that include those terms, but he also tries to write additional ads that he calls "wacky." Instead of mimicking the common approach, the wacky ads focus on asking questions (very eye-catching), responding to competitors' claims shown in other ads, or focusing the pitch on his company's expertise or customer service instead of the more usual claims about price or selection.

Your success with PPC advertising depends on how well you write the tiny little ads it requires. This is more important for this technique than your products, prices, selection, or service. In just 130 characters, you need to attract attention and convince a viewer to click—while also encouraging her to ignore all the other competition on the page.

Visit the discussion forums at ScottFox.com to ask your questions about pay-per-click advertising. Visiting can help save you lots of money by learning more about the latest cost-effective online advertising strategies.

22

AFFILIATE
PROGRAM ADVERTISING
MEET YOUR NEW WORLDWIDE
SALESFORCE

AFFILIATE PROGRAMS are another of the innovative online advertising strategies that are unique to the Internet. From a marketer's perspective, they are a valuable tool because they can help you deploy a worldwide online promotions and sales team on a commission-only basis. That's why affiliate programs are often referred to as "performance-based marketing."

As an affiliate program advertiser, you agree to provide advertising materials (like banner ads, promotional text copy, and tracking links) to "affiliates" who promote your products on their own sites. Then, when an affiliate directs a customer to your site and that customer takes the action you specify, you credit the affiliate's account with a fixed-price bounty or a percentage of the sale.

The premise of affiliate programs is that there are web sites that will promote your products in exchange for a commission from you for each visitor delivered to your site, each visitor that signs up for your mailing list, or each product you sell. This can be a very effective way to spread the word about your products across the Web because it gives owners of small web sites, blogs, and e-mail newsletters incentives to promote your products to their niche audiences.

Administration of an affiliate program can be complex and time-consuming, however. That's why there are many companies that broker affiliate relationships. They help recruit qualified web site publishers to promote your offers, and also provide the tracking codes to measure the clickthroughs, leads generated, and sales resulting from each affiliate's promotion of your products.

So, if this approach appeals to you, here are two approaches for you to consider:

1. Start your own affiliate program with a limited number of participants. If you work only with web sites that you know and trust, it will be easier to track their work and ensure appropriate promotion of your products, transaction reporting, and commission payments. There are many ways to administer such programs yourself. These include software programs specialized for affiliate program management (which you can locate with a Google search), and many shopping cart packages (such as Yahoo! Merchant Solutions stores) include affiliate program management tools today.

2. Join an affiliate program management service like Commission Junction or Linkshare to attract affiliates worldwide. These companies make a business out of helping advertisers like you recruit, provide incentives for, retain, and generate increased revenues from affiliates. These services are usually for companies that are at least medium-sized, however, because they have minimum program sign-up fees of several thousand dollars, and they also add a significant percentage to any affiliate fees paid as their own cut (usually about 30 percent).

While affiliate advertising is clearly an advertising strategy, not simply a marketing one, I thought that it deserved discussion in this marketing-focused book because it offers great viral potential. There are millions of people on the Web each day who have free time on their hands. The millions of blogs, hobbyist web sites, message board forums, virtual worlds, and other online diversions are full of people who wouldn't mind putting some of that free time, and their relationships, to work for you *if you offered to pay them*. This is exactly what affiliate programs do—they can help you find and mobilize lots of foot soldiers to help you win your battle for increased sales.

When a trusted blogger or any niche expert uses his own personal Web soapbox to promote your products, you can easily reach potential customers who would never have encountered your brand otherwise. This can help you not only gain new customers, but also uncover new markets and spread your marketing reach wider and faster than doing it by yourself.

Lots of companies use affiliate programs as part of their marketing strategy. These of course include thousands of small businesses, but they also include lots of big names that you recognize. Allstate Insurance, Macy's, Radio Shack, Time Warner Cable, the *Wall Street Journal*, Apple, Wal-Mart, Capital One, Amazon.com, Office Depot, Foot Locker, Sephora, and Buy.com are all active affiliate program advertisers.

AFFILIATE PROGRAM ADVERTISING
CASE STUDY: BUY.COM

I spoke with Melissa Salas, Director of Marketing at Buy.com, to learn about how that company has successfully deployed an affiliate program to grow its customer base.

Although acting as an affiliate yourself to promote another merchant's products to your audience can be a lucrative business (see the examples in my first book, *Internet Riches*), remember that here we are talking about you acting as the "merchant" or advertiser, not the affiliate merchant. Running an affiliate program as a merchant means recruiting commission-based sales reps to promote your products to their own online audiences. That's part of Melissa's role in promoting Buy.com's affiliate program to its affiliates. Then it's the affiliates' opportunity to promote Buy.com products to their audiences (in exchange for a commission, of course).

Here's my Q&A with Melissa:

Scott: How does your affiliate program work?

Melissa: Any web site owner who is looking to monetize their web site's traffic can join Buy.com's affiliate program by going to www.buy.com/affiliates. Buy.com pays affiliate commissions on over 5 million products. Affiliates partner with us to help customers find quality products at low prices across 13 product categories. Many of our best affiliates focus their promotional efforts on specific product areas, such as digital cameras, software, jewelry, or books.

Scott: Why does Buy.com use an affiliate program as part of its marketing mix?

Melissa: Buy.com's affiliate program plays a pivotal role in the company's overall online marketing strategy. By recruiting and partnering with a select group of affiliates, all of whom have proven records of driving targeted traffic matching Buy.com's customer demographics, we've been able to drive maximum traffic and revenue at an optimal cost.

Scott: How do you attract good affiliates?

Melissa: Buy.com's strong brand, word of mouth in the industry, personal recruitment, and network recruitment all help. It costs them nothing to join Buy.com's affiliate program or to maintain the relationship.

Scott: What kind of support do you offer affiliates to keep them working hard to promote your products?

Melissa: We value our affiliates' time and want to make advertising Buy.com products as easy as possible for them. So we offer affiliates a vast selection of creative (graphic banners, buttons, and so on), plus a variety of promotions including free shipping, coupons, category-related promotions, product-specific promotions, and "deals of the day." This support plays a big role in our mutual success.

Scott: What marketing tactics do you encourage affiliates to use to increase your sales?

Melissa: Buy.com tests various versions of creative to see which banner or text links provide the highest rate of sales conversions. We also perform aggressive affiliate outreach to ensure that each affiliate segment is communicating the right campaign to the right consumer, and to educate affiliates on the importance of posting product-specific deals rather than broad promotion campaigns.

Scott: What do you pay your affiliates?

Melissa: Buy.com offers a baseline commission rate of up to 10 percent (depending on the category) of every sale on all in-stock products purchased on Buy.com. All affiliates are paid this rate, plus they have the potential to earn bonuses based on increased sales.

Scott: Advice for newbies?

Melissa: I think the biggest misconception about affiliate marketing is the idea that affiliate programs offering higher percentage commissions must necessarily be better than programs offering lower percentage commissions. To the contrary, many of the high-percentage-commission affiliate programs have low conversion rates because of lack of product variety, noncompetitive pricing, and deficient customer service practices. Affiliates need to evaluate programs holistically, in terms of brand recognition, conversion, reliability, convenience, security, and guaranteed customer satisfaction.

Melissa recommends affiliate marketing to other companies, large and small. She says, "More and more e-commerce companies are now using affiliate programs because they offer such a win-win model for both the merchant and the affiliate."

I also like affiliate programs because they help to ensure that your products are displayed where customers are most likely to be interested in them. The affiliate publishers take care of this for you because they are given incentives (by the commission payments you offer) to pick and promote the products that are most appealing to their own audiences. As Melissa says, "Consumers want instant access to the products they are looking for. Affiliate web sites provide browsers with relevant product information when and where they want it, therefore helping to convert browsers into buyers at a low acquisition cost."

Of course, your affiliate program doesn't need to start out nearly as big as Buy.com's. That's a big company that has been at it for years.

As I have done with the Scott Fox Affiliate Program, you can start with special commission offers on a few key products, then offer those deals to some of your best customers or fans to promote your business or just post a link on your site to see who writes in to ask to represent your products as an affiliate.

You can administer your own program with a small number of key affiliates and a low number of offers, or you can grow your program to the scale of Buy.com's and generate millions in sales each year.

The important part is to be aware of these strategies as a tool for marketing your products better. If they are properly implemented, affiliate programs can be cost-effective, brand-building, and profitable, too.

Getting Started with Affiliate Programs

If you're looking for an efficient and consistent way to deliver relevant advertising that maximizes new customer acquisition and conversions, affiliate programs may be the answer.

You can Google "performance based marketing" to find dozens of firms and hundreds of consultants that would be happy to help you spend your ad budget.

The leaders in the space are Commission Junction and Linkshare. Both of these companies charge several thousand dollars to get started and have minimum monthly charges of several hundred dollars, however. If you're looking for a solution that you can run yourself, many shopping cart systems (like upgraded versions of Yahoo! Stores) include affiliate program administration tools.

The drawback of a do-it-yourself approach, however, is that you then need to spend time recruiting and managing affiliates yourself. This is a big part of the service that Commission Junction, Linkshare, and others provide for their hefty fees.

ShareaSale.com is a midpriced affiliate program alternative ($550 setup fee plus $100 per month and 20 percent payout commission fees) that looks promising, but I have not yet had time to test it.

For updated recommendations from the world of affiliate marketing or to share your experiences with these strategies, please visit ScottFox.com. I invite you to join the Scott Fox Affiliate Program. You can make money promoting affiliate offers for my products, or you can just check out the tools we use to administer the program. Searching on "affiliate marketing" on ScottFox.com or in our discussion forums will also help you to find a lot of helpful information for both affiliate advertisers and affiliate publishers. For example, my subscription-only coaching program recently spent a whole month on success strategies for entrepreneur publishers interested in promoting affiliate program offers. This resulted in a 100+ page guide, "How to Make Money with Affiliate Programs," two downloadable podcast expert interviews, and more, all of which can help you learn more about making money as an affiliate.

PART EIGHT

YOUR WINNING ONLINE
MARKETING STRATEGY

23

MEASURING YOUR
ONLINE SALES SUCCESS

OKAY, THERE'S obviously plenty for you to do on the path to e-riches. How do you know if all this is working?

It's important that you measure your traffic and other key performance indicators (KPIs). This will help you establish what success means for your business. This sounds simple, but it varies from marketing campaign to marketing campaign—sometimes the objective is merely impressions for "brand building"; other times success is measured by customer conversions or money deposited in the bank.

You should start measuring your KPIs before you even get started with my recommended marketing techniques so that you have a baseline measurement of your site's traffic from which to measure your progress.

Traffic Benchmarking Tools

There are many services available to measure your web site's traffic. These include expensive, enterprise-grade systems like Omniture, Web-Trends, and Coremetrics. They generally require a big budget, a negotiated contract, and serious technical support to implement and use them effectively.

There are also Web-based traffic reporting services like Alexa, Compete, and Quantcast. These services generally offer free introductory traffic reporting and additional detailed reports for fees. They are not always particularly accurate for smaller sites (which are harder to measure because they have less traffic to sample), but they can be useful for researching traffic trends. Where these services excel is in helping you learn about your competitors' traffic. You can enter several URLs of your and competitors' sites to display informative graphs of traffic comparisons.

Google Analytics

If your web site or company does not already have a detailed traffic measurement system installed, Google Analytics is a free service that does a great job (*especially for the low, low price of nothing*). By signing up for a free Google Analytics account, you can obtain a small piece of JavaScript tracking code. You install it by simply copying and pasting this code on each page of your web site.

These free analytics tools will help you determine not only the number of visitors your web site receives, but also the most common entry and exit points on your site, common search terms used to find your web site, the most popular content and/or products you are offering, and much more.

Your own visitor traffic reports are full of actionable information that is available to you for free. Highly recommended.

There are also new services debuting online all the time to help you better measure your site's success. The continued growth of the Web, the growth of online advertising, and improving technology make traffic measurement a hot area for startups that are trying to make reliable data even more available.

24

. . .

DIFFERENTIATION STRATEGIES IN A COMPETITIVE ONLINE MARKETPLACE

Being average has never helped anyone rise above the crowd. Average is average. People don't pay for average. So what makes one think they can have an average business or an average career or an average life and make a difference? Average doesn't make a difference. Average is average.

—John C. Maxwell, author of *The 21 Irrefutable Laws of Leadership* and *Developing the Leader Within You*

YOUR BUSINESS will be more profitable and your marketing also a lot easier if your value proposition is clear to customers. So *differentiation* is an important point for a marketing book, even though it may sound like MBA-speak.

Your e-riches product differentiation strategy can be fundamental—e.g., a new product or service. Or it can be based on better marketing, such as we've been discussing. Or your business can excel over the competition with add-ons like free shipping or after-the-sale features like better customer service. Even if you sell a commodity product, the Web today offers you the opportunity to position yourself as an expert and differentiate your delivery and approach, even if you can't change your product.

Even common products can be differentiated by add-ons like these:

- *Customer service.* Zappos, a top online shoe store, offers the same shoes as other outlets (including loads of well-established offline competition), but it differentiates itself by offering unprecedented customer support. (And the company's CEO, Tony Hsieh, is very active on Twitter, too.)

- *Graphics.* Daily Candy sends daily e-mails full of interesting style and event tips to trendy audiences across the country. While its content and snappy copywriting are clearly critical, the stylized graphics give the company's noozles a visual differentiation that helped propel it to a $125 million acquisition by Comcast.

- *Good storytelling.* Well-written, interesting stories or business advice can create a business with almost no infrastructure or overhead costs. Sign up for Randy Cassingham's "This is True," Joyce Showalter's "Heroic Stories," or Paul Myer's "TalkBiz" noozles. These e-mails are only text, so their differentiation is close attention to content and copywriting.

- *Style.* My wife's SweaterBabe.com design business is a success in a vast sea of online crochet and knitting patterns, many of which are even free. Her business thrives because her fashion sense and design style differentiate it. A younger generation of hip knitters loves her "this ain't your Grandma's knitting" approach.

- *Analysis.* Michael Arrington's Techcrunch offers insight and analysis for the technology startup and venture capital communities. But he's not just repeating the facts; his team digs into the stories and offers informed commentary and product reviews that help readers better understand the business opportunities in Techcrunch's target market.

▲ *Timeliness.* Being first with a story always helps get attention. "Breaking News" alerts from the *Wall Street Journal* or CNN get attention. You can, too, if you are the first to discover or publicize information that is valued by your audience.

▲ *"Inside" info.* All Hip Hop, Ned Sherman's Digital Media Wire, and ArtFairInsiders.com prove that there are niches where your industry expertise can differentiate you, too.

Analyzing Your Online Competition

Strength lies in differences, not in similarities.

Stephen R. Covey, author of *The 7 Habits of Highly Effective People*

If you take advantage of the Web's many free research tools (including Alexa, Google Analytics, Compete, and others detailed in the previous chapter), you can learn a lot about your competitors and find new ones, too. Analyze their products, content, copywriting, marketing style, e-mail strategy, customer support, and SEO approach to see what does and doesn't work.

I often find it helpful to create a matrix like the one shown. It can help you compare your marketing strategies versus your competitors'.

MARKETING STRATEGY	COMPETITOR A	COMPETITOR B	COMPETITOR C
E-mail marketing			
▲ Address collection	None	Yes, but small	Prominent
▲ Design	None	Nice	Text-only e-mails
▲ Frequency	None	Weekly	Never?
Blog	None	Not updated	Weekly
Social networks			
▲ MySpace	None	Yes	No
▲ Facebook	None	No	No
▲ LinkedIn	None	No	Yes

Analysis like this can help reveal your best opportunities for profitable differentiation of your products and marketing strategy. Then you can use the Internet's communications platform to expand on those competitive advantages to differentiate and brand yourself in customers' minds.

In this example, it appears that you could reach many potential customers online with little competition by expanding your product presence on social networks or with an active blog. It also looks as if Competitor A is stuck in the old school brochure-ware phase of online marketing.

E-RICHES TIP: LOCAL BUSINESS DIFFERENTIATION!

Amazingly, for local businesses, being online at all can still often be a differentiator.

Many of your local competitors are probably not marketing effectively online. Many of them probably still don't even have web sites. By establishing your web site, distributing your product presence, and nurturing your reputation cloud across the Web, you can probably leapfrog them.

This means that your listings will show up first in the search engines, attract the most customers looking online for a local provider of your products, and increase your revenues.

The sooner you start establishing the authority of your site with the search engines, collecting e-mail addresses of local customers, and building relationships with your potential customer audience online, the longer it will take your competitors to catch up.

The *Other* Major Differentiator for Your Business: You

If you are insecure, guess what? The rest of the world is, too. Do not overestimate the competition and underestimate yourself. You are better than you think.[1]

Timothy Ferriss, author of *The 4-Hour Workweek*

The other major differentiator that will determine the success of your online marketing is *you*. You are the engine that drives your marketing, and it's quite likely that those marketing efforts are what drive your whole company.

It's certainly true that the potential of any product or company is largely dependent on the quality of its marketing. I've written a whole book here to try to help you.

Now, what are you going to do about it?

Staffing for Online Evangelism and Community Organizing

To succeed at a distributed engagement marketing strategy you also are likely to need "foot soldiers." Many of the Web 2.0 and social media marketing opportunities are based on "many-to-many" interactive communications. So instead of broadcasting one-size-fits-all marketing messages, you're seeing the fragmentation of mass media into niche channels that are more targeted. Add to that the interpersonal communication and communities that are facilitated by these platforms, and you've got real live people who are open to hearing about your products, but who insist that the information be presented in a relevant, appropriate-to-the context way.

This requires staff.

For tips on hiring "virtual assistants" that can help you outsource your workload, I recommend Tim Ferriss's book *The 4-Hour Workweek*, as well as the ongoing discussions at ScottFox.com.

Successful management of a Web 2.0 reputation cloud also requires letting go of your brand control in ways that can be unsettling for marketing personnel who previously made a career out of tightly controlling the brand message.

You need to start by setting clear guidelines for communication about your products and brands. Then you need to train the heck out of the junior people (or outsourced contractors) whom you place in front of the keyboards to spread your product presence. They will rapidly become specialists in the communities you send them to, so you'll need to trust their judgment about how best to position your brand evangelism to attract, and not piss off, the online community members you're targeting through distributed engagement.

As discussed earlier, this strategic imperative also suggests that you need to reprioritize your marketing resources and budgets. You are likely to need more online community evangelists and fewer broadcast TV or radio ads, for example.

These folks can spread your distributed engagement campaigns by:

▲ Responding to comments received across multiple platforms and channels

▲ Posting articles to your blog

▲ Publishing noozles

▲ Submitting updates and articles to social bookmarking sites

▲ Updating your status on Facebook or Twitter

▲ Sourcing and uploading photos

▲ Moderating any interactive areas sponsored or promoted by your company

▲ Producing teleseminars or podcasts

Obviously, interacting with and nurturing customers and fans online can easily be a full-time job!

Redeploying your staffing budgets this way can really shake up a company, but hopefully by now you recognize the importance of prioritizing this online marketing work.

. . .

CONCLUSION

LET'S MAKE IT HAPPEN

I believe through learning and application of what you learn, you can solve any problem, overcome any obstacle, and achieve any goal that you can set for yourself.

Brian Tracy, author of books including *Maximum Achievement*, *Speak to Win*, and *Advanced Selling Strategies*

Creating a Constant Stream of Traffic Is Your Goal

All the new media and marketing opportunities on the Internet can make your head spin—I get it. That's why I wrote this book. Hopefully, after reading it, you have a better idea of how the best new online marketing strategies work, and how they can help you sell more products.

Having started with the strategic repositioning discussed at the beginning of the book and having gone through all the top strategies

I recommend now makes you one of the best-educated marketers on the planet! The combination of these techniques, the worldwide reach of the Internet, and your clever hard work can turn your online marketing into a success story, too.

The key is careful implementation of multiple reinforcing marketing strategies. You want to attract an ongoing stream of visitors to your product presence. By executing a strategy of distributed engagement you should have marketing messages displayed all across the Web where your most likely customers can encounter them. The detailed e-mail, blog, social network, social news, online broadcasting, PR, and other tactics discussed in *e-Riches 2.0* should empower you to do this. You then want to convert your new visitors into long-term fans.

So, as a modern marketer, your job is no longer just attracting customers. You need to extend your skill set to encouraging the customer loyalty that leads to profitable repeat business.

Why?

The problem you're facing is that your online store is effectively *invisible* to customers once they click away from your web site or unsubscribe from your mailing list. I call this the *Invisibility Principle*. This is a key difference between online business and traditional brick-and-mortar retailing. Unlike in the "real" world, former customers will not drive past your shop each day or naturally return to your neighborhood to buy groceries.

> *You MUST understand that every retail outlet is a click away online. In real life, location and convenience and price matter. Online, everybody's in the same neighborhood and everybody's got a low price, comparison shopping can be done by bot! You distinguish yourself by the extras.*
>
> —from Bob Lefsetz, music industry commentator, "Online Monopolies," The Lefsetz Letter, September 9, 2008

If your product presence does not actively and consistently reach out to customers across the Web today, your company is effectively invisible to most customers.

Even when you have attracted customers into visiting your site, there is no friction to prevent them from leaving. Unlike in the real world, where you may have the advantage of a local neighborhood location, online competition is always just a mouse click away. And it's often cheaper, too.

So nurturing your audience is a critical new marketing success skill because your customer relationships *are* your business in the online world.

The permission you have from your opted-in subscribers and purchasers, their trust in you to deliver the products you promise, and their attention to your marketing messages are 100 percent of both your present and your future revenues.

Without their loyalty, you'll have nothing—zero repeat traffic, a minimal (or negative) reputation cloud, and zero repeat sales.

Relying solely on new customers and one-time purchases is very expensive. It's also unnecessary if you embrace these Internet marketing strategies that can help you work smarter, not harder.

Warning: Don't Stop Now!

Nobody has ever earned a black belt from reading about martial arts.
—Steve Pavlina, author of *Personal Development for Smart People*

Reading this book is not enough by itself.

You need to embrace at least a few of the many modern online marketing tools we've discussed. Not doing so neglects critical areas of your product presence and leaves your reputation cloud open to damage from your neglect. It also means that you have wasted the time you invested in reading this book.

If you don't market yourself online, who is going to? All that will be left in your reputation cloud will be comments by your customers, disgruntled employees, and your competitors. Yikes!

But if you bought this book, it's clear that you know you need to be doing more online. By reading this far, you've demonstrated a rare and valuable commitment to improving your marketing expertise.

Join Me in Choosing to Succeed Online

Much of the stress that people feel doesn't come from having too much to do. It comes from not finishing what they've started.

—David Allen, author of *Getting Things Done: The Art of Stress-Free Productivity*

Now you're faced with a choice.

You now know that you can use the Internet to grow your business online. The dozens of examples in this book have showed you many ways in which your business can profit from distributed engagement with your audience.

You also know that you don't need to drown yourself trying to do everything—the Web is bigger than you are. But taking small steps into online marketing each day can expand your product presence, lead to a positive and far-reaching reputation cloud for your products, and encourage rapid growth in both your online and offline sales.

Now that I've armed you with all of these tools, as well as free updates from my blog and a free membership in my online community at ScottFox.com, it's up to you to put the tools to work to make some money online. *The value of this book doesn't come from reading it. It comes from acting on what you've learned.*

Are you going to put this book down and forget what you learned? Or maybe put off taking action by buying more books and doing some more "strategizing"?

Or, are you going to get started?

Knowing something and doing it are different. If you've read this far, you now know more about modern marketing than 99 percent of the population. Now you need to *do* it.

As Tony Robbins (author of *Awaken the Giant Within*) says, "If you keep doing what you've always done, you'll get what you've always gotten." Is that enough for you?

Much of success in both life and business is about *momentum.* Right now, you have momentum toward becoming a better marketer. You've rolled through more than 300 pages to get here. Keep that going by taking action *now.*

Taking action is the key to your e-riches success. Reading, talking, meeting, researching, analyzing—none of these is a substitute for getting started.

If you're still in the researching stage, give yourself a deadline. You need to move past "analysis paralysis" if you expect to grow your business. To find the additional info you need, visit the many web sites and blogs mentioned throughout this book. Sign up for the free noozles and e-books that many of them offer. Reading just an e-mail or two each day on a topic can help you learn it almost effortlessly over time.

If you're ready to get started, try testing the tools that I've discussed to find those that give you the best return on investment for your business. For example, why not pick one of the marketing techniques I have detailed and try it for 90 days starting today?

Lastly, visit ScottFox.com to redeem your free trial membership. Join me, my team, and fellow online marketers worldwide in sharing expertise that can help grow your business online now. Put down this book and go to your PC—get on with it!

Since you've gotten this far (whew!), I know that you're one of the folks who's really listening. How about if we agree right now that you're going to be one of the success stories in my next book?

Visit ScottFox.com today to let us help you continue your e-riches quest. Come to leave comments, ask questions, meet people, and share updates from your experience, too. I look forward to hearing from you!

Let's make it happen!

APPENDIX
RECOMMENDED RESOURCES AND WEB SITES

The following sites and blogs are all well-established resources for the online marketing community. I read, use, and recommend them personally.

Awake at the Wheel: http://www.jonathanfields.com. A well-written and often inspiring blog from a former yoga teacher turned social media expert and author of *Career Renegade*.

Chris Brogan's Blog: http://www.chrisbrogan.com. Chris is an active and insightful social media professional. His blog covers the latest trends in online community and social media. His book is called *Trust Agents*.

CopyBlogger.com: http://www.copyblogger.com. Brian Clark is a master of online copywriting. Read this blog and watch your writing (and your sales) improve.

Darren Rowse's Problogger: http://www.problogger.net. The leading blog (and book) teaching how to make money as a blogger. Darren's advice is practical and down-to-earth.

FreeTeleseminarList.com: I designed this site to offer free promotions for teleseminar and webinar hosts. If you are promoting such an event, you can post it here for promotion by email to subscribers worldwide interested in teleconference and webinar education.

HARO: http://www.helpareporter.com. The free press leads e-mail service profiled in Chapters 9 and 15 of this book.

InternetMillionaireDomains.com: http://www.internetmillionaire-domains.com. Here I offer domain names just above cost, basic web site hosting, and the tools to help get your Web presence moving cost-effectively.

Joan Stewart's Publicity Hound: http://www.publicityhound.com. Joan Stewart's always informative and entertaining free noozle offers public relations tips, tricks, and strategies.

PRLeads.com: http://www.prleads.com. Dan Janal's affordable repackaging of the ProfNet service that includes custom coaching and personal training on how to work with reporters.

RadioGuestList.com: http://www.radioguestlist.com. My free service that helps radio, podcast, and teleseminar hosts find expert guests.

Rich Brook's Web Marketing Blog: http://www.flyteblog.com. An informative resource for both online marketing strategy and tactics.

ScottFox.com: http://www.scottfox.com. My web site offers free e-mail newsletters, downloads, and my blog about e-commerce entrepreneurship and online marketing. Use the search box on the site to find more info on any topic that interests you. Search on "Web design," "affiliate marketing," "SEO," or "podcasting," for example. ScottFox.com is also home to the Scott Fox forums. This membership community is focused on mentoring and sharing online marketing expertise. Your purchase of this book entitles you to a free trial of the service, too!

ScottFoxRadio.com: http://www.scottfoxradio.com. The home of my online radio show and podcast, *The E-Commerce Success Show*. Visit the archives for free downloadable MP3 recordings of my interviews with experts, authors, and online entrepreneur success stories.

Web Strategy by Jeremiah Owyang: http://www.web-strategist.com. The informative and insightful blog of Forrester Research's social media and Web marketing analyst.

NOTES

CHAPTER 1
1. Deborah Fallows, "Browsing the Web for Fun," Pew Internet Project Data Memo, February 2006; http://www.pewtrusts.org/uploadedFiles/wwwpewtrusts org/Reports/Society_and_the_Internet/PIP_Surf_0206.pdf.

CHAPTER 2
1. "U.S. Consumers Increasingly Going Online and Calling Stores to Research Product, Availability and Price, Accenture Survey Finds," Accenture Newsroom, April 4, 2007; http://accenture.tekgroup.com/article_display.cfm?article_id=4529.

CHAPTER 3
1. Jack Loechner, "Daily Search Engine Users Closing In on Email Users," MediaPost Research Brief, August 14, 2008;
http://blogs.mediapost.com/research_brief/?p=1771.

2. "The Ins and Outs of Online Sharing," Forrester Research, quoted in "New Independent Study Highlights Differences in How and Why Adults and Youth Share Online," ShareThis, September 15, 2008; http://sharethis.com/press?pr=7.

3. "Email Sender Authentication Checks on the Rise, According to Lyris' EmailAdvisor Deliverability Study," Lyris press release, August 29, 2007; http://web0.lyris.com/news/pr/pr-082907.html.

4. Ibid.

CHAPTER 8
1. "Cone Finds That Americans Expect Companies to Have a Presence in Social Media," September 25, 2008, http://www.coneinc.com/content1182.

CHAPTER 9
1. "Global Survey Shows 58% of People Don't Know What Social Networking Is, Plus Over One-Third of Social Networkers Are Losing Interest," Synovate press release, September 1, 2008; http://www.synovate.com/news/article/2008/09/global-

survey-shows-58-of-people-don-t-know-what-social-networking-is-plus-over-one-third-of-social-networkers-are-losing-interest.html.

2. eMarketer e-mail, June 13, 2008.

3. "Global Survey Shows," Synovate.

4. http://www.quicksprout.com/2007/09/19/build-a-Facebook-profile-you-can-be-proud-of.

5. "Unrepentant on Facebook? Expect Jail Time," Associated Press, July 18, 2008; http://www.cnn.com/2008/CRIME/07/18/facebook.evidence.ap/index.html.

CHAPTER 13
1. Jonathan Fields, "Grab Attention of Top Editors and Producers with Social Media," Small Business Trends, July 15, 2008; http://www.smallbiztrends.com/2008/07/get-access-social-media.html/#comment-593358.

CHAPTER 17
1. Many sources, including Hillel Italie, "Free Business Book Is Web Sensation," Associated Press, February 16, 2008; http://www.boston.com/ae/books/articles/2008/02/16/free_business_book_is_web_sensation/.

CHAPTER 18
1. Mary Madden, "Online Video," Pew Internet & American Life Project, July 25, 2007; http://www.pewinternet.org/pdfs/PIP_Online_Video_2007.pdf.

2. "Daily Hours Watching Video and TV to Match Sleep by 2013," PRNewswire, June 11, 2008;
http://www.prnewswire.com/cgi-bin/stories.pl?ACCT=104&STORY=/www/story/06-11-2008/0004830501&EDATE=.

3. http://news.yahoo.com/s/afp/20080926/tc_afp/usinternettelevisonbroadband, September 26, 2008.

4. "Law Firms Find Business Through Online Video," FindLaw, May 21, 2008; http://company.findlaw.com/pr/2008/052108.video.html.

CHAPTER 20
1. "HD Radio vs. Internet Radio—Which Is Radio's Future?" Bridge Ratings, August 8, 2007; http://www.bridgeratings.com/press_08.08.07.HDvsInternet.htm.

2. Mary Madden and Sydney Jones, "Podcast Downloading 2008," Pew Internet & American Life Project, August 28, 2008; http://www.pewinternet.org/PPF/r/261/report_display.asp.

CHAPTER 21
1. Jack Loechner, "Daily Search Engine Users Closing In on Email Users," MediaPost Research Brief, August 14, 2008; http://blogs.mediapost.com/research_brief/?p=1771.

2. "Small Businesses Intimidated by Search Marketing," http://www.marketingvox.com/small-businesses-intimidated-by-search-marketing-042523/. December 8, 2008.

CHAPTER 24
1. Timothy Ferriss, *The 4-Hour Workweek: Escape 9–5, Live Anywhere, and Join the New Rich* (New York: Crown, 2007), p. 50.

INDEX

ACKNOWLEDGMENTS

To find myself writing the acknowledgments for a second book is a great pleasure. Thanks to all my readers who have helped to make *e-Riches 2.0* possible by purchasing my first book, *Internet Riches.* Your confirmed interest in hearing from me has not only helped me find unexpected success as an author but it has also (more importantly) allowed me to help thousands of aspiring entrepreneurs worldwide.

e-Riches 2.0 would not have happened without the ongoing patience, love, and support of my wife, Katherine. Thank you for believing in this project, believing in me, and taking care of our beautiful girls every day. (Yes, girls, daddy really was writing another book!) Family from all sides (Phil, Ti-ta, Shun-jong, Jonathan, Carie, and especially my mother Connie) has also been very supportive of both my creative process and the unexpected career path that my writing has led me down. Thank you also to Jay and Jacki Bilsborrow for your help.

I'd also like to recognize Frances Hamburger, for teaching me how to speak, and Professor Don Cameron, for teaching me how to write with purpose.

My agent Shannon Marven of Dupree-Miller (and her team) helped bring this book to market. Thanks, Shannon, for your help and for believing that the world really was ready for more Internet books after all!

The AMACOM books team, led by my editor Jacquie Flynn, has once again been a pleasure to work with. Thank you to all, especially Hank Kennedy, Jenny Wesselman, Rosemary Carlough, Kama Timbrell, Penny Makras, Barry Richardson, Jennifer Holder, Jim Bessent, and Vera Sarkanj for helping me put together another educational and inspiring blockbuster.

Thanks also to Therese Mausser, Tara Boodoo, and our international publishing partners for the U.K., Turkish, Polish, and other foreign editions of my books, too.

Thank you to Brilliance Audio's Michael Snodgrass, Eileen Hutton, Joe McNeely, Colleen Rockey, Laura Grafton, Laura Stahl, Steve Woessner, Kimberly West, and the rest of the Grand Haven team for the great job they've done of expanding my work into audio editions.

I have also learned a lot from many other top marketers and bloggers whose generously shared expertise is reflected in this book. They include Seth Godin, Guy Kawasaki, Brian Clark, Darren Rowse, Jonathan Fields, Joel Comm, Gary Vaynerchuk, Andy Sernovitz, Joan Stewart, Frank Kern, Shawn Collins, Jeff Walker, and Paul Myers.

My many friends in radio have also contributed greatly to the promotion of *Internet Riches* and the ScottFox.com approach to online success. Bob Sullivan and Russ Stolnack, my hosts on Business Talk Radio Network's *Big Biz Show* each week, are at the top of this list. My thanks goes out to them and Peter Anthony Holder, Kate Delaney, Jim Blasingame, Dave Graveline, Mike Butts, and the many, many other radio personalities who have generously shared their air time to hear about my approach to e-commerce success.

Thanks for their support of my work as a writer also goes to Bryan Perez, Michael Rapino, my Live Nation team, Bill O'Reilly, Robert Kiyosaki, David Bach, Darren Hardy of *SUCCESS* magazine, Ken Evoy, Rick Frishman and Jeff Nordstedt of Planned Television Arts, Scott Dinsmore, Uri Blackman, Catrina Luedtke, Deanna Yick at Google, and my partners at the Learning Annex (especially Kathi Khoury and Oliver Waller).

At the end of the day, it is readers who make an author successful. So I'd especially like to thank everyone who reads and comments at

ScottFox.com, my thousands of e-mail newsletter subscribers, and the 1,000+ people who took my surveys online. Your input truly helped shape the direction of this book. I hope you like it!

Thanks to all of my Facebook fans, MySpace friends, LinkedIn connections, Twitter followers, and especially frequent Commenters on my blog. These include David Peters, Jim Vickers, Mireya Pizarro, Eddie Lewis, Ron Vinnedge, Candis Crocker, Linda Smith, Karl Jennings, Himanshu Sheth, Molly Sandquist, Eric Pratum, Andrew Selvaggio, Bob Russel, Abby Brown, and Susan Emmer.

I especially appreciate the support of the Charter Subscribers of Instant Internet Business Secrets: David Peters, Laura Murray, Elliot Feldman, Tamara Snell, Traci Hayner Vanover, Taide Zamora, LaBarbara Dhaliwal, Peter Conradie, John Kirsch, Charlotte Dixon, Brian Cadieux, Caroline Christl, Robert Hill, Tim Atkinson, Moses Mauricio Chacham, Richard Hamil, Mark Lane, Mark Wilson, Toni Bihm, Charles Rayman, Doug Naujeck, Terence, David Green, Skuli Thorhallsson, Ron Vinnedge, Elena Zoueva, Steven Barrett, Robert Russel, James Moncur, Doran Haynie, Jim Ludzieski, Tom Hickok, Jason Harthun, Devan Persaud, Shane Robinson, Gary Wolff, Darren Smith, John Higgins, JS Goyette, Kip Fleury, Irwin Manes, Justin Minns, Renee Buffington, Robert Lord, Al White, Sidney Williams, and Eric Windless.

The entrepreneurs and experts profiled in this book were helpful and inspiring. Thank you to all of you who participated in my interviews. Your participation, inspiration, and expertise made this book a reality. Together we are changing lives for the better.

I am very grateful for the opportunity to share my vision and inspire people to realize their own potential. Please come join me at ScottFox.com and invite your friends, too. I'd love to hear what you want me to write about next!

Thank you for reading.